THE ORIGINS OF PHOTOGRAPHY IN SALISBURY 1839–1880

To my wife Katharina

THE ORIGINS OF PHOTOGRAPHY IN SALISBURY 1839–1880

Anthony Hamber

THE HOBNOB PRESS

2019

First published in the United Kingdom in 2019

by The Hobnob Press,
8 Lock Warehouse, Severn Road, Gloucester GL1 2GA
www.hobnobpress.co.uk

British Library Cataloguing in Publication Data
A catalogue record for this book is available from the British Library

ISBN 978-1-906978-73-0

Typeset in ITC New Baskerville 11/14 pt.
Typesetting and origination by John Chandler

CONTENTS

FOREWORD

THIS STUDY OF the history of photography in Salisbury between 1839 and 1880 arose from a case study undertaken as part of my doctoral research published in 1996 as *"A Higher Branch of the Art" – Photographing the Fine Arts in England 1839-1880.* The research took place in the late 1980s and early 1990s and primarily consisted of scrolling through the microfilm of the *Salisbury and Winchester Journal* (henceforth abbreviated to *SJ*) held in Salisbury Public Library. The Internet and Web has, of course, transformed the ability of researchers to access, filter and share vast amounts of information in digital form, and local histories of photography have greatly benefitted from this.

Many people have helped or encouraged me to research and complete this study. These include Adrian Green and Peter Saunders, respectively director and past director of the Salisbury Museum, Jane Howells, Steven Joseph and Michael Pritchard. Alan Clarke has been most helpful in locating photographs from the Salisbury Museum's rich and diverse collections. I also wish to thank Larry Schaaf and Geoff Batchen for answering a number of questions.

While this study may be considered a contribution to an understanding of photography in Salisbury during the mid-19th century, it should not be considered as definitive. Hopefully others will be encouraged to undertake further research on the individuals and events mentioned together with the numerous other activities that helped define the city and its progress.

I continue to be grateful to my family for there tolerance of the time taken to undertake my research for this study and to write up the text of this book.

Anthony Hamber
Clapham
2019

INTRODUCTION

In 1839, the year of the announcements of the photographic processes of the Frenchman Louis-Jacques-Mandé Daguerre (1787–1851) and William Henry Fox Talbot (1800–1877) of Lacock Abbey near Chippenham (henceforth referred to as Henry Talbot), Salisbury was a comparatively small market city with a population recorded in the 1841 census of 10,086 inhabitants.[1] Largely dependent on the fact that it acted as the centre of commerce for a largely rural community, the city was also a resting-place on the stagecoach from London to Exeter. It was estimated that, in the year 1839, 37,000 passengers travelled through Salisbury on the Exeter to London stagecoach.[2] The city was also strategically placed on the route from Bristol to Southampton, and historically had prospered during the latter part of the Middle Ages as a centre for the wool trade based on Salisbury Plain.

The expansion of the British railway network during the 1840s brought significant benefits to Salisbury, though there were some to suffer. The number of horse-drawn coaches from Salisbury to London declined and the last horse-drawn coach was to leave the city in October 1846. The city was to see much railway development during the next decade or so. The London and South Western Railway (LSWR) opened its Milford station on the east side of the city on 1st March 1847 and in the following year the rail connection between Salisbury and London was completed via Bishopstoke. On 30th June 1856 the Great Western Railway (GWR) opened its Salisbury branch from Westbury and the connexion to Warminster and Bristol was made in 1856. The GWR built a station to the north of the future and current mainline station. The LSWR opened its extended main line from London and Andover on 1st May 1857, and this at first stopped at the Milford station.

The LSWR continued its expansion and opened on 2nd May 1859 a station on the south side of the GWR station west of Fisherton Street. This was to coincide with the opening of the first section of the Salisbury and Yeovil Railway. At the same time the terminus of the Andover line moved to the new LSWR station, having been linked from Milford across the city by way of a 405 metre tunnel. The Yeovil and Exeter line opened in 1860 putting Salisbury on a direct line of rail communication between London and the west country.[3] In 1857 the more direct line to London through Andover was opened.

The impact of the expanding railway network on Salisbury was noted in 1867 at the opening ceremony of William Blackmore's purpose-built eponymous museum behind the Salisbury and South Wilts Museum in St Ann Street. Horatio Bolton Nelson, 3rd Earl Nelson (1823–1913) pointed to Salisbury's emerging position as a transport hub, stating that the city was 'so generally connected by railways with almost every other place in England' that the establishment of the Blackmore Museum in the city 'might really be called a boon to the nation at large.'[4] Passenger statistics support the sociological impact. On average, there were 0.65 railway journeys per head of population in 1841, while in 1881 there were 20 per head of population.[5] Railways also improved the transport of animals and other goods to the Market Place in Salisbury. This was enabled by the construction of a spur railway from the main line in Fisherton to the new Market House opened in May 1859 and now the site of Salisbury Public Library.

The Gothic Revival had taken off around 1840. Salisbury had been the place of the reception of the architect Augustus Welby Northmore Pugin (1812–1852) into the Catholic Church in 1835 and in 1848 his Roman Catholic church of St. Osmund was completed in Exeter Street. The interest in the Gothic coupled with the increased number of visitors to the city resulted in Salisbury Cathedral becoming one of the most photographed buildings in Great Britain. The building was to help sustain many of Salisbury's commercial photographers and drew a number of the leading contemporary photographers to document the building, including Roger Fenton (1819–1869).

Salisbury offers a view of a typical British Victorian provincial city in which to examine the rise and impact of photography. However, a key question underpinning this study is just how representative Salisbury actually was in terms of its inhabitants' knowledge and use of photography; the scale of local amateur and commercial photographers' exploitation of the medium and its applications; and the size of the market for photographs in and around the city.

To form a view, this study has closely examined two contemporary Salisbury newspapers, the *Salisbury and Winchester Journal* (henceforth abbreviated to *SJ*) and the *Salisbury Times* (henceforth abbreviated to *ST*). There were a number of other newspapers published in Salisbury during the period 1839 to 1880 and these were discussed a century ago in several articles in the *Wiltshire Archaeological and Natural History Magazine.* The first of these was by J.J. Slade, from 1914 until 1935 the editor of the *Wiltshire Gazette,* published in Devizes, and several others followed by Mrs Herbert Richardson.[6] The following list of newspapers other than the *SJ* and *ST* points to the vibrant market for newspapers in Wiltshire during the mid-19th century, many of which focussed on the area around Salisbury:

Hampshire Advertiser and Salisbury Guardian. (1831–1860), then continued as *The Hampshire Advertiser* (1860–1923)
Salisbury and Wiltshire Herald (1833–1852)
Wiltshire Independent (1836–1874)
Wiltshire County Mirror and Express (1852–1887)
Salisbury Advertiser and South Wilts Miscellany (1854)
Salisbury Times and Wilts Miscellany (1854)
South Wilts Express, Salisbury Standard, and General Advertiser (1855)
Salisbury Examiner (1862)
The Wiltshire County Telegram (1863–1865) continued as *The Wiltshire County Telegram and Salisbury Advertiser* (1865–1869)
Salisbury Standard and Wilts Advertiser (1869–1870)
South Wilts Express (1869)

Future research of these newspapers may add further to our knowledge of the rise of photography in Salisbury.

Other national, regional and local newspapers, together with a variety of periodical and serial publications, including the professional photographic press, provide other insights to early photography in Salisbury. However, significant and detailed contemporary personal accounts of photography in the city during the period covered have yet to be unearthed. This fact masks the scale and scope of both amateur and commercial photography in and around Salisbury during the first four decades of the medium's existence.

This study was significantly influenced when the author purchased a copy of *Photographers in Wiltshire* by Martin Norgate assisted by Judith Blades and Pamela Slocombe. Published in 1982 this handlist of some three hundred photographers in Wiltshire up to 1939 was compiled largely from a number of local trade directories coupled to information transcribed from some of the (then) 35,000 or so photographs in the collections of Wiltshire Library & Museum Service, together with associated collections in ten museums receiving 'pastoral care' from the Service. The study included some significant caveats; that the trade directories gave a 'reasonably trustworthy return of data for effort spent' and that 'at least five years of uncertainty should be allowed on the beginning and end of the date spans actually noted.'

The Internet and Web has transformed the study of early photography, particularly the understanding of the first four decades of the medium's existence. The digitisation of national, regional and local newspapers has opened up a rich seam for photographic historians to mine. This study has benefited from this new resource, though forming a comprehensive history of early photography in Salisbury remains problematic, since it is currently largely dependent on a few regional and, particularly, local newspapers.

The leading source is the *SJ,* which had been founded in 1729 by William Collins (1705–1740), a bookseller of Silver Street. On his death, his brother Benjamin Collins (1715–1785) took over the business. The paper was later run by Collins's son Benjamin Charles (1758–1808), and by the 1780s its circulation was claimed to exceed 4,000.

Historically, the *SJ* represented landed, agricultural and commercial interests.[7]

At his death in 1808, and having had no children, ownership of the paper passed to Benjamin Charles Collins's nephew William Bird Brodie (1780–1863) who also took over the banking business begun by his grandfather Benjamin senior in the 1770s. Politically active, William Bird Brodie was Whig MP for Salisbury, 1832–1843, wrote pamphlets on slavery, and his strong Whig and pro-reform views were reflected in the newspaper.

Brodie went bankrupt in 1847 and the *SJ* was sold in 1848 to James Bennett (*c.* 1798–1859). Under Bennett, the paper became more politically neutral. The Bennett family managed the business for over 100 years before selling it to Berrow's Organisation Ltd. in the 1960s.

In combination, newspapers offer multiple viewpoints of the rise of photography before 1880. These range from photographers' advertisements; reviews of photographs of, or exhibited in, Salisbury; the application of photography to a wide variety of local events; and news of the development and application of photography on a local, regional, national and international level. These newspapers also give an indication of the pre-existing market for print selling in Salisbury and the transition of local book and print dealers to stocking photographs, photographically-illustrated publications, and themselves becoming photographic publishers. However, while the *SJ* and *ST* are valuable sources on the origins and early history of photography in Salisbury, they should not be considered as providing a comprehensive account.

Browsing through the advertisements in the *SJ* one cannot but be struck by the diverse range of products and services offered by the shops and businesses in the city. Booksellers, such as Brown & Co. of the Canal also acted as agents for insurance companies. The selling of various patent medicines was another feature. In 1866, Witcomb, the photographer of Catherine Street, even rented out rooms every Tuesday to a dentist from Southampton! See Appendix 2 - Salisbury Photographers and Commercial Photographic Studios.

From the advertisements in local newspapers it is possible to date and locate – though not necessarily conclusively – when and where photographers operated within the city, and thus help date extant photographs.[8] Such advertisements not only provide details such as the products and services offered and their costs, but in some instances tit-bits about the background of the photographers; where they had trained, which studios they had worked in or operated. However, some professional photographers working in Salisbury did not advertise in either the *SJ* or the *ST*. This begs the question as to what strategy such photographers followed and where else they advertised and marketed their services.

The editorial stance of the *SJ* seems to have included a significant interest in photography from the earliest announcements of Daguerre and Talbot. Readers of the *SJ* were informed at a very early date of the arrival of photography, and in its issue of 8th February 1839 the announcement of the daguerreotype process was reported in an article entitled 'Permanent Camera Obscura Views', that provided an account of the presentation of Daguerre's invention by François Arago (1786–1853), French mathematician, physicist, astronomer and politician, at the séance of the French Academy of Sciences [Académie des sciences] held on the 7th January.[9]

Whether this coverage of photography in any way reflected the interests of the *SJ*'s owner, Brodie, is unclear. On Brodie's bankruptcy, the new owner, of the *SJ*, James Bennett, employed James Smith (1820–1910) as editor from 1848 until 1854, at which point Smith emigrated to Australia where he became a well-known journalist and encyclopaedist, leader-writer and dramatic critic for the Melbourne newspaper *The Age*. Smith's editorship coincided with the period in which photography took off following the 1851 Great Exhibition. This saw the establishment of commercial photography in Salisbury, though again, what specific interest Smith had in photography – if any – has yet to be established.

From the second half of the 1850s several commercial photographic studios were established in the city, some surviving until the end of the century and beyond. In parallel, the availability of photographs to buy through a variety of outlets in the city increased, as did accessibility to photographic equipment and materials. The affordability and democratisation of photography in the city largely took place in the 1860s and 1870s. By 1880, photography was embedded in Salisbury and widely employed to record the city, its inhabitants, architecture and social activities. Ironically, one of the key issues facing this study has been the paucity of examples of many of these mid-Victorian photographs identified through printed sources. Perhaps one outcome of this study will be that such photographs may surface and thereby provide a fuller picture of the medium's rise in the city.

1 The population of Salisbury recorded by the censuses undertaken during the period covered by this study are:

YEAR	POPULATION
1841	10,086
1851	11,657
1861	12,278
1871	12,903
1881	14,792

Source: https://history.wiltshire.gov.uk/community/getcensus.php?item=Salisbury
Variations in the figures between sources frequently depends on which wards have been included in the total, and also boundary changes.

2 John Chandler, *Endless Street: A History of Salisbury and Its People*, Hobnob Press, Salisbury, 1983 p. 137.

3 'Salisbury: Economic history since 1612', *A History of the County of Wiltshire*: Volume 6, ed. Elizabeth Crittall, Victoria County History, London, 1962 pp. 129–132.

4 *Some Account of the Blackmore Museum – Part I. The Opening Meeting*, H.F. &E. Bull, Devizes; Bell & Daldy, London ; J.R. Smith, London 1868 p. 35.

5 Dan Bogart, Leigh Shaw Taylor and Xuesheng You, 'The development of the railway network in Britain 1825–1911' in *The Online Historical Atlas of Transport, Urbanization and Economic Development in England and Wales c.1680–1911.* https://www.geog.cam.ac.uk/research/projects/transport/onlineatlas/railways.pdf

6 Slade, J. J. 'Wiltshire Newspapers: Past and Present. Part I.', *WAM*, No. CXXVII, Vol. XL, December 1917 pp. 37–74.

7 Mrs Herbert Richardson, 'The Old "Salisbury Journal" and early newspaper enterprise in Salisbury' in Frank Stevens (ed.), *The Festival Book of Salisbury. Published to commemorate the Jubilee of the Museum.* Salisbury, South Wilts & Blackmore Museum, Salisbury, 1914 pp. 83–98. Richardson subsequently published several articles on the newspapers of Wiltshire in *WAM*. These are listed in the bibliography.

8 Advertisements in the *SJ* may provide a *terminus post quem*. However, quite how early photographers in Salisbury advertised and marketed their businesses remains to be established. For instance, printed notices might be placed in the windows of accommodating shops; business cards might be distributed; and word of mouth could also be effective.

9 *SJ*, Monday 8th February 1839 p. 2.

1 PICTURE MAKING IN SALISBURY BEFORE PHOTOGRAPHY

SALISBURY HAD PROVIDED a suitable source for illustrations for a number of publications dating back to before the c. 1672 views of the cathedral made by Wenceslaus Hollar (1607–1677).[1] In the years leading up to the announcements in 1839 of the respective photographic processes of Daguerre and Talbot the city had not established a picture-making industry of any significance. There was no heritage in the matrix of professions involved in image making; professional artists, engravers, etchers, plate makers, lithographers and graphic arts printers.

Evidence in the *SJ* points to there being no resident portrait artists – 'limners' or 'miniaturists' – during the first decades of the 19th century. Visiting miniature portrait painters advertised in the newspaper, some displaying their works in the premises of Brodie & Dowding in the Canal. In 1820 'Mr. Gray', describing himself as 'Artist, Portrait and Miniature Painter, & Drawing-Master, a Student the Royal Academy and British Institution', set himself up in business in Rollestone Street.[2] It is unclear whether Gray's business flourished, and no other advertisement subsequently appeared in the *SJ*.

In June 1840, a mere year after the announcements of the photographic processes of Daguerre and Talbot, M. H. Froste, SRA [*sic*] of Edinburgh, advertised that he would make 'excellent likenesses, in a bold, free, accurate Style, suitable for Miniature-frame, Scrap-book, or Album'. He had set up a temporary studio at Mrs Ann Nicklen's, High Street milliners and dress makers.[3] Froste's published charges are significant in that they act as a benchmark for those Salisbury citizens who would in the next few years be considering having their photographic portrait taken.

Coloured Profiles, on Board...7s. 6d.
Highly finished...10s. 6d.
Front Face, large size, on Board... £1 1s.
Miniatures of Ivory, front face...£1 11s. 6d.
Portraits in Oil, cabinet size...£3 3s.

From around 1844 Walter Francis Tiffin (1817–1890), was active in Salisbury as a miniaturist and landscape painter, exhibiting two landscapes at the Royal Academy in 1844, and miniatures at the Royal Academy, the British Institution and the Suffolk Street Gallery from 1844 to 1867. Tiffin is significant in that he was to adopt and adapt photographs to create his work, specifically a view of the Peace Pageant held in May 1856 to celebrate the conclusion of the Crimean War. This is discussed in more detail in Chapter 5, on applications of photography.

Frederick Tatham (1805–1878), an English artist who was a member of the Shoreham Ancients, a group of followers of William Blake, advertised in the *SJ* in August 1846 that 'after the Season is over in London' he would be visiting Wiltshire and Dorsetshire and offer 'portraits in water colours, miniatures, locket portraits, &c.'[4] Tatham appears to be just one of the itinerant artists who plied their trade in the provinces during the 1840s, though quite how much competition these artists faced from the earliest photographers is unclear.

Architectural and topographical views of Salisbury also offered publishing opportunities during the early decades of the 19th-century. There were several publications of the English antiquary, author and editor John Britton (1771–1857) that documented the cathedral and the city. The first two volumes of *The Beauties of Wiltshire* by Britton were published in 1801.[5] Volume one included an engraving of the west front of the cathedral and volume two an exterior view from the east end. Both were frontispiece engravings by James Sargant Storer (1771–1853) after drawings by Britton.

Another example is *Britton's Picturesque Antiquities of English Cities* published from 1819,

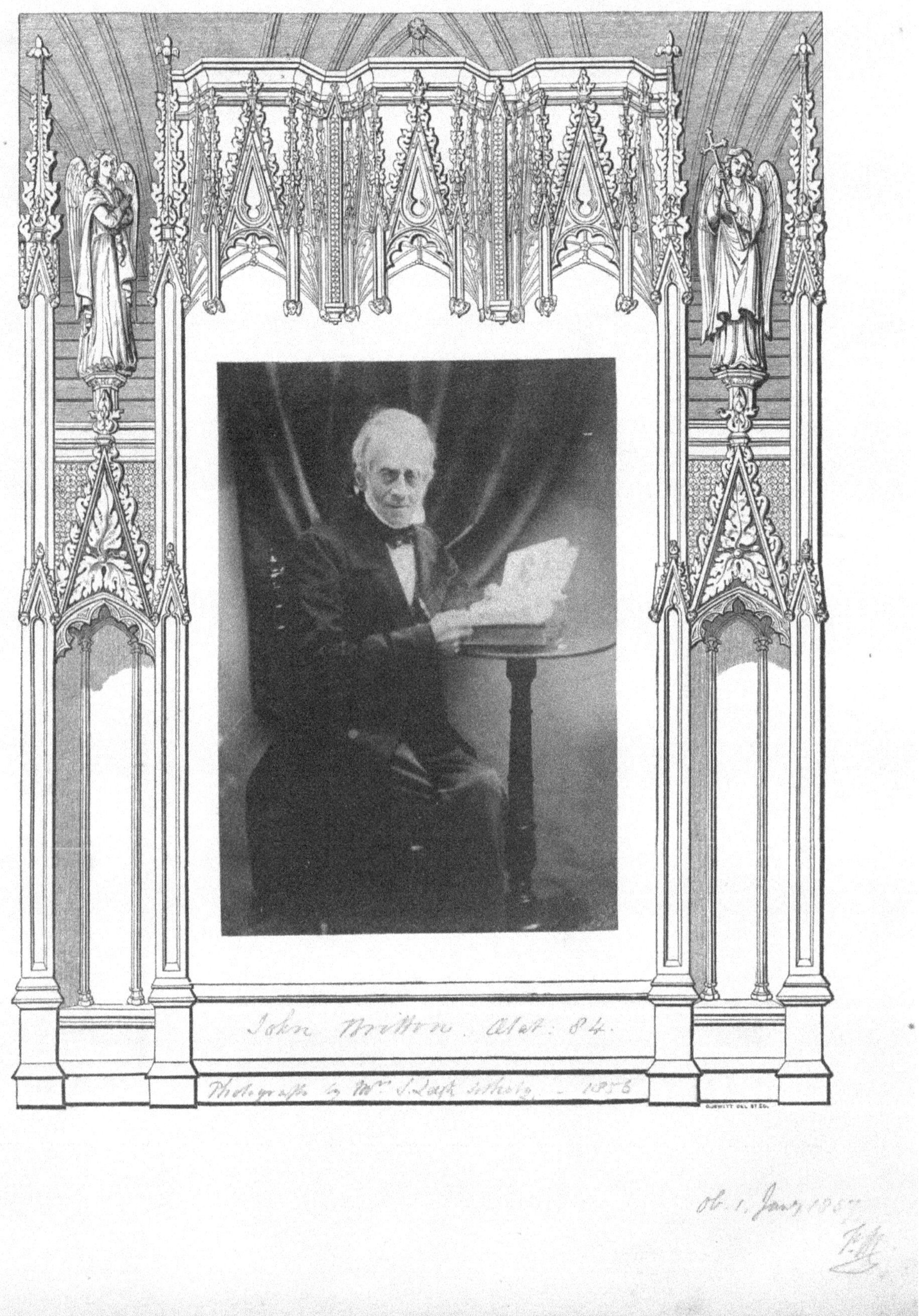

Julia Emma Sotheby. Portrait of the antiquary John Britton. July 1856. Albumen print. The frame is taken from the title page of Britton's *Architectural Antiquities of England and Wales*. The Salisbury Museum.

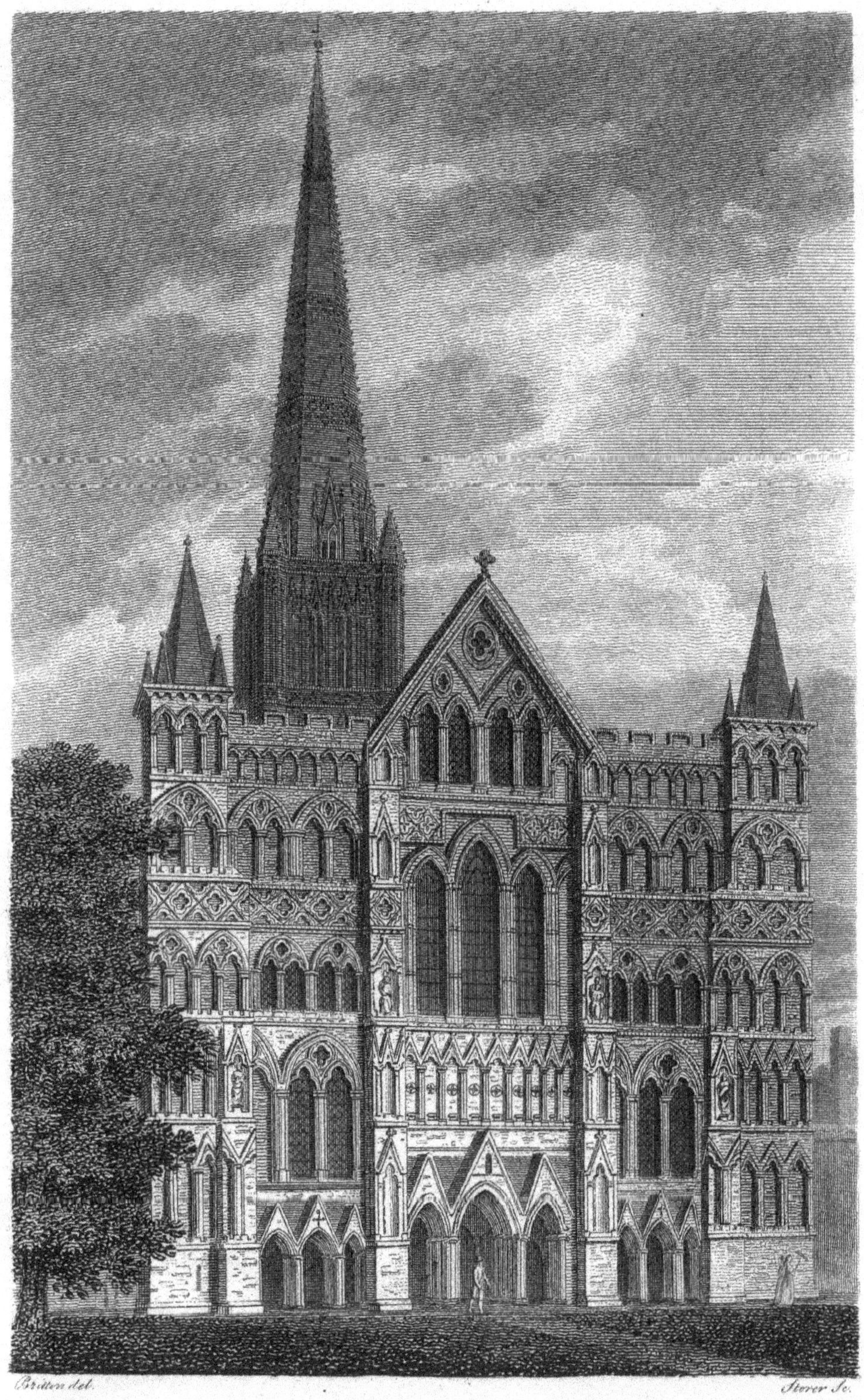

Salisbury Cathedral West Front. 1801. Copper plate engraving by James Storer after a drawing by John Britton. Dated April 1801 from *The Beauties of England and Wales: or Delineations Topographical, Historical and Descriptive.* Vol. I. London, 1801. Anthony Hamber collection.

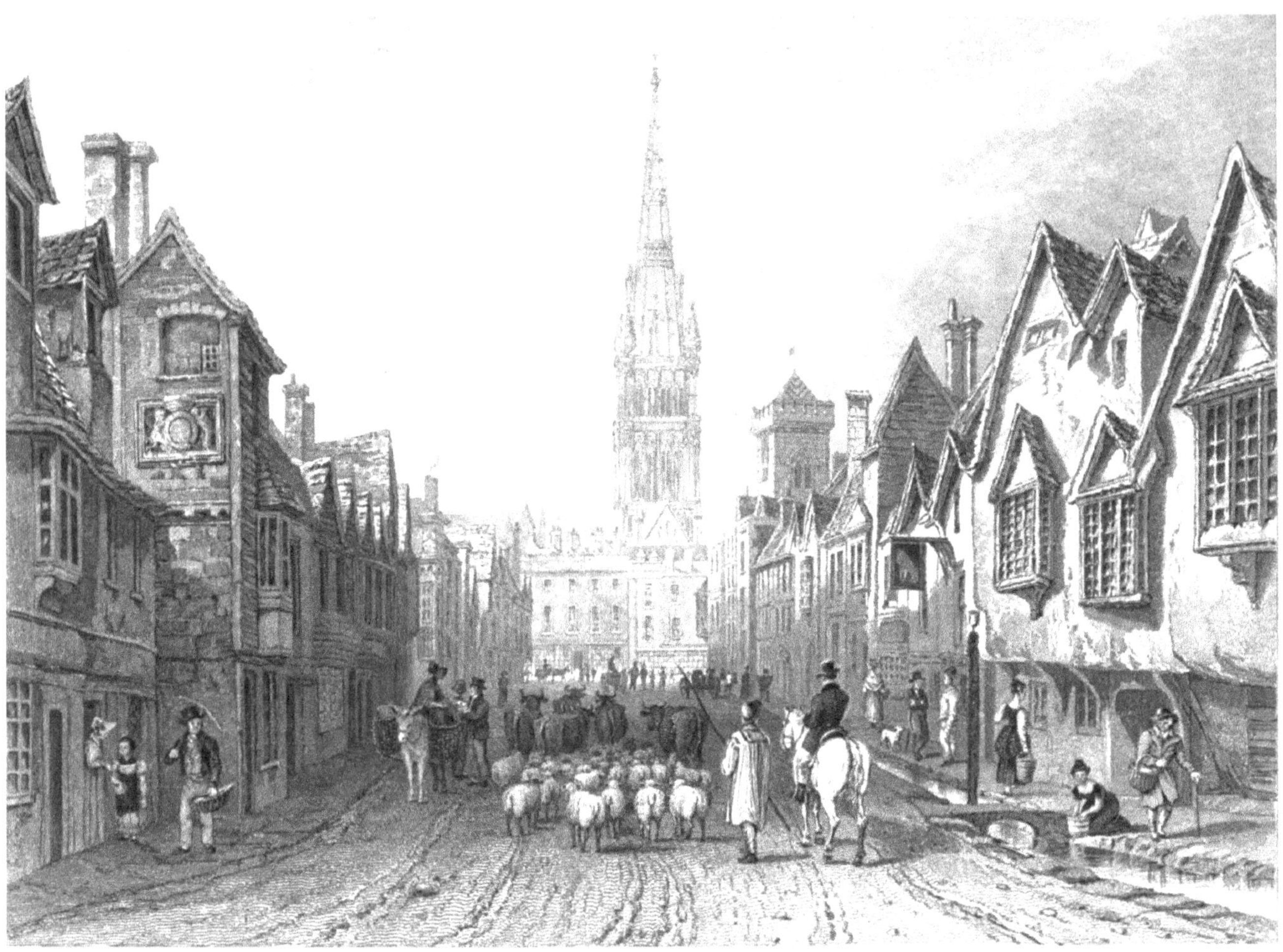

View in Castle Street, looking South. Etching by John Charles Varrall after a drawing by William Henry Bartlett. From John Britton, *Picturesque Antiquities of the English Cities,* M. A. Nattali, London, 1836. Private collection.

which included an etched view by John Charles Varrall (1795–1855) of the cathedral from Castle Street after a drawing by William Henry Bartlett (1809–1854), one of the foremost illustrators of topography of his generation. However, such publications were often not the result of the work of local artists, engravers or printers.

Joseph Mallord William Turner (1775–1851) first visited Salisbury in 1795 and he subsequently received a commission from the local antiquarian Sir Richard Colt Hoare (1758–1838). Turner made watercolour views of buildings in the city, including St Edmund's church, the Council House, the unrestored Poultry Cross, and another ten of the exterior and interior of the cathedral.[6] A view of the city from Old Sarum engraved by William Radclyffe (1783–1855) illustrated *Picturesque Views in England and Wales,* published between 1827 and 1838.

William Dodsworth (*c.*1761–1826) was the cathedral verger and in 1792 his unillustrated *A Guide to the cathedral church of Salisbury* was first published, being printed by Benjamin Collins. It ran into several editions by the end of the decade. In 1814 his landmark book *An Historical Account of the Episcopal See, and Cathedral church, of Sarum, or Salisbury: comprising biographical notices of the bishops; the history of the establishment, from the earliest period; and a description of the monuments. Illustrated with engravings* was published. It forms an important milestone in the study of the cathedral and had been printed by the local printer Brodie and Dowding for the author. Containing twenty-one engraved plates by sixteen engravers it was described in a contemporary study as 'by far the most accurate, complete, and even elegant [publication], which has hitherto appeared.'[7] This publication, a copy of which was presented to Queen Victoria in 1856 when she visited the city, became another potential template for views that the first generation of photographers might consider following. It was, however, a *deluxe*

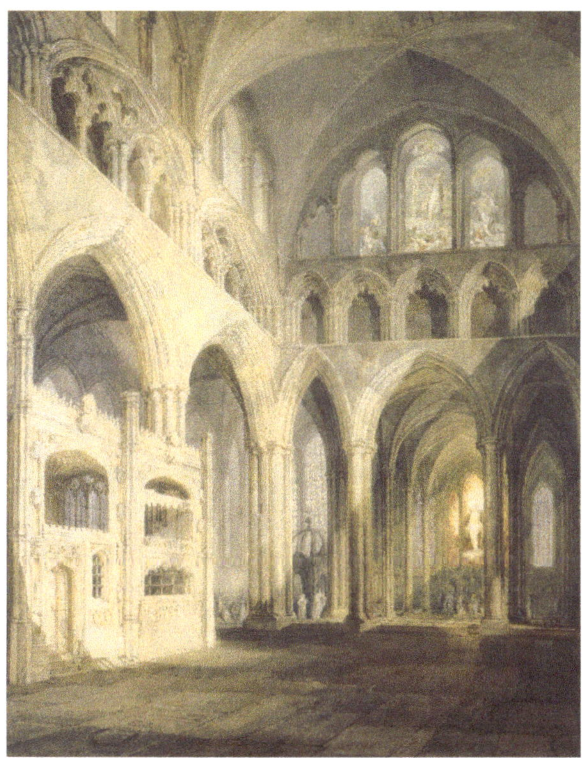

Joseph Mallord William Turner, Choir and Lady Chapel, Salisbury Cathedral. 1797. Watercolour. The Salisbury Museum.

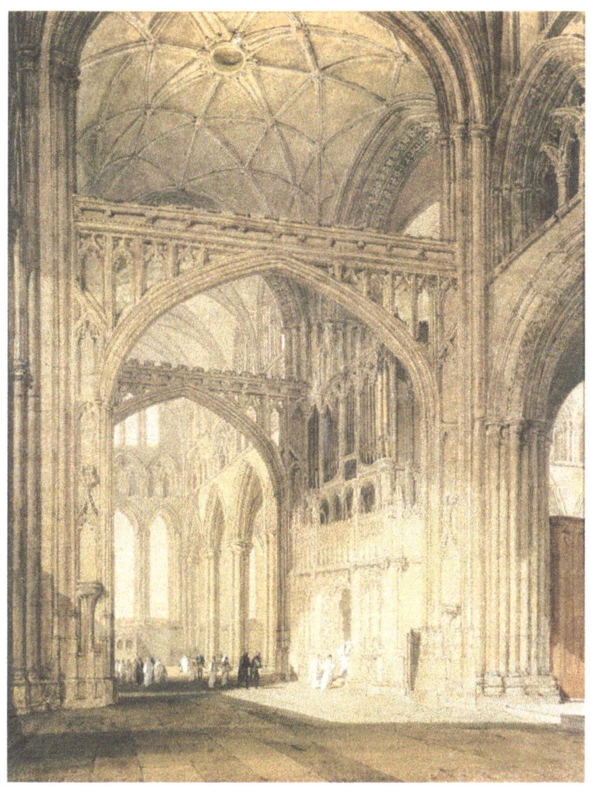

Joseph Mallord William Turner, Interior of Salisbury Cathedral, Looking towards the North Transept. 1802–1805. Graphite and watercolour on paper. The Salisbury Museum.

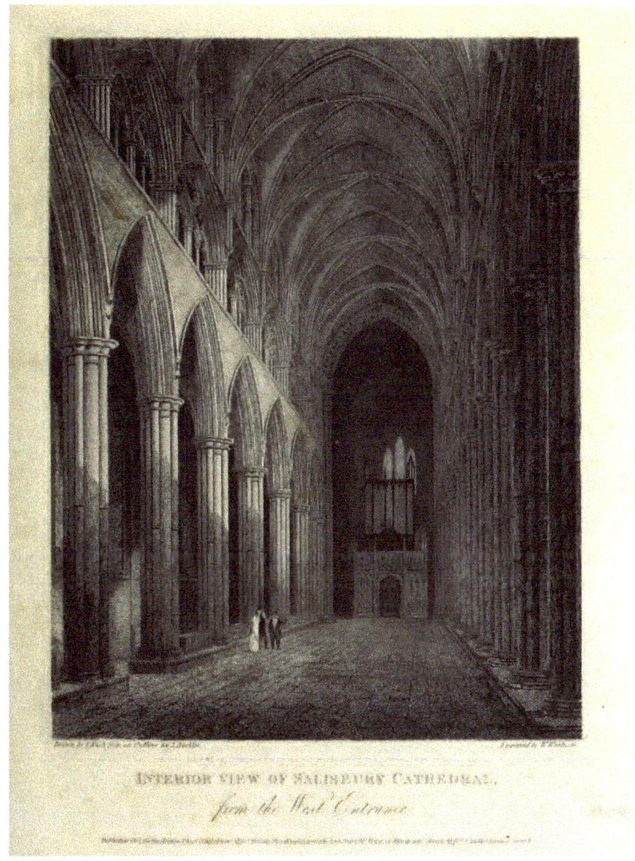

Interior View of Salisbury Cathedral, from the West Entrance. Engraving by William Woolnoth after a drawing by John Nash. 1812. From William Dodsworth, *An Historical Account of the Episcopal See, and Cathedral church, of Sarum, or Salisbury*, Printed by Bennet and Dowding for the Author, Salisbury, 1812. Private collection.

publication which appeared in several formats;

Royal 4to	£3 13s. 6d.
Imperial 4to	£6 6s.
Imperial 4to, India proofs	£8 8s.
Atlas 4to, gilt leaves	£10 10s.

The cost of production necessitated the securing pre-publication of around 650 hundred subscribers. These included the Prince Regent, the Prince Royal of Bavaria and numerous members of the British aristocracy. John Britton subscribed for two copies while George Hayter, Clerk of the Works at Fonthill Abbey, subscribed for no fewer than six copies.[8]

Guide books provide another insight to the available prints of the city and its environs. As early as 1770 James Easton (d. 1839) had begun publishing annually his *The Salisbury Guide* as early as 1770. It was not extensively illustrated. The thirty-first edition of 1830 was priced at 2s. 6d. and contained three very crude woodcuts; one of the West front of the cathedral, a view of the Council House and one of the Poultry Cross. An insight into the availability of images of the city was provided through an advertisement for eight prints of Salisbury and environs; a view of the cathedral by the artist, architect and antiquary John Buckler (1770–1851), probably dating to *c.*1816, cost 10s., though the remainder cost either 1s. or 6d. each.

PRINTS.

North-West View of Salisbury Cathedral, by Buckler.—10s.
North-East View of ditto, and Belfry.—6s.
North View of Salisbury Cathedral, quarto.—1s.
North-East and South-West Views of Stonehenge, 1s. each.
Three small Views of ditto, printed together.—6d.
West View of Salisbury Cathedral, and Poultry-Cross.—6d.
South-East View of Old Sarum in its present State, and the Castle as in the Reign of King Stephen.—6d.
Antient Coins found at Old Sarum.—1s.

Advertisement from *The Salisbury Guide*, James Easton, Salisbury, 1830. Private collection.

W. B. Brodie and Co., of the Canal, was the leading publisher of locally produced engravings and prints during the 1830s. Peter Hall's *Picturesque Memorials of Salisbury. A Series of Original Etchings and Vignettes Illustrative of the most Interesting Buildings and Other Remains of Antiquity. To which is prefixed A Brief History of the Old and New Sarum by The Rev. Peter Hall. With 28 copper-engravings of views* was published by subscription by Brodie in ten parts from January 1832, and then issued as a complete volume in 1834. J. Fisher, of Salisbury, engraved a number of the plates after his own drawings and those of J. Biddlecomb. There were also etchings by C. Castle. The work was issued in a variety of formats; Plain and India 4to, and also India Folio. An 1854 advertisement in the *Wiltshire Archaeological and Natural History Magazine* (WAM) stated that the title – 'proof impressions on India paper, large paper' - had been published at £4 10s.[9] In 1874 Brown and Co, the successor to Brodie and Co., was selling the book for 12s. 6d.

The selection of subject matter to illustrate confirmed, in Hall's mind at least, the 'most Interesting Buildings' in the city 'not only to preserve a faithful record of the venerable remains of Salisbury, as they at present stand, but to rescue from oblivion many traces of beauty and curiosity, which the lapse of ages, the fluctuations of taste, and the love of comfort and convenience, have already swept away.'[10] Hall's selection may have influenced subsequent photographers. The views include:

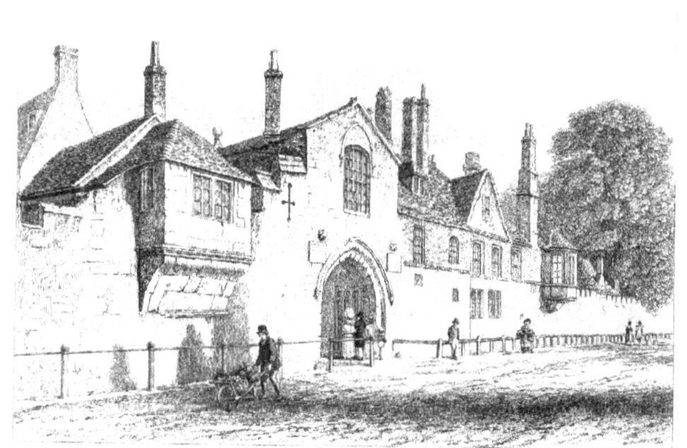

St. Anne's Gate, Copper plate engraving. From Peter Hall, *Picturesque Memorials of Salisbury. A Series of Original Etchings and Vignettes Illustrative of the most Interesting Buildings and Other Remains of Antiquity. To which is prefixed A Brief History of the Old and New Sarum by The Rev. Peter Hall. With 28 copper-engravings of views*, W. B. Brodie and Co., Salisbury, 1832–1834. Private collection.

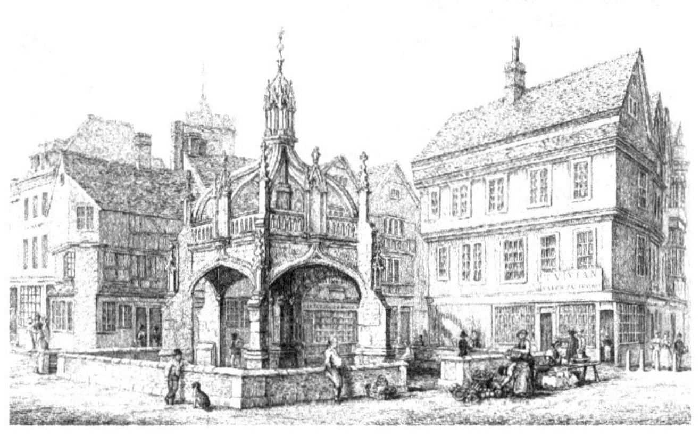

The Poultry Cross, proposed restoration design. Copper plate engraving. Peter Hall, *Picturesque Memorials of Salisbury. A Series of Original Etchings and Vignettes Illustrative of the most Interesting Buildings and Other Remains of Antiquity. To which is prefixed A Brief History of the Old and New Sarum by The Rev. Peter Hall. With 28 copper-engravings of views*, W. B. Brodie and Co., Salisbury, 1832–1834. Private collection

St. Anne's Gate
St Martin's Church
Joiner's Hall exterior
The Work House, Crane Street
The Poultry Cross, proposed restoration design
The interior of Halle of John Halle (referred to as 'Ancient Refectory on the Canal')
The Bishop's Palace
Harnham Gate
View of St Anne's Street, looking towards the Cathedral
The Council Chamber

together with exterior views of several local parish churches.

Brodie and Co. were uncredited co-publishers of *Winkles's Architectural and Picturesque Illustrations of The Cathedral Churches of Great Britain* published in 1836. Issue numbers 1 and 2 contained six views of Salisbury Cathedral drawn and engraved by Henry Winkles (1801–1860) and Benjamin Winkles (1805–1856).

A significant consideration is that none of these publications were aimed at a mass market. They were expensive and had limited print runs. Hall's *Picturesque Memorials of Salisbury* was published by subscription. The printed list of subscribers numbered a total of 467 and included many citizens of Salisbury, local nobility such as the Earl of Pembroke and the Earl and Countess of Radnor, together with the Archbishop of Canterbury, the Bishop of Winchester, and more far-flung individuals, such as James Woolls of Kingston, Jamaica and William Woolls of Sidney, Australia.

Antiquarian recording of the antiquities of Salisbury was also undertaken by local amateurs, and one of the most significant was Elizabeth Wickens (*c.*1788–1866), a rich spinster listed as a 'fundholder' in the 1851 census. She lived at 25 The Close, in Rosemary Lane off the North Walk. The house was the first home of the Godolphin School from 1784 to 1788. Wickens was an amateur topographical artist who had a 'zeal in antiquarian research in relation to Salisbury.'[11] One of her projects was to record 'Remains of Antiquity in the City of Salisbury. All Drawn on the Spot.' Sufficiently skilled as an artist, she was confident enough to submit work to the Royal Academy. She helped document important architecture of Salisbury that was disappearing as a result of urban development.

Quite when Elizabeth Wickens began to record her native city is unclear though her initial recognition seems to have been for her drawing the doom painting in St Thomas's church after it was initially uncovered in 1819, following centuries under whitewash. In his 1834 history of Salisbury, Henry Hatcher stated of this painting;

> This curious painting has been rescued from oblivion, by the correct and ready pencil of Miss. Wickens of the Close. To this Lady, who to many elegant accomplishments, adds an enlighted taste for antiquities, the public are indebted for graphic representations of many architectural remains, now destroyed.[12]

Her sketch was subsequently engraved and published in Hatcher's *The History of Modern Wiltshire. vol.1, Old and new Sarum, or Salisbury* of 1843.

Wickens continued to document the city and at the 1854 WANHS meeting held in Salisbury she exhibited at the Temporary Museum held on 13th September in the Council Chamber:

> Volume containing a large number of drawings of antiquities in Salisbury and the neighbourhood.
> Copy of an ancient Fresco Painting in St. Thomas' Church, Salisbury, representing the Last Judgment.

In 1860 it was noted in *WAM* that Elizabeth Wickens had donated a photograph of her drawing of the painting in St Thomas's to the library of the WANHS.[13] The identity of the photographer of this photograph was has yet to be established.

From the early 1830s there was a growing movement towards cheap illustrated periodicals aimed at the working classes and illustrated with wood engravings. *The Penny Magazine* commenced publication in March 1832 and ran until October 1845. It was published by Charles Knight (1791–1873), one of the most prominent English publishers of the mid-Victorian era, for the Society for the Diffusion of Useful Knowledge. Extraordinarily successful, it was selling over 200,000 copies in 1832, with an estimated nearly one million readers. The use of illustration was key to its success as many of its working-class readership were illiterate. In 1841 it was estimated that over

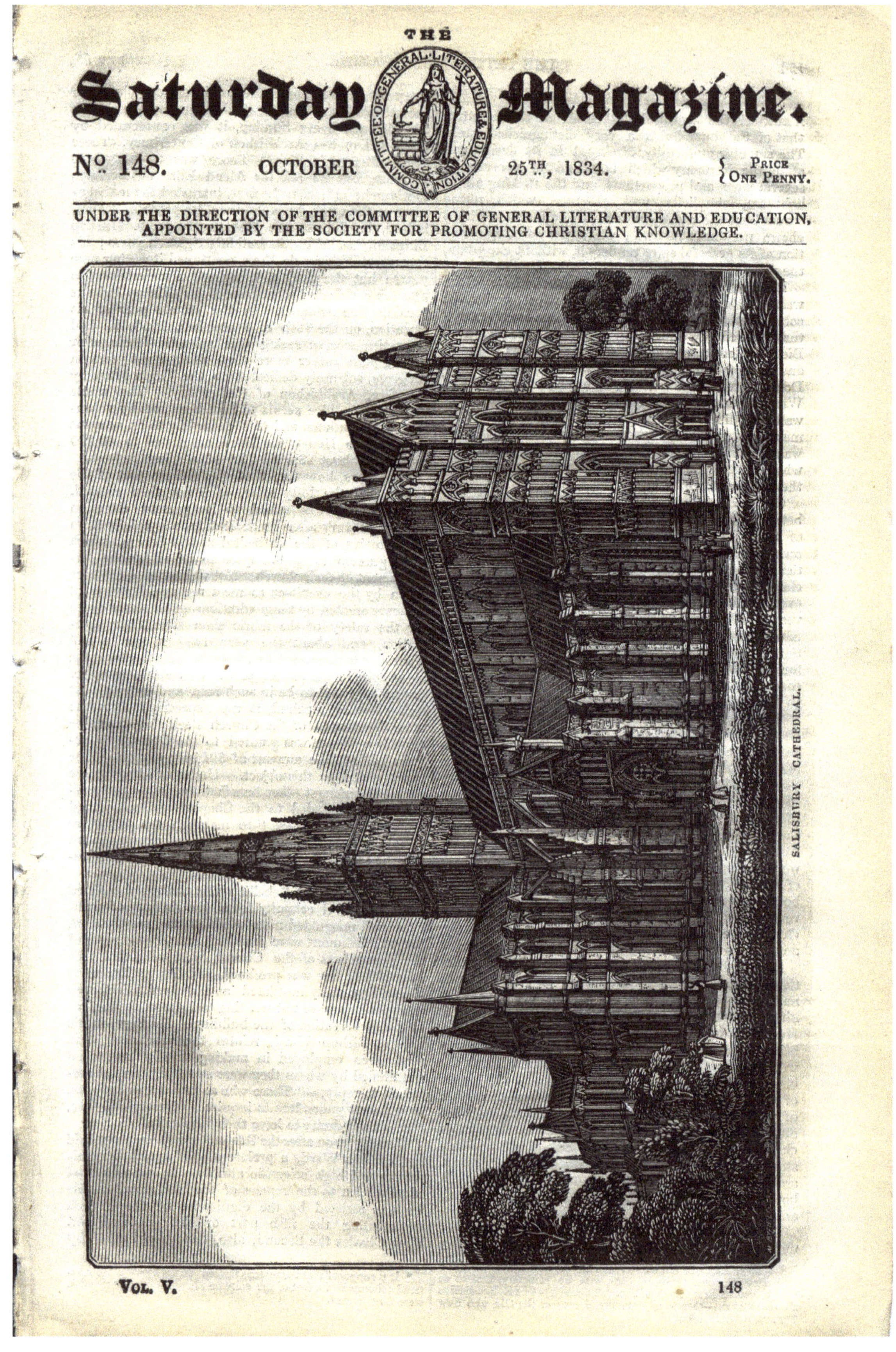

THE
Saturday Magazine.

COMMITTEE OF GENERAL LITERATURE & EDUCATION

Nº 148. OCTOBER 25TH, 1834. { PRICE ONE PENNY.

UNDER THE DIRECTION OF THE COMMITTEE OF GENERAL LITERATURE AND EDUCATION, APPOINTED BY THE SOCIETY FOR PROMOTING CHRISTIAN KNOWLEDGE.

SALISBURY CATHEDRAL.

VOL. V. 148

Salisbury Cathedral. Wood engraving by Mary Byfield. Front cover of *The Saturday Magazine,* 25th October 1834 p. 148. Anthony Hamber collection

30% of males and nearly 50% of females were still illiterate.[14]

The Saturday Magazine commenced publication in July 1832 and ran until December 1844. It was an Anglican church rival to *The Penny Magazine*, being published by the Committee of General Literature sponsored by the Society for Promoting Christian Knowledge. It was widely sold, including by the bookseller Brodie in the Canal. Both magazines included full page illustrations of Salisbury Cathedral in early issues.[15]

Another family business in Salisbury that published both illustrated books and loose prints was that of the Clappertons. Kenneth Clapperton (*c*.1793–1859), a bookseller, bookbinder, printer, publisher and manufacturer of picture frames, traded in the city from 1820 when he bought premises in Catherine Street. He launched the short-lived *Wiltshire Standard* newspaper in 1833, and in the following year Clapperton published, together with Whittaker & Co. of London, the Salisbury historian Henry Hatcher's *An historical and descriptive account of Old and New Sarum, or Salisbury,* though it was unillustrated. During the 1850s Clapperton published several views of Salisbury and was to play a significant role in the development of photography in the city, selling photographs and acting as a photographic publisher.

Booksellers, Stationers and Printers

Trade directories provide some insights into the professions operating in Salisbury that created and sold images of the city. *Pigot's Commercial Directory* of 1822 lists several Salisbury 'Booksellers, Stationers and Printers' collected under one heading:

Brodie & Dowding, (& publishers, &c. of the Salisbury & Winchester Journal, Sunday) Canal

Fellowes, Charles.	Catharine Street
Gilmour, James A.	Market Place
Holloway, James H.	Catharine Street
Wilks, Richard.	Market Place

The 1841 census gives some indication of those involved in creating printed images in Salisbury during the earliest years of photography. Thomas Burrough (born in 1786), living in Blue Boar Row, was described as an 'engraver.' Elizabeth McCullam (born in 1816) was listed as a 'Stationer & Engraver', together with Reuben Nichols (born in 1826), cited as an 'engraver.' Both were living at the same address in the High Street. William Halpin of Silver Street, who had been born in Ireland in 1796, was listed as a 'printer'. In the Close we find the 'printer' Francis Gilmore (born in 1821) whose premises were in the High Street.

Pigot's Commercial Directory for 1842 separates 'Booksellers & Stationers' from 'Printers':

BOOKSELLERS & STATIONERS.

Brodie, Wm. Bird & Co.	New Canal
Clapperton, Kenneth.	Catherine Street
Cullam, Elizabeth.	(stationer) High Street
Gilmour, Francis.	High Street
Hearn, John.	(and library) Queen Street
Pittman, Charles Henry.	(stationer) Silver Street
Saunders, Thomas Aubry.	(& circulating library) Winchester Street

PRINTERS - LETTER-PRESS.

Brodie, Wm. Bird, & Charles George.	(and stamp office) New Canal
Clapperton, Kenneth.	Catherine Street
Cullam, Elizabeth.[16]	High Street
Hearn, John.	Queen Street
Gilmour, Francis.	High Street

What is significant is that these printers are listed as offering 'letter-press' services, that is printing texts and stationery. This suggests that commercial services offering 'fine-art' printing of graphic images were not available, or well established, in Salisbury.

That Salisbury lacked commercial printing services to print graphic fine art images is evidenced by the career of David Charles Read (1790–1851), an English painter and etcher who lived and worked in Salisbury from 1820 until 1845. Read primarily used the dry-point etching process to make his own plates. He sent his earliest plates to be printed in London, but then obtained a press and made the impressions himself. Read created a significant number of etchings, and in 1832 W. B.

Brodie & Co. published *A catalogue of etchings, after his own designs, by D. C. Read: dedicated to his friends, and the lovers of the fine arts: to which are appended, extracts from the letters of Göethe, and other distinguished individuals.* This twenty-four page catalogue was presumably a form of marketing tool, though Read sold few of his etchings. One of his 'friends' was the artist John Constable who, while initially supportive of a struggling artist and his aspirations, by 1823 was to write to Bishop John Fisher (1748–1825), 'the truth...is that he [Read] is ignorant of every rudiment of art – without one grain of original feeling – without one atom of talent.'[17] Read presented to the British Museum in 1833 and 1842, two volumes containing 168 of his etchings. In 1845, however, he destroyed sixty-three of his plates; the rest were destroyed by his family after his death in London in 1851.

The scale of amateur artists, draughtsmen, engravers, etchers, and lithographers active in and around Salisbury in the decades immediately before the advent of photography remains to be established. This cohort acts as a link with those who were to become professional and amateur photographers in the city during the 1850s. As will be shown, while traditional graphic illustration – both in terms of illustrated publications and loose prints – continued to be a significant activity during the second half of the 19th century, photography introduced a new commercial market and had a fundamental impact on expanding existing image making in the city.

1 Richard Pennington, *A Descriptive Catalogue of the Etched Work of Wenceslaus Hollar 1607–1677*, Cambridge University Press, Cambridge, 1982 p. xxxvii. Hollar's view of Salisbury Cathedral appeared in William Dugdale, *Monasticon Anglicanum*, Vol. III, London, 1673, p. 375.
2 *SJ*, Monday 12th June 1820 p. 4.
3 *SJ*, Monday 15th June 1840 p. 4. See *Pigot and Co.'s Royal National and Commercial Directory...*, I. Slater, London, and Manchester, June 1844, p. 33.
4 *SJ*, Saturday 1st August 1846 p. 1.
5 [John Britton], *The Beauties of Wiltshire displayed in Statistical, Historical, and Descriptive Sketches*, Vernor and Hood; J. Wheble, J Britton, London, 1801.
6 Ian Warrell, *Turner's Wessex: Architecture and Ambition*, The Salisbury Museum, Salisbury, 2015 p. 48 and Appendix pp. 184–193.
7 *History and Antiquities of the Cathedral Churches of Great Britain*, Rivingtons; Murray; Hatchard; Clarke; Taylor; and Sherwood, Neely, and Jones, London, 1814, vol. II., [p. 7.]
8 See https://www.salisburycathedral.org.uk/news/many-versions-dodsworths-history by Dawn Wilson.
9 *WAM*, Henry Bull; G. Bell, Devizes; London, 1854, vol. 1.
10 This quotation, from a positive review that appeared in *The Literary Gazette and Journal of Belles Lettres*, Saturday 14th January 1832 p. 27, appears to have been part of a text used to market the publication and may have been on the paper wrapper of the first part.
11 Thomas Joseph Pettigrew 'On the Antiquities of Wiltshire', *Journal of the British Archaeological Association*, J. R. Smith, London, 1859 p. 20.
12 Henry Hatcher, *An Historical and Descriptive Account of Old and New Sarum, or Salisbury*, Walter Clapperton; Whittaker & Co, Salisbury; London, 1834 p. 90.
13 *WAM*, Henry Bull; G. Bell, Devizes; London, 1860, vol. 6., p. 120.
14 Sally Mitchell, *Daily Life in Victorian England.* Greenwood Publishing Group, Westport, 1996 p. 166.
15 *The Penny Magazine* had a full-page wood engraving on the front cover of the issue for 22nd June 1833.
16 Elizabeth Cullam (née Nichols), had married John Cullam, an engraver of Catherine Street, in 1833. He died in 1841, and was described as a 'very clever and ingenious man.' *SJ*, Monday 24th May 1841 p. 4.
17 Letter dated 1st February 1823. R. B. Beckett (ed.), *John Constable's Correspondence - VI - The Fishers*, Suffolk Records Society, Volume XII, 1968 p. 108.

2 PHOTOGRAPHY AND SALISBURY IN THE 1840S

DURING THE 1840S news of the application and advance of photography was to be found in the columns of national newspapers such as *The Times* and *Morning Chronicle*, and periodicals such as the *Athenæum* and *Art-Union* (from 1849 retitled the *Art-Journal*). More locally, relatively detailed explanations of Talbot's calotype process appeared in the *Wiltshire Independent* in October 1842.[1]

Establishing the actual level of interest shown in photography by readers in Salisbury and any photographic activity in the city during this decade has yet to be established. There were significant and diverse mentions of the medium in the editorial columns of the *SJ* and this points to interest by the editor, who perhaps considered the readership had either expressed an interest or were likely to be attracted to such news.

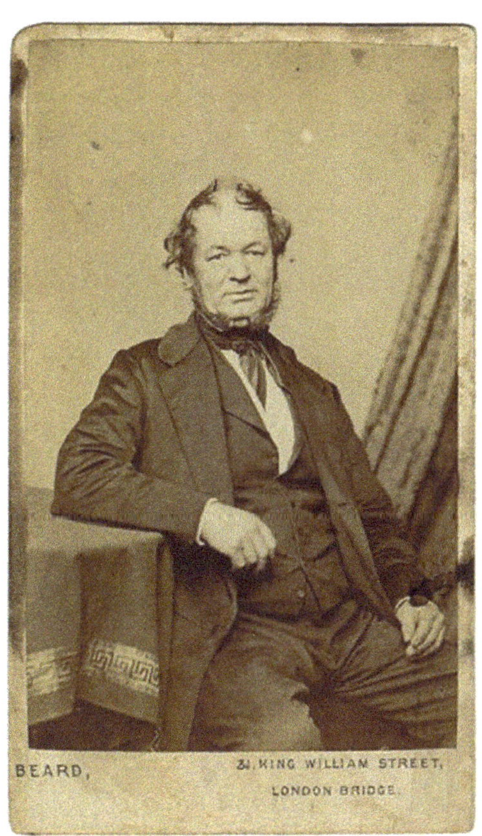

Studio of Richard Beard. Portrait of Richard Beard. c. 1860s. Carte de visite. Albumen print. Courtesy of Professor Geoffrey Batchen.

It seems likely that there were amateur photographers in Salisbury during the 1840s. These were a hallmark of the rise of the medium during this and the following decade. Unfortunately, we know little about those citizens of Salisbury and its environs who experimented with the metal-based daguerreotype and paper-based calotype (also known as talbotype) process. Who they were and what they photographed remains to be discovered. A portrait photograph of James Oates and his family of Britford dated to 1847 has been previously published. However, examination of the Oates family details found in the censuses of 1841 and 1851 indicates that the photograph is more likely to date to around 1852.[2]

What can be said with some confidence, is that there was only one commercial photographer active in the city during the 1840s, and this studio failed almost immediately. However, as discussed below, the photographer behind this studio was none other than Richard Beard (1802–1885), a London coal merchant and entrepreneur, who was a key player in the commercial development of daguerreotype portrait photography across England and Wales during the 1840s.

In the summer of 1840 Richard Beard began to prepare to develop what was to become a substantial commercial photography business. According to his first business partner, the American photographer John Johnson (1813–1871), Beard paid some £7,000 for the patent rights for England and Wales to use the first commercial portrait camera that had been developed by Johnson and his partner Alexander S. Walcott (1804–1844).[3] On 23rd March 1841 Beard opened the first commercial photographic studio in Great Britain on the roof of the Royal Polytechnic Institution overlooking Cavendish Square, London. Three months later, on 23rd June 1841, Beard purchased for £800 the patent rights for the daguerreotype, originally sealed by the patent agent Miles Berry in August 1839 as British Patent 8194. Almost immediately Beard was issuing licences for the establishment of photographic portrait studios outside London, either by county or by individual town. He attempted to charge over £1,000 for each licence, primarily in order to recoup his colossal initial outlay for patents. Those who were issued licences were required to indicate on their cases holding their daguerreotypes the fact that they were Beard's licensee. Towards the end of July 1841, William Bishop, a carver and gilder, opened England's first provincial photographic studio at his business premises at 44 Union Street, near the Royal Hotel, Plymouth, which in 1841 had a population of some 36,000.[4] By the end of 1841, Beard had licensed twelve other studios in towns including Bristol, Cheltenham, Liverpool, Nottingham, Southampton, Brighton, Bath, Manchester, Norwich and Guildford.

Beard attempted to consolidate his grip on commercial photography in England. Henry Talbot had been issued a patent for his paper calotype process. entitled 'Photographic Pictures', Patent No. 8,842, on 8th February 1841. In late 1841 Beard contacted Talbot, proposing that he act as Talbot's agent for issuing calotype licences for England, Wales and Berwick upon Tweed. Talbot's patent agent William Carpmael (1804–1867) met with Beard and opened negotiations. Carpmael went so far as to write out a complete contract, making Beard Talbot's agent for 14 years for England, Wales and Berwick upon Tweed.[5] However, by April 1842 Beard had been unable to agree what he considered a reasonable percentage of the licence fees to cover his costs, and he discontinued the negotiations.

The risks involved in setting up the earliest daguerreotype portrait studios are illustrated by the career of Alfred Barber (1809–1884). In October 1841 he set up a daguerreotype portrait studio in Bromley House in Nottingham.[6] A native of the town, Barber perhaps concluded that with a population in 1841 of some 52,164, his home town would be capable of sustaining his innovatory daguerreotype portrait business. Barber was asked by Beard to pay £1,200 for his daguerreotype licence: £500 to be paid immediately and the remainder in three quarterly instalments by Bills of Exchange of £240 each. With this method of payment, the total became £1,220. However, Barber's business was to fail, probably due to the gap between the hyperbole of Beard's sales pitch in terms of potential earning versus the actuality of the revenue generated. Beard sued Barber in late 1842 and early 1843 over his failure to pay the last instalments on the licence, and he also took legal action to stop Barber using the process. Michael Pritchard has postulated that during the 1840s a population of at least 30,000 was needed to support a permanent Beard daguerreotype licensee, with the exceptions being Cambridge, Oxford and Southampton, all of which had large visiting and transient populations which would have provided additional trade for a photographic studio.[7]There is, however, no simple characterisation of the relationship between population, demographics, disposable income and the prevailing economic situation underpinning the success or failure of the first studio photographers.

In the autumn of 1841, a licence for a daguerreotype studio in Southampton was issued by Beard to John Frederick Goddard (1797–1866), a lecturer and chemist. At this date Southampton had a population of 27,744, almost three times that of Salisbury, and this grew to 34,098 by 1851. The building of this studio, the Photographic Institution in Portland Terrace, commenced in November 1841, though it did not open until May the following year.[8] The studio seems to have been successful since, at the end of May, the *Hampshire Advertiser* reported, 'The number of visitors to the Photogenic and Daguerreotype Portrait Establishment, in Portland Terrace, has been very great.'[9] It remains unclear whether the term 'Photogenic' actually referred to Talbot's photographic process and that Goddard was using it. Goddard is known to have been trained by Talbot since on 8th April 1842 he had visited Talbot at his home, Lacock Abbey, and undertaken experiments with Talbot and Nicolaas Henneman.[10]

Goddard played a central role in establishing a number of photographic studios in Hampshire during the 1840s, largely due to his business relationship with Beard. A science lecturer at the Adelaide Gallery (also known as the National Gallery of Practical Science) in London, Goddard had been employed by Richard Beard and John Johnson, the co-designer of the camera used in Beard's early photographic studios, to improve the process. During the summer and autumn of 1840 Goddard experimented and began to take portraits, probably the first of their type in Great Britain. In December 1840 he introduced his modifications to the photochemistry of the daguerreotype that increased the sensitivity through the use of silver iodo-bromide. On 18th February 1841 Goddard exhibited portraits, including one of his father, at a meeting held at the Royal Society in London. Goddard became a camera operator in Beard's London studio and he may have been responsible for the initial set up of the studio, a role he appears to have filled in a number of other provincial daguerreotype studios set up as a result of Beard issuing a licence.[11]

Thus, by the time Goddard had purchased his licence to set up a studio in Southampton he had already acquired considerable knowledge of commercial photography from photo-scientific development work coupled to practical experience within the leading London photographic studio. He retained these contacts and in early 1843 was back in London managing the studio at the Royal Polytechnic Institution at 309 Regent Street. Goddard then set up a photographic business with the Jersey photographer Henry Mullins (1818–1880) around the beginning of August 1844. In 1847, while retaining control of the Southampton studio, Goddard then entered into partnership with Alfred Barber, the daguerreotype artist who had set up the first daguerreotype studio in Nottingham. A new studio at 48 Above Bar was constructed though may not have been a success, since by 1849 the Post Office Directory did not list either Goddard or Barber as being in business in Southampton though it did list a George Marks as having a daguerreotype studio on the premises of a booksellers and printers at 180 High Street. In March 1849 Marks announced that he had moved his studio to 68 Marland Place, a terrace on the west side of Above Bar.[12]

Wiltshire did not deliver commercial success for Richard Beard. It is relevant to examine the demographics of the county, mindful of Pritchard's 'population of 30,000' metric of sustainability. The censuses held during the period covered by this study indicate that there was no city or town in the county of a size anywhere near Pritchard's metric.

	1841	*1851*	*1861*	*1871*	*1881*
Salisbury	10,086	11,657	12,278	12,903	14,792
Trowbridge	11,050	11,148	10,487	11,672	11,040
Warminster	6,211	6,285	5,995	5,786	5,640
Devizes	4,631	6,554	6,638	6,839	6,645
Marlborough	3,391	3,908	3,684	3,660	3,343
Swindon	2,459	4,879	6,856	11,720	19,904

Figure: Tabulated population of the Salisbury and the most populous towns in Wiltshire as recorded in the censuses of 1841, 1851, 1861, 1871 and 1881.

We know something of Beard's proposed daguerreotype licence for Wiltshire since a copy of his three-page printed prospectus, titled *Photographic, or Daguerreotype Portraiture* survives in the archives of Henry Talbot held in the British Library.[13] This circular was addressed 'To Capitalists' for the licence to operate the daguerreotype process in Wiltshire, setting out terms that were '£700 down/£450 + 15% on gross receipts/£350 + 20% ditto'. It dates to 1842, the year in which Beard placed advertisements in local newspapers across England,

MR. BEARD'S PHOTOGRAPHIC, or DAGUERREOTYPE PORTRAITS! To SMALL CAPITALISTS. The above wonderful Invention, which is a momentary and simple process for taking Likenesses, unerringly true to nature—forming indeed exact *Reflections in Miniature*, full lengths, busts, and groups (coloured if required), with all the elaborate finish of Fine Engravings—offers, at the present time, a most eligible oppertunity to small and enterprising Capitalists in the purchase of the *USE of the PATENT* for provincial Cities, Towns, and Districts. From the immense known success of this Invention in London, It may readily be conceived that most extensive patronage will greet the introduction of the Patent into the Country. The amount of consideration for using the Daguerreotype Apparatus will be made dependent upon the populousness of the City, Town, or District applied for; but every reasonable facility will be afforded Purchasers, who will only be required to deposit one moiety of the sum agreed upon,—the other half to be secured upon actual profits made—or other arrangements, mutually advantageous, may be entered into. For full particulars, apply to MR. BEARD (the sole Patentee for Great Britain), at either of his London Establishments—Royal Polytechnic Institution, Regent Street; 34, Parliament Street, Westminster; or 85, King William Street, City, where the apparatus is daily worked.

The following form a few of the hundreds of eulogiums bestowed by the Press upon Mr. Beard's Daguerreotype Portraiture:—

"The likenesses are admirable, and closely true to nature."—*Times*.

"One of the most beautiful and gratifying inventions that has ever done honour to human ingenuity."—*Morning Herald*.

"The portraits taken by this means are really extraordinary likenesses."—*Morning Chronicle*.

"It is nature herself."—*Advertiser*.

"Altogether this is a most wonderful and extraordinary exhibition."—*Observer*.

"Every line, every touch in the picture produced, is from the pencil of nature without flattery or fallacy."—*Courier*.

"We were delighted with the exhibition."—*Court Journal*.

"It is bodily and personally the individual who is the sitter."—*Bell's Weekly Messenger*.

"The most incomparably perfect resemblance imaginable."—*Argus*.

"The effigy of a relative or friend delineated with such faithfulness, is indeed a treasure."—*Court Gazette*.

Advertisement for daguerreotype licenses by Richard Beard. *Gloucestershire Chronicle*, Saturday 25th June 1842 p. 1.

A PROFITABLE BUSINESS.

MR. BEARD, sole Patentee of the DAGUERREOTYPE, or PHOTOGRAPHIC PORTRAITURE, offers, upon terms highly advantageous to the purchaser, the EXCLUSIVE PATENT RIGHT, for the unexpired Term of 10 Years, to exercise the above much-admired Invention, in the whole or any part of the County of WILTS.

The unerring and incomparable fidelity, and beautiful effect which the recent valuable improvements impart to Photographic Portraits—the extensive patronage bestowed—the trifling cost of the productions (being obtained chiefly by the agency of light)—and the high ready-money prices it commands, are among the many features which commend this invention to the notice of those who may be desirous of a light genteel employment, or of blending such with any other pursuit.

85, *King William-street, City, London.* [1085

Advertisement by Richard Beard for the unexpired license for County of Wiltshire. *Salisbury Journal*, Saturday 20th April 1844 p. 1.

and sets out the basis for profitability, including notices for the public outlining the attractions of daguerreotype portraiture, giving prices and 10 extracts from press comments lauding the daguerreotype portrait.[14] Who acquired the licence is unknown and in April 1844 an advertisement by Richard Beard appeared in the *SJ* and the *Wiltshire Independent.* This was for the 10 years unexpired for the daguerreotype licence for 'the whole or any part of the county of Wilts.'[15] It is not clear whether Beard had previously sold a licence for Wiltshire to a third party which he had somehow regained or the term reflected the period left on his patent for the daguerreotype. However, Beard began placing regular advertisements for his London studio in the *SJ* from June 1846[16] and continued to do so in this newspaper up until the mid-1850s. His adverts also appeared in the *Wiltshire Independent* up to 1860, by which time he was about to give up his photography business. The 1861 census records him as describing his profession as a 'coal merchant.'

The year 1846 saw Richard Beard undertake a focussed campaign to develop commercial photographic studios in Hampshire and Wiltshire. The March 1846 editions of the *Hampshire Telegraph* included an advertisement for the photographic studio of Richard Dowle (1802–1869) at 13 King Street, Portsea Island, at that date incorporating Portsmouth, which in 1841 had a population of 53,036.[17] In Winchester in May of the same year, John Frederick Goddard and Alfred Barber announced their photographic 'Glass House' at

PHOTOGRAPHIC PORTRAIT-ROOMS, *CLOSE-GATE, HIGH-STREET, SALISBURY.*

MR. BEARD has the honour to announce, that at this Establishment the recent improvements of the Patentee are being fully carried out at moderate charges, and Amateurs instructed in the art at Two Guineas each.

Likenesses taken. Small sizes for Brooches, Lockets, &c.

By the Improved System, sitters are detained but a few seconds, and a truly faithful likeness is produced, defying the pencil of the most skilful artist for truthfulness, proportion, &c. [8833

Advertisement by Richard Beard for the Photographic Portrait-Rooms in the High Street. *Salisbury Journal*, Saturday 6th June 1846 p. 4.

No. 12 St. James's Terrace, Winchester.[18] While Winchester was already significantly larger than Salisbury and the census of 1851 indicated that the population was some 13,000, a figure that Salisbury (with a population in 1851 of 11,657) was only to achieve in 1871, it fell far short of the 30,000 figure considered by Pritchard to be the benchmark of sustainability.

The next stage in Beard's campaign was to include Salisbury. The first commercial photographic studio in Salisbury opened for business in June 1846. An advertisement in the *SJ* placed by Beard announced the Photographic Portrait Rooms, next to the Close Gate in the High Street. The advertisement did not name the resident photographer, and these Portrait Rooms may have been a Beard branch studio, rather than run by an independent licensee.[19] Portraits in small sizes for brooches and lockets were taken for 'moderate charges.' It is perhaps significant that Beard did not specify the prices charged, perhaps waiting to see what the nascent commercial photography market in Salisbury could sustain. Beard noted that 'sitters are detained but a few seconds, and a truly faithful likeness is produced, defying the pencil of the most skilful artist for truthfulness, proportion, &c.' Other services were available and 'Amateurs instructed in the art at Two Guineas each.' This studio appears to have failed immediately. Beard placed no more adverts for it in the *SJ* during the summer of 1846 and no other reference to this studio has been found. This single, enigmatic reference in the *SJ* seems to indicate that in 1846 there was not a sufficient market to support commercial photography in Salisbury, nor significant numbers of citizens who wished to learn photography. It is worth noting that in the same issue of the *SJ* announcing the High Street studio, Beard also advertised his London studio.

Alfred Barber represents an interesting case study since he had already experienced the challenges of setting up daguerreotype studios in a number of towns and cities and was to try and build trade from neighbouring Salisbury using an innovative tactic. Following the forced closure of his Nottingham studio, Barber had moved to the Channel Islands where the patent restrictions to take daguerreotypes did not strictly apply. There, a busy summer tourist trade from Southampton, coupled to a significant ex-patriot population, provided a reasonable living for Barber since he did not have to pay Beard for the exorbitant licence fees, and therefore could charge less for a portrait. In April 1843, three months after Beard's injunction against him, Barber advertised in the *Guernsey Star*. In September he announced his arrival in Jersey. He rather disingenuously stated his intention to operate a process 'precisely the same as Mr Beard's ... having purchased the right of using the patent.' Barber set up an 'Operating Room on the roof of Lozy's Hotel de Paris on the Pier' in St. Helier, on the site of the present-day Royal Yacht Hotel.[20] How long Barber remained in Jersey is unclear, though by 1846 he was back on mainland England, perhaps due to an invitation by Richard Beard.

In an attempt to entice Salisbury residents to his Winchester studio, in September 1847 Barber placed an advertising in the *SJ* in which he stated 'In order to afford the Inhabitants of Salisbury an opportunity of availing themselves of the unerring process in securing a faithful likeness, Mr Barber will deduct the Second Class Railway fare, One way, to all Parties taking a Coloured Portrait, on receiving One Day's notice, and a satisfactory Likeness guaranteed.' It is significant that Barber mentioned 'coloured' portraits, since these were premium products, being hand-coloured daguerreotypes affording a higher price, that could help offset the cost of a rail ticket from Salisbury. Barber also mentioned that his terms could be sought at Messrs Brodie and Co., of the Canal, where specimens of his work might also be seen.[21] Significantly, on the same page, there was a short editorial comment on Barber's advertisement and the quality of his portraits. 'We beg to recommend Mr. Barber and his establishment, satisfied that in doing so we are at once serving them and performing a duty in recommending to public notice a clever and deserving man.'[22] How many customers from Salisbury Barber may have received in his Winchester studio, or the temporary studio he set up in 1848 at Mr. Cottle's, bookseller, in Winchester Street, Basingstoke, remains unknown.[23] What seems clear is that in the later 1840s neither itinerant photographers nor photographers wishing to set up new permanent studios appeared to have considered Salisbury a

TO PERSONS VISITING LONDON.
Portraits, Landscapes, Copies of Paintings, &c., by the Agency of Light.

MR. BEARD'S recent IMPROVEMENTS in the DAGUERREOTYPE INVENTION have been honoured with the following among a variety of other notices by the leading public Journals:—

" We witnessed with great gratification the improvements Mr. Beard has lately effected."—*Morning Herald.*

" The Portraits are now fixed on the plate in all their natural hues of colour."—*Britannia.*

" They exhibit a degree of boldness, and stand out with a relief, greatly desiderated in all the earlier specimens."—*Times.*

" The fidelity of the likeness is wonderful, and the effect imparted by Mr. Beard's new process of colouring is extremely beautiful."—*Critic.*

" As Family Portraits, these Miniatures are invaluable."—*Church and State Gazette.*

Portraits taken daily from Nine till Six, and Licences to exercise the Invention in London or the Provinces, granted by Mr. Beard (sole Patentee), at 85, King William-street, City, 34, Parliament-street, and the Royal Polytechnic Institution, London. [8773

Advertisement by Richard Beard for his London daguerreotype studio. *Salisbury Journal*, Saturday 6th June 1846 p. 1.

PHOTOGRAPHIC OR DAGUERREOTYPE PORTRAITS,
With all the recent Improvements in COLOURING, &c., are taken, Daily, by MR. BARBER, at No. 12, SAINT JAMES'S-TERRACE, WINCHESTER.

IN order to afford the Inhabitants of SALISBURY an opportunity of availing themselves of this unerring process in securing a faithful Likeness, Mr. BARBER will deduct the Second Class Railway fare, One Way, to all Parties taking a *Coloured* Portrait, on receiving One Day's notice, and a satisfactory Likeness guaranteed.

Particulars, as to terms, &c., may be known by applying to Messrs. BRODIE and Co., Canal, Salisbury, where Specimens may be seen. [4429

Advertisement by Alfred Barber for his Winchester studio. *Salisbury Journal*, Saturday 4th September 1847 p. 4.

large or financially lucrative market. While Barber's Winchester studio survived the 1840s, in April 1851 he announced that his studio would be closed for 'some months.'[24] He reopened his studio in December for the 'winter season only' though the studio appears to have finally closed in 1852.[25]

Those citizens of Salisbury and its environs wishing to practice photography as amateurs needed to acquire a detailed knowledge of photographic processes. They could purchase one of a number of photographic manuals that began to appear soon after the announcements of Daguerre and Talbot. By the end of the 1840s some of these manuals had been published in several editions.[26] *Photogenic Manipulation: Containing the Theory and Plain Instructions in the Art of Photography, Or the Production of Pictures Through the Agency of Light* was first published by George Knight in London in 1843 and by 1850 was issued in its seventh edition. Whether these were stocked by bookshops in Salisbury, or needed to be ordered through them, remains unclear.

AGRICULTURAL CHEMISTRY.

GEORGE COX, OPTICIAN and PRACTICAL CHEMIST, 128, Holborn Hill, London. Established 120 years.

	s.	d
SPECTACLE SECRETS, second Edition, price	1	0
CHEMICAL DELECTUS, ditto..................	1	0
AGRICULTURAL CHEMISTRY, cloth boards	2	6

Agricultural Test Chest, complete, 3*l*. 3*s*—5*l*. 15*s*. 6*d*. with book; Chemical Laboratories, with book, 7*s*. 6*d*., 12*s*, 21*s*., 30*s*., and 42*s*.; Chemical Tests and Re-agents, Apparatus for Photogenic, Electrotype, and Daguerreotype Manipulations; Electro-magnetic Machines, 18*s*. to 3*l*. 3*s*.; Spectacles, Telescopes, Microscopes, Thermometers, Hydrometers, Micrometers, &c.

Guano and other Manures and Soils analysed. Terms, 1*l*. 1*s*.—A complete quantitative analysis of a Soil (en detail), with an opinion as to its future culture, 4*l*. 4*s*.; ditto (en masse), 3*l*. 3*s*.; ditto, for estimating the amount of Phosphates, &c., 1*l*. 1*s*.; ditto Refuse of Manufactures, 1*l*. 1*s*. Instruction given in every branch of Analytical Chemistry, and arranged to meet the views of the Student.

Webster's Patent Hand-tile Machine, 25*l*.; Draining-level, giving the rise and fall of Land, as well as its level, and used without an assistant, price 2*l*., packed in a box 18 in. by 4, with familiar instructions; improved beam Draining Level, on Tripod Legs. In addition to the above advantages, it is adapted for a variety of purposes besides draining and tile-laying, 3*l*. 10*s*.

Mathematical, Optical, and Philosophical Instruments, in great variety. [7949

Advertisement of photographic equipment and materials by George Cox of London. *Salisbury Journal*, Saturday 21st March 1846 p. 1.

During the 1840s, amateur photographers in Salisbury would have needed to purchase equipment from specialist London dealers who placed advertisements in daily newspapers such as *The Times*, or locally in the *SJ*. These enthusiasts needed a combination of a good working knowledge level of optics and chemistry coupled to a significant level of manual dexterity, since they had to mix their own chemicals and prepare daguerreotype plates or paper negatives. Perseverance was also a necessity, since experimentation and refinement of the working combination of equipment and chemicals was a hallmark of early photographic processes and their practitioners. As a result, those readers of the *SJ* interested in becoming photographers might have been interested in an advertisement placed in the issue of 21st March 1846 by George Cox, Optician and Practical Chemist, of 128 Holborn Hill, London, who offered 'Apparatus for Photogenic, Electrotype, and Daguerreotype Manipulations.'[27] This may have assisted members of the local scientific community to engage in experimentation and to start to take photographs, though the failure of Beard's Photographic Portrait Rooms that summer did not bode well.

One conduit for a knowledge and appreciation of photography were the literary, scientific and mechanics' institutes that had proliferated during the 1830s and 1840s. It was estimated that in 1850 in Great Britain there were some seven hundred mechanics' institutes, literary institutes, athenæums, mutual improvement societies and kindred organizations, and these had a total membership of one hundred and twenty thousand. Six hundred of these were in England. Their libraries held some eight hundred thousand volumes, with an annual issue of books of over two million. Between five and six thousand lectures were delivered during the year, and over eighteen thousand of the members were attending evening classes.[28]

The Salisbury Mechanics' Institution was founded in early 1833, there being 74 subscribers. The first annual meeting was held on 21st May in the School Room in Salt Lane.[29] Subsequently the Institution met in the Assembly Rooms, on the corner of the High Street and the Canal. In 1840 at the annual meeting it was stated that there were some 234 members and its library held almost 1,000 volumes; 40 of these members were categorised as mechanics by profession, 194 as 'other' and

26 were under 21 years of age.[30] The Rev. Lewis Tomlinson (1806–1880) and his brother Charles Tomlinson (1808–1897) ran a day school in Brown Street and were listed as lecturers. They covered astronomy, natural philosophy and navigation.[31] However, in 1840 there was also an indication that there were some financial problems facing the Institution and an editorial comment in the *SJ* that 'the inhabitants [of Salisbury] will surely not suffer it [the Institution's Reading Room] to be closed for want of a trifling pecuniary aid.'[32] The Institution collapsed later that year and the books from its library together with furniture and equipment were sold.[33]

The collapse of Salisbury Mechanics' Institution removed a key environment for the display, discussion and promotion of photography during the 1840s. It is reasonable to assume that during the 1840s those interested in the new photographic medium met and discussed in informal gatherings (in conversaziones or soirées) in their private homes. It was only in 1849 that another organisation that might promote photography, the Salisbury Literary & Scientific Institution(SLSI) was founded, which remained active until 1885. However, the SLSI did not adopt and promote photography in any significant way and no local photographic club or society was formed in the city during the 19th century.[34]

As the decade drew to a close, preparations were under way for the 1851 Great Exhibition of the Works of Industry of All Nations. Housed in the innovative Crystal Palace in London's Hyde Park, the exhibition was to have a significant effect on the rise of photography. Salisbury was to benefit from this and the 1850s saw the rapid growth of commercial photography in the city, and probably a rise in the number of local amateur photographers whose history remains to be discovered. Nevertheless, the actual scale, scope and significance of amateur photography in Salisbury during the 1840s has yet to be unearthed.

1 *Wiltshire Independent*, Thursday 4th August 1842 p. 4 and Thursday 20thOctober 1842 p. 4.

2 See Peter Daniels, *Around Salisbury in Old Photographs*, Alan Sutton Publishing, Stroud, 1989 p. 138. I thank Professor Larry Schaaf for confirming that a *c.*1852 date seems likely.

3 On 9th November 1842, John Johnson obtained from Beard the patent rights for the daguerreotype process in the counties of Lancashire, Cheshire and Derbyshire and took control of Beard's Photographic & Daguerreotype Portrait Gallery in Manchester. He subsequently set up a studio in Derby in July 1843. He returned to the USA in 1844. See http://freepages.rootsweb.com/~brett/genealogy/photos/jjohnson.html

4 An advertisement, dated 18th July, published in *Devonport & Plymouth & Stonehouse Gazette*, 31st July 1841.

5 The unsigned indenture forms part of the Fox Talbot Collection, the British Library, MS 88942/4/1/9NTA 34876. LA(B)42–1. Eleven pieces of related correspondence can be found on *The Correspondence of William Henry Fox Talbot* website. www.foxtalbot.dmu.ac.uk.

6 *Nottingham Review and General Advertiser for the Midland Counties*, Friday 1st October 1841 p. 4. See also R. Derek Wood, 'The Daguerreotype in England: Some Primary Material Relating to Beard's Lawsuits', *History of Photography*, October 1979, Vol. 3, No. 4, pp. 305–9.

7 Michael Pritchard, *A Directory of London Photographers 1841–1908. Revised and expanded edition*, Photo Research, Watford, 1994 p. 19.

8 A large advertisement for the opening of the studio on the 9th May 1842 appeared in the *Hampshire Advertiser & Salisbury Guardian*, Saturday 7th May 1842 p. 2. See Keith Adamson, 'More Early Studios', *The Photographic Journal*, January, 1988 pp. 32–36. A Daguerreotype studio was opened at the Horticultural Rooms in Bristol on 10th August 1841 and Thomas Sharp opened his studio at Royal Victoria Park, Milsom Street in Bath by 11th November of the same year. See Bernard & Pauline Heathcote, *A Faithful Likeness. The First Photographic Portrait Studios in the British Isles 1841 to 1855*, Lowdham, 2002 p. 11.

9 *Hampshire Advertiser*, Saturday 28th May 1842 p. 2.

10 See See Larry J. Schaaf, *Sun Pictures Catalogue 9: William Henry Fox Talbot, Friends & Relations*, Hans P. Kraus, Jr., Inc., New York, 1999 pp. 22–29. Goddard referred to setting up a calotype studio at the 'Western Establishment' [in London] in a letter to Talbot dated 14th April 1842. Talbot letter Doc. No. 4486 at *The Correspondence of William Henry Fox Talbot* at foxtalbot.dmu.ac.uk.

11 See Helmut and Alison Gernsheim, *L.J.M. Daguerre – The History of the Diorama and the Daguerreotype*, 2nd revised edition, Dover Publications, New York, 1968 pp. 151–152. See Steve Edwards, 'Beard Patentee': Daguerreotype Property and Authorship', *Oxford Art Journal*, Vol. 36 No. 3, 2013 pp. 369–394.

12 *Hampshire Advertiser*, Saturday 17th March 1849 p. 4. Goddard appears also have set up a studio in Chester in 1844. See Keith Adamson, 'More Early Studios' Pt. 2,' *The Photographic Journal*, July1988 p. 305.

13 A copy of a variant prospectus was offered by Jarndyce, *The Museum. Jarndyce Miscellany.,* Catalogue ccxvii. Winter 2015–2016, Cat. No. 231. This prospectus records (in manuscript) that the cost for the licence in East Riding and York would be an initial payment of £1,200 plus 15% of gross receipts or £600 laid down and 20% of gross receipts. The licence for West Riding is advertised at £3,000 (plus 15%) or £2,000 (plus 20%). This seems to indicate that Beard made estimates of the value of the market on a region by region basis.

14 *Correspondence of William Henry Fox Talbot* document number 5520. Letter from West Audry, a solicitor in Chippenham, to Talbot dated Wednesday 3rd August 1842. Richard Beard had sent this circular to Audry to pass onto Talbot.

15 *Wiltshire Independent,* Thursday 18th April 1844 p. 2 and *SJ,* Saturday 20th April 1844 p. 1. It is not clear whether Beard was able to sell this licence, and if so, to whom.

16 *SJ,* Saturday 6th June 1846 p. 1.

17 *Hampshire Telegraph,* 21st March 1846 p. 4. Dowle referred to 'larger than usual' portraits and a colouring process he had introduced from France.

18 *Hampshire Chronicle,* 23rd May 1846 as cited by Raymond V. Thurley, *ibid,.*

19 *SJ,* Saturday 6th June 1846 p. 4. It is possible that John Frederick Goddard was involved in the setting up of this Salisbury studio.

20 https://www.theislandwiki.org/index.php/The_beginnings_of_photography_in_Jersey

21 *SJ,* Saturday 4th September 1847 p. 4. No advertisement by Brodie confirming these samples were on display has been found.

22 *SJ,* Saturday 4th September 1847 p. 4.

23 Barber advertised his services 'for a few days only' in the *Hampshire Chronicle,* Saturday 16 September 1848 p. 1.

24 *Hampshire Chronicle,* Saturday 19th April 1851 p. 4.

25 *Hampshire Chronicle,* Saturday 13th December 1851 p. 4.

26 See Helmut Gernsheim, *Incunabula of British Photographic Literature 1839–1875,* Scolar Press, 1985.

27 *SJ,* Saturday 21st March 1846 p. 1.

28 *House of Commons Select Committee on Public Libraries,* 1849.

29 Monte Little, *Salisbury Mechanics Institution 1833–41,* Wiltshire Library & Museum Service, 1982.

30 *Report of the State of Literary, Scientific, and Mechanics' Institutions in England,* Society for the Diffusion of Useful Knowledge, London, 1841 p. 100.

31 Charles left Salisbury and had a distinguished academic career. In the 1861 census Lewis was living with Maria his wife and two children in New Street and was recorded as the Chaplain of the City Workhouse.

32 *SJ,* Monday 10th February 1840 p. 4.

33 *SJ,* Monday 14th December 1840 p. 4. Four hundred volumes remained unsold at this date.

34 The Salisbury Camera Club was formed in the summer of 1904.

3 RISE OF PHOTOGRAPHY FROM THE 1850s TO 1870s

THE GREAT EXHIBITION *of the Works of Industry of All Nations,* which ran from 1st May to the 17th October 1851, was the first international display of manufactured products. It has been credited consistently by historians as being a pivotal point in mid-19th century industrialisation, presenting a view of the world as seen from a primarily British perspective. Significantly, contemporaries also saw the display of photographs and photographic equipment in the Crystal Palace in London's Hyde Park as a defining moment in the progress of photography; an advance from being a comparatively small-scale commercial activity to a more mainstream part of mid-Victorian image making. The official *Report by the Juries,* published in 1852, remarked that 'never before was so rich a collection of photographic pictures brought together, the products of England, France, Austria and America'.[1] Significantly, Henry Talbot, the very inventor of photography on paper, publicly stated in July 1852, 'Ever since the Great Exhibition I have felt that a new era had commenced for photography.'[2]

The 1851 Great Exhibition and Salisbury

AROUND ONE THOUSAND photographs were exhibited at the Crystal Palace Great Exhibition.[3] Although not photographic, a small number of exhibits were sent from Salisbury manufacturers. These included the cutler William Beach, Thomas John Holloway, rope manufacturer, George Churchill clock maker of Downton, and Mary Ann Uphill, from Fonthill Bishop, who was an embroiderer.

Some citizens of Salisbury availed themselves of the special excursions organised by rail companies and some local companies sent their employees. The banking firm of Messrs Everett and Smith of Endless Street gave their clerks £5 each, and a week's holiday, to enjoy and educate themselves at the Great Exhibition. There was also mention of Lord Radnor 'and some neighbouring landowners' enabling workers from their estates to visit the exhibition.[4] Local schoolchildren also visited the Great Exhibition. Nineteen children from the free school in Wilton visited the Crystal Palace in Hyde Park on 10th September.[5] However, how many citizens of Salisbury travelled to London's Hyde Park and saw and were influenced by the photographs on display may never be known.

Amateur Photographers

THE THREE DECADES of the 1850s, 1860s and 1870s formed the building blocks of the rise of photography in Salisbury. Currently, the role of amateur photographers in Salisbury during these decades is almost completely unknown. That such individuals existed is reasonable to assume. While the evidence for this study is primarily concerned with commercial photography in Salisbury it is worth, at this point, to provide an overview of the role of amateur photographers and the environment they worked in during the period from the 1850s to the late 1870s.

While the 1840s had been a decade for a limited number of enthusiasts for photography – some commercial portrait photographers and others being amateurs – the 1850s were to see some fundamental changes to the photographic landscape.

During the 1840s two photographic clubs had been set up in Great Britain. The Edinburgh Calotype Club had been founded around 1843 and is considered the first photographic society.[6] In the autumn of 1847 a dozen or so keen amateur photographers formed the Calotype Club in London. From 1848 it was referred to as the Photographic Club. The group appears to have had no laws, office-bearers or formalities of any kind, and no publications have been identified.[7] These clubs evidenced the need for primarily amateur photographers to gather to discuss and promote the photographic medium. Unsurprisingly, Salisbury had no connection with either of these.

The distinction between the commercial portrait photographer and the amateur became increasingly blurred during the 1850s. While in practical terms the equipment and materials used by the amateur was little different from that used by commercial photographers, the concept of making money from photography being the differentiator began to become fragmented. There were gradations of earnings from photography that complicated matters. For some traditionalists simply selling a few prints or allowing a photograph to be reproduced as an engraving or lithograph might justify the removal of amateur status. There were photographers who straddled the boundaries of such a rigid definition. One was Roger Fenton (1819–1869), who started as an amateur but then undertook paid work for the British Museum (1852–1859) and sought to commercialise his photographs of the Crimean War (1854–1856) and those of Salisbury Cathedral (1857–1858).[8]

Estimating the number of amateur photographers that practised in Great Britain during the 1850s is notoriously difficult. Through study of the 1851 census for England using online genealogical resources, it is possible to identify over 200 men and women who stated their occupation as 'Daguerreotypists', 'Photographic Artists', 'Photographists', and 'Heliographic Artists'. This was from a total population of nearly 28 million.[9] No resident in Salisbury stated their occupation as one of these, though any amateur photographers would have given their primary occupation rather than their 'hobby'. In reality there were probably more than five hundred – perhaps as many as a thousand – active photographers, both professional and amateur, in Great Britain in 1850.[10] Only significant further research will determine whether there were amateur photographers in Salisbury at this date, and evidence is likely to be the result of a combination of serendipity and archival research.

The formation of a number of photographic clubs and societies provided a range of opportunities for photographers during the 1850s and beyond. They created forums within which photographers met to discuss processes and equipment. Photographs could be displayed and discussed either within meetings of the members of such clubs and societies, or at exhibitions that they organised and that might be open to non-members. The 1850s also saw the rise of the photographic press.

The Photographic Society was formed in London in January 1853 and became the Royal Photographic Society in 1894. It had the largest membership by far of any photographic society during the period covered by this study, with approximate 360 members by mid-1854. The 1859 membership list records 2,534 and by 1871 this had almost doubled to 4,715.[11] It is also striking that there were 168 female members of the Photographic Society in 1859 and 694 by 1871. Significantly too, no Salisbury photographer, either commercial or amateur, became a member of the Photographic Society until Charles John Witcomb(1835–1913), whose studio was at 10 Catherine Street, was elected in November 1877. He is recorded as only being a member during the years 1878 and 1879 though quite why this was the case is unclear.

A number of regional photographic societies subsequently sprang up during the 1850s. The Devon and Cornwall (1854), Norwich (1854), Brighton and Sussex (1855), Birmingham (1856) reformed in 1885, Chorlton (1857), Blackheath (1857), Greenwich (1857) and Macclesfield (1858), the North London Society (1857), Nottingham (1858), the South London Society (1859), and Bradford Society (1860). These British photographic societies had memberships numbered in tens rather than hundreds with, for example, Blackheath Photographic Society, having 23 members in 1857. There were no photographic societies founded near Salisbury during the 1850s, indeed not even during the period covered in this study. The Southampton Camera Club was founded only in 1896 and the Salisbury Camera Club was formed in the summer of 1903.

At least three specifically amateur photographic organisations existed during the 1850s: the Photographic Exchange Club and two groups inside the Photographic Society of London: the Photographic Society Club, founded in 1856, and the Exchange Club of the Photographic Society' (sometimes called the Photographic

Club) that was restricted to twenty-one members and met five times a year. These organisations existed to facilitate exchanges of photographs and information between members.[12] Again, unsurprisingly, no Salisbury photographers were members.

The photographic press rapidly developed during the 1850s. The *Liverpool Photographic Journal* began publication in January 1854 and continued through to December 1856; then continued as the *Liverpool & Manchester Photographic Journal* from January 1857 to December 1858; then continued as the *Photographic Journal* from January to December 1859 (vol 6) and then as *The British Journal of Photography* from January 1860; *Photographic Notes* (the Journal of the Photographic Society of Scotland and the Manchester Photographic Society) began publication in 1856; *The Photographic News* was founded in 1858 and from its first year of publication was quoted from in the *SJ*.[13]

By the end of the 1850s the demographic of practising photographers had changed. There were more commercial photographers and increased numbers of amateurs. In 1860, Thomas Sutton (1819–1875), the English photographer, author, inventor and editor of *Photographic Notes,* looking back to 1851, described the approach of the amateur to photography as:

> rational enthusiasts, and not men to take up a hobby in a hurry and give it up in a pet. The amateur of 1851 was a man who first considered the cost of the apparatus and the artistic value of the results, and who after having weighed the matter in his mind and determined to become a [amateur] photographer, worked steadily at it…. But since the introduction of collodion, [on glass negatives] photography has got out of its good old sensible path, and everything has become too easy, too quick, and consequently too harum-scarum.[14]

By the late 1860s the number of commercial photographers in Great Britain had also reached a plateau and this was reflected in Salisbury.

Although there was growth in the number of amateur photographers from the early 1850s, this number had started to decline by the 1870s. Yet the amateur played an important role in photography's first foundational period up to the 1880s and this was widely acknowledged at the time, primarily through the photographic press. From the 1870s the situation gradually reversed so that it was no longer the amateur but commercial firms that began to make technical improvements to a medium that was increasingly rooted in science, theory and commercial industrialisation rather than practical empiricism. The story of Salisbury's early amateur photographers has yet to be written.

1850s

The rise of photography in the decade following the Great Exhibition built on several facets of the industrialisation of the medium. These included the economies of scale of standardised mass production coupled with widespread increases in disposable income. Photographic processes moved from the daguerreotype and the paper negative to the glass negative using collodion as the support for the photosensitive chemicals. Camera and lens technology advanced in parallel. In terms of photographic prints, the albumen print replaced the salted paper print and was to remain the most widespread print process for the remainder of the century. However, permanent photographic prints (the carbon print) and photomechanical processes (including photolithography, collotype, woodburytype and photogravure) were introduced during the 1850s and 1860s.

The first generation of commercial photographers in Salisbury came from a variety of backgrounds. Some were itinerants who travelled around the provinces plying their trade from temporary studios during the summer months, sunlight being the only form of illumination for the taking of photographs. Advertisements placed in the *SJ* by these itinerants follow a marketing formula; to announce imminent arrival in the city, try and maximise the potential of the market in Salisbury, and then move on to another neighbouring town or city. So, advertisements in the local press would mention the photographer's 'last week' in the city, only for the set date to be passed as more trade compelled the photographer to extend his stay.

Some photographers had gained (or claimed to have) experience elsewhere – primarily the major London photographic studios, such as Richard Beard or Antoine Claudet – and set up permanent

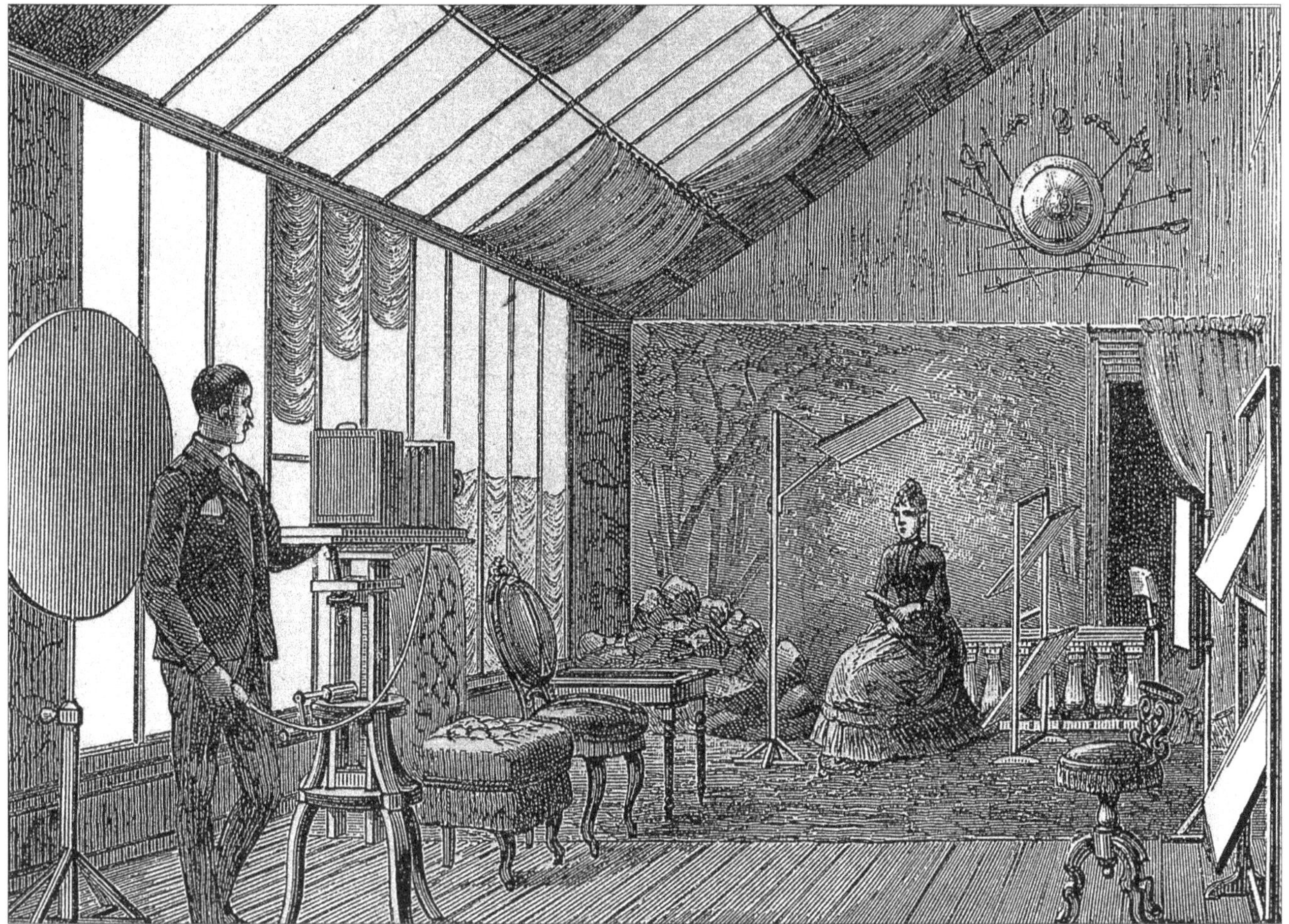

View of a typical photographic portrait studio. Engraving from Adolphe Miethe, *Lehrbuch der praktischen Photographie*, Wihelm Knapp, Halle, 1902.

studios in Salisbury. These photographers would sometimes mention in their advertisements in the *SJ* their professional connection with such metropolitan studios.

A small number of the first generation of the city's commercial photographers were born in Salisbury, though exactly how and where they learned photography remains unclear. Most had had an existing profession before taking up photography and might continue to offer other commercial services. A significant number of these photographers referred to themselves as 'artists' and 'photographers', though it is unclear whether the also provided painted or drawn portraits as part of their services. One notable exception was the photographer Henry Brooks, who gave up photography in order to return to painting portraits.

While the primary form of income of the commercial photographers working in Salisbury from the 1850s through to the 1880s and beyond was that of portraiture, their advertisements indicated that they were generalist and would photograph a wide range of subject matter, from the homes of residents, through fine and decorative arts, to animals. Studio portraiture dominated the services of these photographers and the examination of carte de visite portraits taken by Salisbury photographers documents the fixtures and fittings of their studios and the various styles of portrait photography.[15]

Photographic studios were invariably built specifically to enable portraiture. They were north facing to prevent direct sunlight and with top and side lighting through glazed windows. Light was controlled by adjustable blinds. In the first generation of studios blue glass was mistakenly thought to improve the quality of the light within the studio.This was used in an attempt to correct the over-sensitivity of early photographic emulsions to blue light.[16] By 1880 such use of blue glass had largely disappeared.

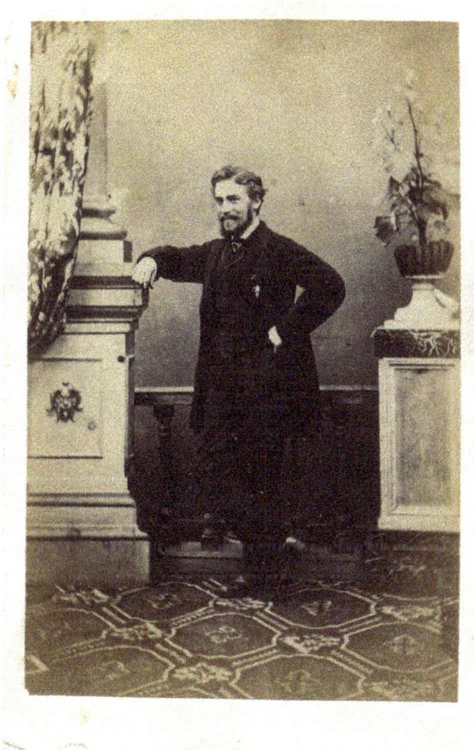

James Miell. Full-length standing portrait of a man leaning against a balustrade. c. 1865. Carte de visite. Albumen print. Anthony Hamber collection.

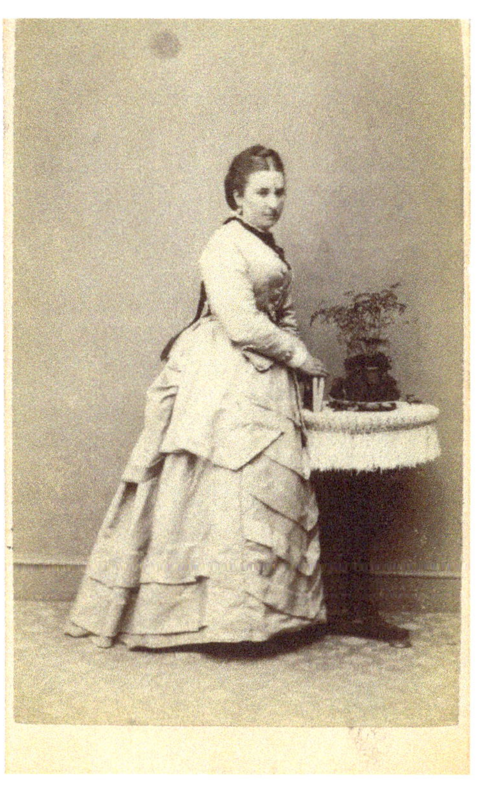

Edward Sanger. Full-length standing portrait of a woman with a side table. 1877–1880. Carte de visite. Albumen print. Anthony Hamber collection.

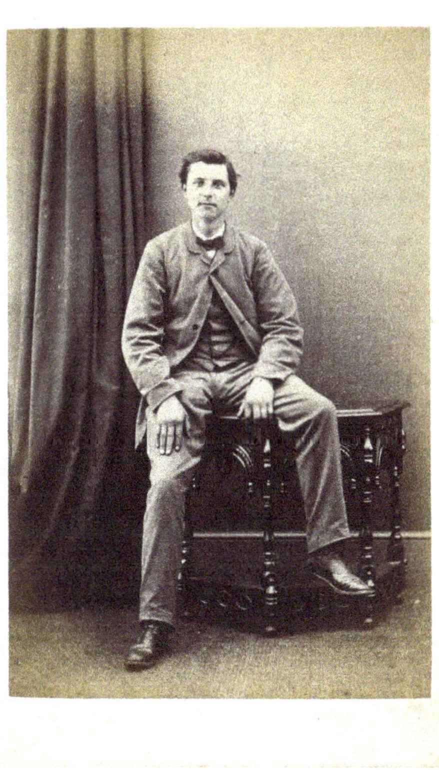

Henry Brooks. Casual portrait of young man seated on a side table. c. 1870. Carte de visite. Albumen print. Anthony Hamber collection.

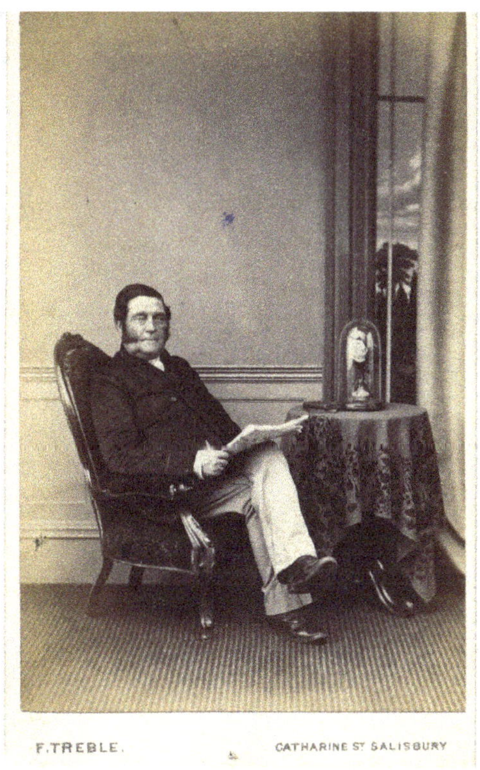

Frederick Treble. Seated man with newspaper. c. 1864, Carte de visite. Albumen print. Anthony Hamber collection.

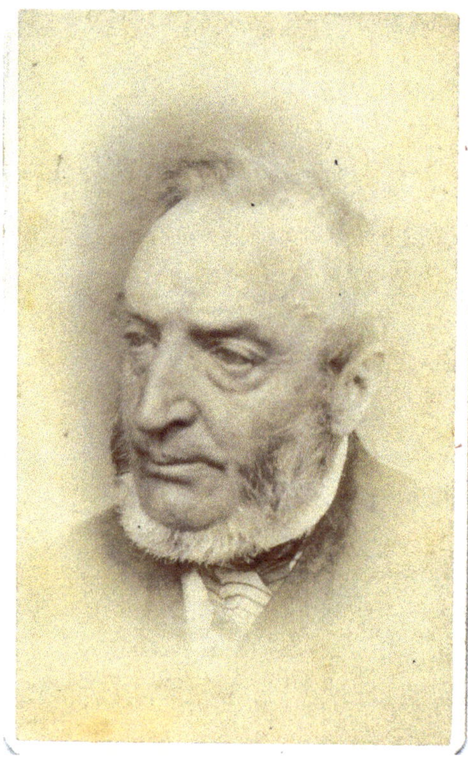

Edwin Macy. Portrait head of a man. c. 1875. Carte de visite. Albumen print. Anthony Hamber collection.

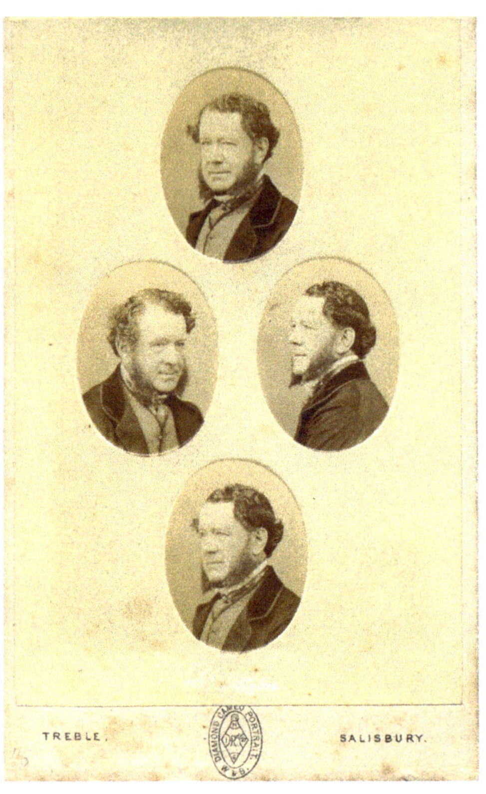

Frederick Treble. Four head and shoulder portraits of a man. c. 1865. Diamond Cameo Portrait. Albumen prints. Anthony Hamber collection.

Studios had a variety of painted backdrops. Some depicted elegantly furnished interiors, such as drawing rooms, or views of rustic or idealised landscapes. Furniture props included chairs, tables, desks, pedestals, carpets and architectural components such as sections of balustrade or decorative skirting boards. Other props included drapery, books, sculptures, and plants.

A variety of photographic styles was used for portraits. They followed stylistic conventions formed by centuries of portraits created by manual graphic processes. Photographic poses included full-length standing portraits, three-quarter length standing portraits, full view seated portraits, half-length seated portraits and head-only views. Edwin Macy, for instance, included head-only portraits from unusual viewpoints, perhaps influenced by the celebrated portraits made by Julia Margaret Cameron (1815–1879) during the 1860s. Victorian photographers often followed prescribed and formal poses. Men were seemingly allowed a greater variety of poses than women. The physical appearance of the photographs also evolved, such as vignette effects introduced from the late 1860s. The Diamond Cameo Portrait was introduced by the photographer Frederick Richard Window (1824–1875) of the London photographic firm of Window & Bridge in 1864. It consisted of four small oval portraits of the sitter arranged in the shape of a diamond. These were pasted on the carte de visite that had four embossed convex shapes which resembled a cameo.

Fixed costs were a primary consideration for all Victorian photographers, particularly up to the mid-1850s before which payments to patent owners were required; Richard Beard for the daguerreotype and Henry Talbot for the paper negative calotype process. Following the Great Exhibition pressure to relax photographic patents grew. In August 1852 the two leading institutions representing the science and the arts in Great Britain combined forces. *The Times* of 13th August 1852 published an open letter from the Earl of Rosse (1800–1867), the president of the Royal Society, and Charles Lock Eastlake (1793–1865), the president of the Royal Academy, written to Talbot 'to inquire whether it might not be possible for you, by making some alteration in the exercise of your patent rights, to obviate most of the difficulties which now appear to hinder the progress of art in England'. Talbot's response was also published in which he agreed to waive licensing fees for amateurs, but, crucially, not for commercial photography. This correspondence was also published in August 1852 in *The Mechanic's Magazine, Register, Journal and Gazette.*[17]

The momentum for the freeing up of the progress of photography from patent constraints gained traction in August 1853 when the patent rights for the daguerreotype process for England and Wales (British Patent No. 8194) expired. Richard Beard had been the sole patentee of the daguerreotype process in England and Wales, which he had purchased in June 1841. For whatever reason, Beard, who in 1853 had some 12 photographic studios operating in London under his licence, decided not to apply for an extension to his patent. Thus the daguerreotype process became free to use by the rapidly emerging cohort of commercial photographers.

Meanwhile, Talbot continued to pursue professional portrait photographers who had failed to obtain a licence and take them to court if they did not. 1854 saw probably the most significant development in terms of patent expiry. Having filed several lawsuits against photographers he considered acting without the necessary licence, Talbot applied for an extension of his 14-year calotype patent (British Patent No. 8842). He also took legal action against the London photographer Martin Laroche, the professional name of William Henry Silvester (1814–1886), in a court case heard in December 1854.[18] Talbot's claim was that the commercial use of the collodion on glass negative process infringed his calotype (paper negative) patent. The court decided otherwise and, disappointed by the outcome, Talbot chose not to continue his application to extend his patent.

Talbot's response to the Laroche court case coupled to the ending of Beard's daguerreotype patent in August 1853 resulted in a step change in commercial photography and by the late 1850s all photographers – whether amateur or professional – had exploited the relaxation of patents and the rise of practical and affordable photographic processes, equipment, materials and accessories.

Photographic processes

THE 1850S SAW a significant change in the photographic processes used by both professional and amateur photographers. See Appendix 1 for an overview.

The publication of Fredrick Scott Archer's wet collodion process in the March 1851 issue of *The Chemist* was later described by an early photographic historian as 'the announcement of the birth of an infant Hercules, that was destined to slay a beautiful youth [the daguerreotype process] whose charms had only arrived at maturity.'[19] In this process liquid collodion was poured on to a glass plate, then photographically sensitised before camera exposure and subsequent chemical processing. Following the relaxation of Talbot's paper negative process (calotype, also known as talbotype) collodion on glass negatives rapidly rose to become the predominant photographic negative process, and by the end of the decade

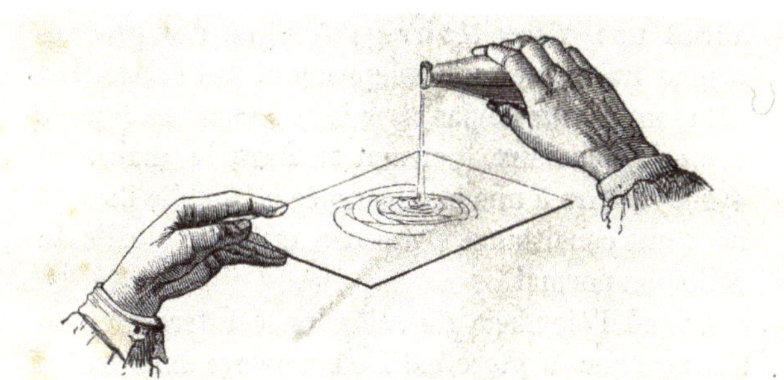

Fig. 19. —Manière d'étendre le collodion. Première position des mains.

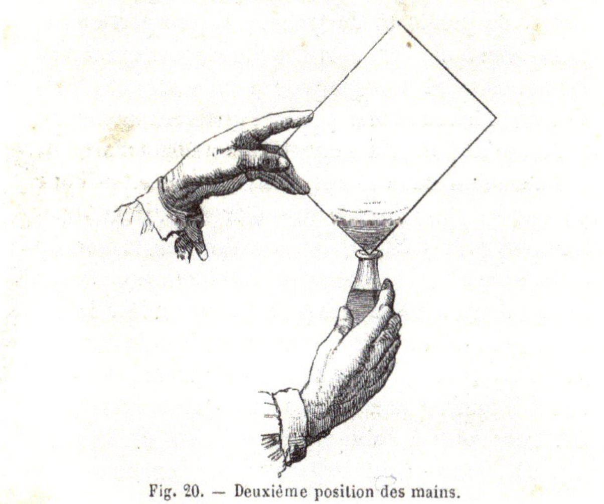

Fig. 20. — Deuxième position des mains.

Two positions of pouring collodion onto a glass negative, Figure 20 in Gaston Tissandier, *Les Merveilles de la Photographie,* Librarie Hachette, Paris 1874. Anthony Hamber collection.

had displaced fully the daguerreotype across Great Britain. However, there was a transitional phase; in March 1856 Mr Monson, whose studio was in St Ann Street, advertised that he practiced the daguerreotype, collodion and talbotype process, and in December the same year Miell stated that he practised both the collodion and talbotype process.[20]

Coupled to the rise of the collodion on glass negative process was the replacement of the salted paper photographic print – in which the image was formed in the paper fibres themselves – with the albumen print, in which the photochemicals were held in an albumen coating supported by a paper base. The albumen print was to remain the key photographic print process throughout the nineteenth century.

The stability of photographic print processes became a major concern during the mid-nineteenth century. In 1856 in France, Honoré Théodoric d'Albert, duc de Luynes (1802–1867), offered a prize for a process to reproduce photographs in permanent printer's ink. This spawned a number of permanent photographic processes (the carbon and woodburytype) and the advent of photomechanical process, such a photolithography and photogravure.

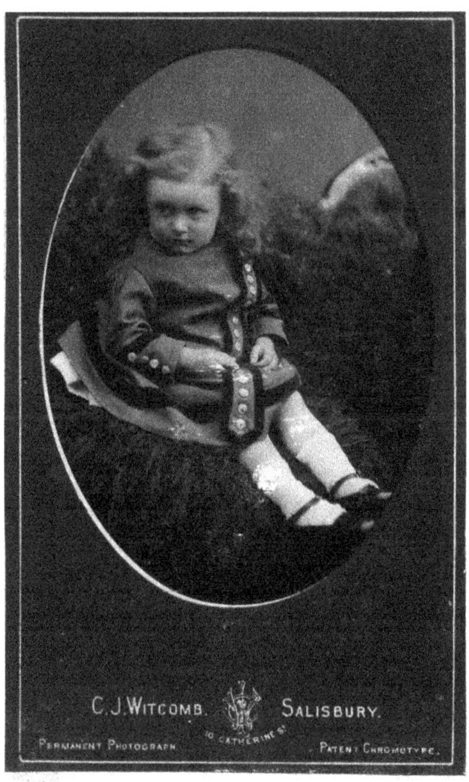

Charles Witcomb. Portrait of Master Southly. 1876.
Carte de visite. Chromotype (carbon process).
Anthony Hamber collection.

One Salisbury photographer was to take a prominent role in the commercial application of two photographic processes. In July 1876 Charles John Witcomb(1835–1913), who ran a studio in Catherine Street, was advertising that he had purchased the sole rights for the Lambertype Patent Process.[21] The Lambertype was a method of retouching negatives and positives invented by Claude Leon Lambert of Paris. Lambert also produced his own version of the carbon print process which he christened 'Chromotype' and Witcomb also purchased a 13-year licence for this process. In an editorial piece, the *SJ* stated it had inspected some examples of Witcomb's Chromotypes and that

> These specimens, which are permanent in character, are of great beauty and exquisite finish, and it appears as if the new process was about to revolutionise the art of photography. The portraits are very superior in brilliancy of tone and effect to anything yet produced by the ordinary modes.[22]

In December 1876 Whitcomb had an article entitled 'Hints on Permanent Chromotype Printing' published in the *British Journal of Photography* in which he stated that he had been trained on the Chromotype at the Autotype Company, who held the British licence for the process. In the same issue an editorial note stated that Witcomb had sent to the journal's editor 'three charming *cartes*.'[23]

During 1876 Witcomb's Chromotypes gained a high profile through mention in the national photographic press. The *British Photographic Journal* for the 1st December 1876 stated 'We are favoured by Mr. Witcomb, of Salisbury, with charming card portraits printed in chromotype.' 'Thanks for the portraits; they are brilliant, and the tone excellent.' G. Wharton Simpson (1824–1880), the editor of the *Photographic News*, stated in the issue of 15th December 1876. 'The success of Mr. Witcomb is apparent enough in his communication, but the confirmation he sent us in examples of his work is in the highest degree satisfactory; they are among the best chromotype we have seen.'

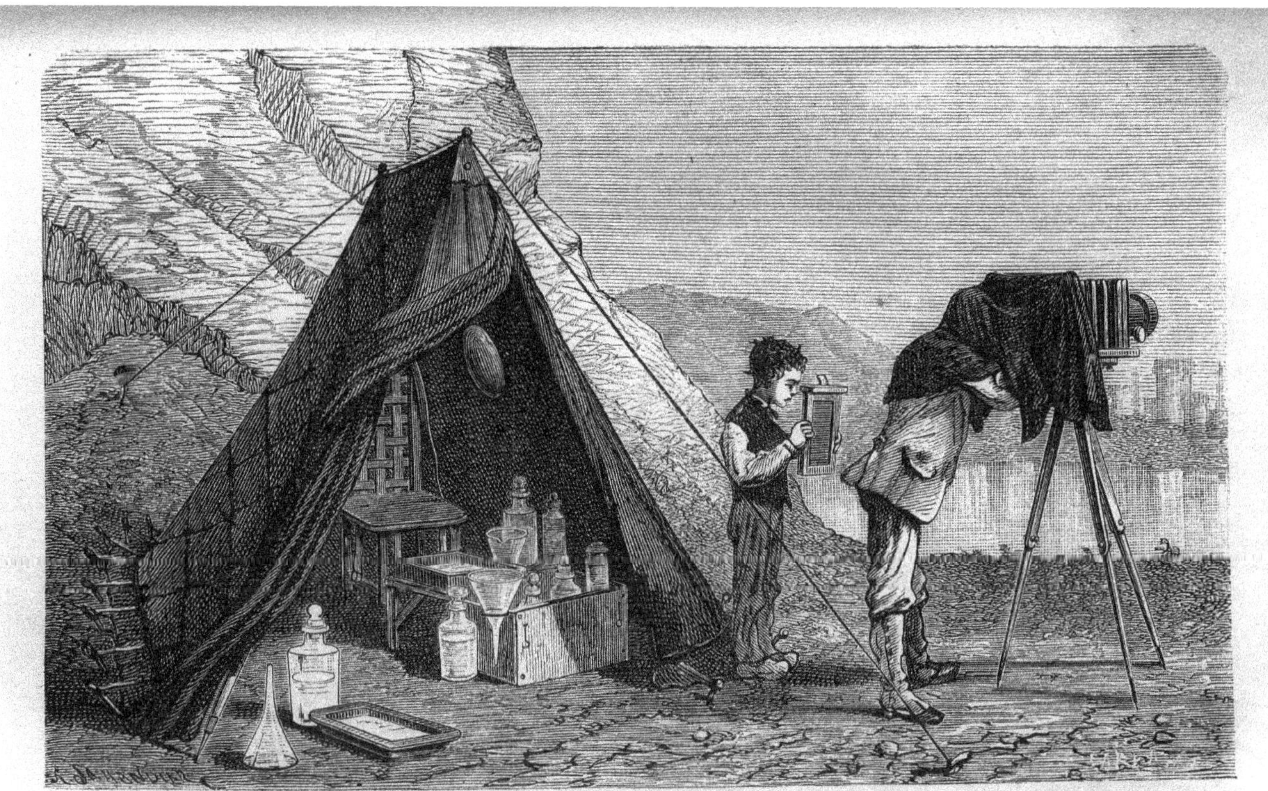

Fig. 63. — La photographie dans les voyages d'exploration.

A portable wet collodion photographer and assistant at work. Figure 63 in Gaston Tissandier, *Les Merveilles de la Photographie*, Librarie Hachette, Paris 1874. Anthony Hamber collection.

The issue of the *Photographic News* for 9th March 1877 included a letter from Sir Thomas Parkyns, who lived on Harnham Cliff and had visited Witcomb's Salisbury studio to see how easy it was to make carbon prints using the Autotype Company's carbon tissue. He found that 'A youth of sixteen years of age had management of the production of the prints'. Significantly, Parkyns noted that 'a young lady' had taken the negatives.' It is not clear who this female photographer was, but this is a rare mention of the significant role played by women in photography during the mid-Victorian era. The prints were put in the printing frame at 10.55 and Mr Witcomb delivered them to Sir Thomas by 12.12. The prints were judged successful. There was much fuss going on amongst professional photographers at the time as the Autotype patents were about to expire. Many were saying that the process was difficult to operate, Sir Thomas delivered fine carbon prints to the *British Journal of Photography*'s editorial offices where anyone could examine them, while a gentleman from Ceylon, where he was making 11 x 14 inch enlargements in tropical conditions, pointed out that in order to get the process to work properly, all one had to do was follow the instructions.

Photographic equipment and supplies

During the 1840s those wishing to practice photography had limited options regarding commercially available equipment. There were few camera and photographic lens manufacturers, and those that did exist were primarily metropolitan based. Some Salisbury photographers of the 1850s provided a portfolio of services to meet the emerging demand. In 1856 James Miell advertised that he would give lessons on photography and was able to supply 'Apparatus'.[24] By 1858 he was offering to supply amateurs with 'Apparatus and Materials at London Prices'.[25] He was also offering to take stereoscopic portraits producing plain or coloured portraits on paper prints, or positive images on glass. By 1859 Miell was advertising 'English,

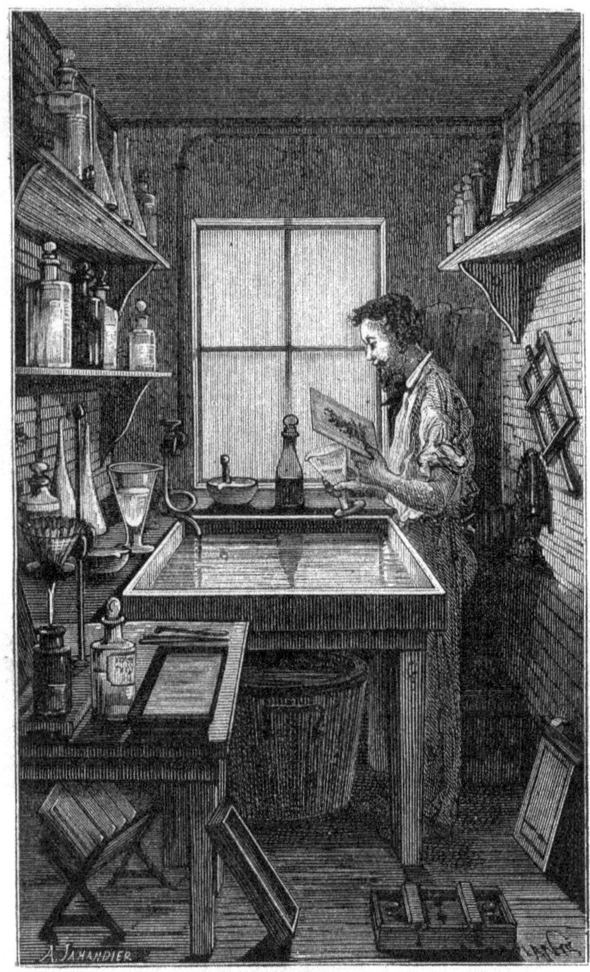

A dark room, Figure 9 in Gaston Tissandier, *Les Merveilles de la Photographie,* Librarie Hachette, Paris 1874. Anthony Hamber collection.

French, German, and American Photographic Goods of every description.' These includes the 'Celebrated American excelsior, and Mawson's Positive, and Scovill Manufacturing Company's negative collodions.'[26]

A range of specific chemicals was required for photography, both to coat photographic plates and to process these plates and photographic prints both in the field and in a darkroom. By the end of the 1850s the demand from amateur and professional photographers in and around Salisbury saw the rise of 'photographic chemists'. Advertisements by photographers in the *SJ* frequently indicate the use of proprietary photographic chemicals, sometimes under exclusive licences. These advertisements gave the readers an insight to the progress of photography, though how much they understood of the significance of the details of different chemical formulae seems less clear.

Possibly the first chemist to advertise photographic chemicals was Samuel R. Atkins of 47 Catherine Street. Atkins advertised in the 1858 edition of *Brown's Stranger's Handbook and Illustrated Guide to Salisbury Cathedral* that he could supply photographic chemicals and apparatus and may have already been selling these products the previous year. An advertisement in *The Photographic Journal* issue for 16th August 1859 for 'Ponting's Iodized Negative Collodion' mentioned that stoppered bottles of the collodion could be had from Atkins; 5 oz. costing 4s., 10 oz. 7s. 6d., 20 oz 15s. and 40 oz. 30s. By October 1859 Atkins was advertising that he could supply three different types of photographic collodion; Ponting's, Ramsden's and Thomas's.[27] In January 1860 Atkins was listed in an advertisement in the '*Photographic Journal* for Leeds-based J. W. Ramsden's collodion, varnish, &c.' as being an appointed agent.[28]

In November 1864, another outlet for photographic chemicals arrived at 29 High Street, when William Frowd Young (born *c.*1833 in Warminster) began trading as a 'Photographic Chemist.' He had traded from around 1860 as a chemist and druggist in the High Street. Young advertised in the *SJ* that he was the sole agent for Keene's collodion, 'unquestionably the most sensitive ever prepared, and from its extreme rapidity is peculiarly adapted for use during the Winter Season'.[29] It is relevant that Young made reference in his advertisements to both the 'profession' and to 'amateur' photographers. He also stated that he was an agent for Schering's, Spencer's, &. Bosch's albumenized papers.

How long Young traded as a photographic chemist is unclear. By 1869 he was no longer advertising himself as a 'Photographic Chemist' and appears to have concentrated on supplying Salisbury's medical profession. In 1874 he relocated his premises to 29, Canal, one door from the Post Office, and was described as an 'Operative Chemist'.[30] Young was still trading in Salisbury in the early 1890s.

The evidence, from the advertisements in the *SJ,* is that there was a significant professional and amateur photographic market in Salisbury during

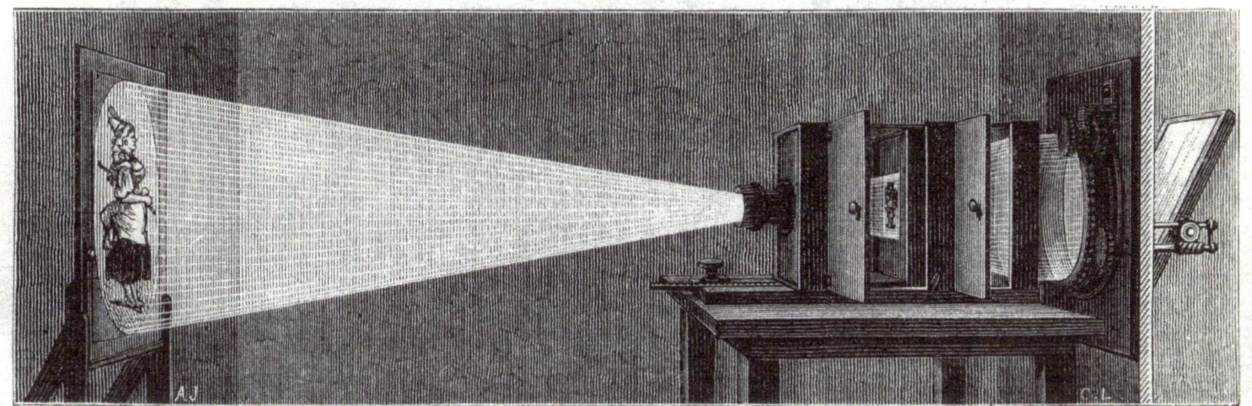

Solar enlarger by Desire van Monckhoven (1834–1882), Figure 32 in Gaston Tissandier, *Les Merveilles de la Photographie*, Librarie Hachette, Paris 1874. Anthony Hamber collection.

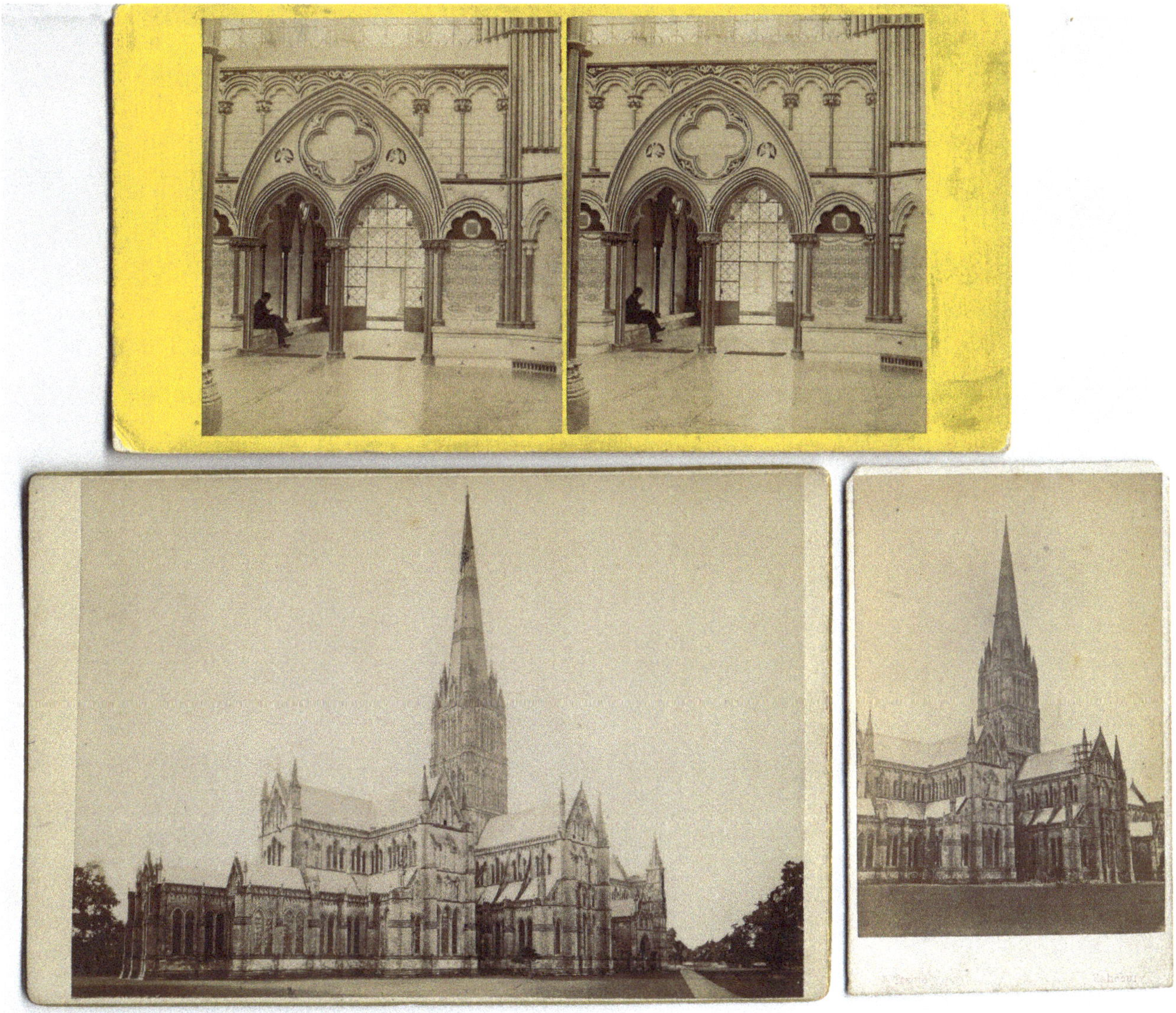

The three popular photographic formats. Clockwise from the top; stereoscopic view, carte de visite and cabinet. Anthony Hamber collection.

the 1860s supported by well stocked local dealers in equipment, chemicals and other photographic materials.

Photographic Formats

During the decades following the Great Exhibition, a wide range of photographic formats appeared.

The daguerreotype formed a unique image on a silvered metal plate. Seven standard sizes were commonly used, ranging from ninth-plate (7 x 5.5 cm) to full plate (21.5 x 16.5 cm).

Paper photographic prints had an even wider range of formats from postage stamp sized paper prints (often used as border decorations on album pages) up to life size portraits, such as those

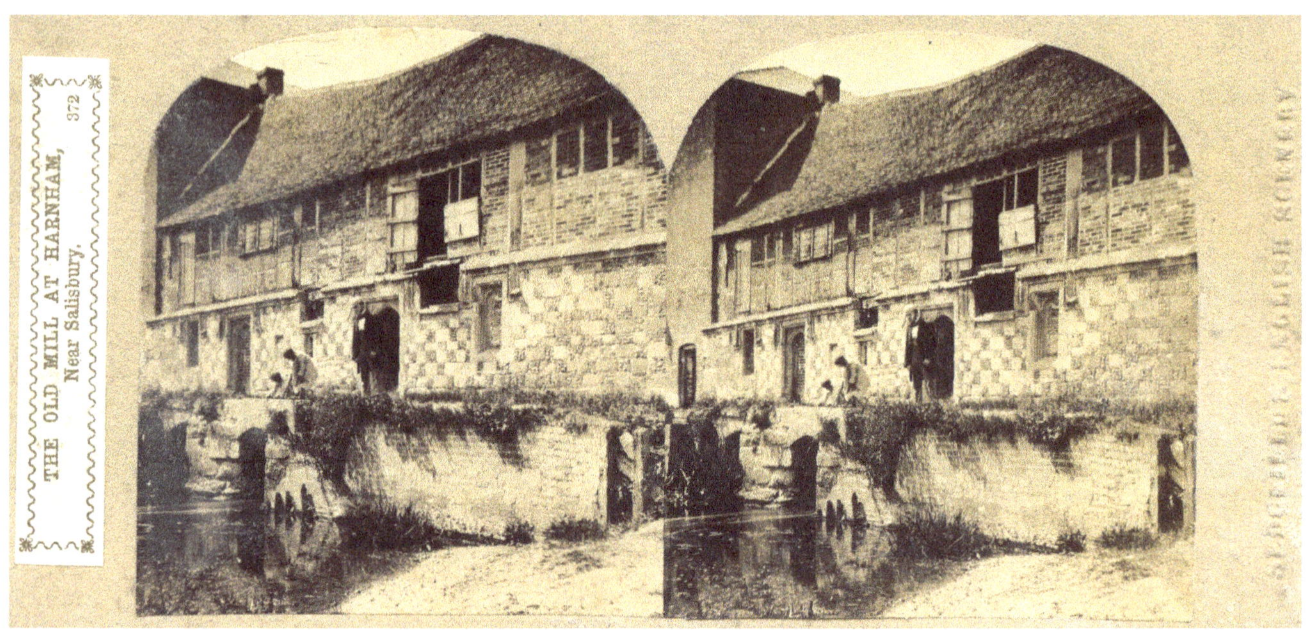

William Russell Sedgfield. *The Old Mill at Harnham, near Salisbury. 372.* Stereoscopic view. Albumen print. The Salisbury Museum.

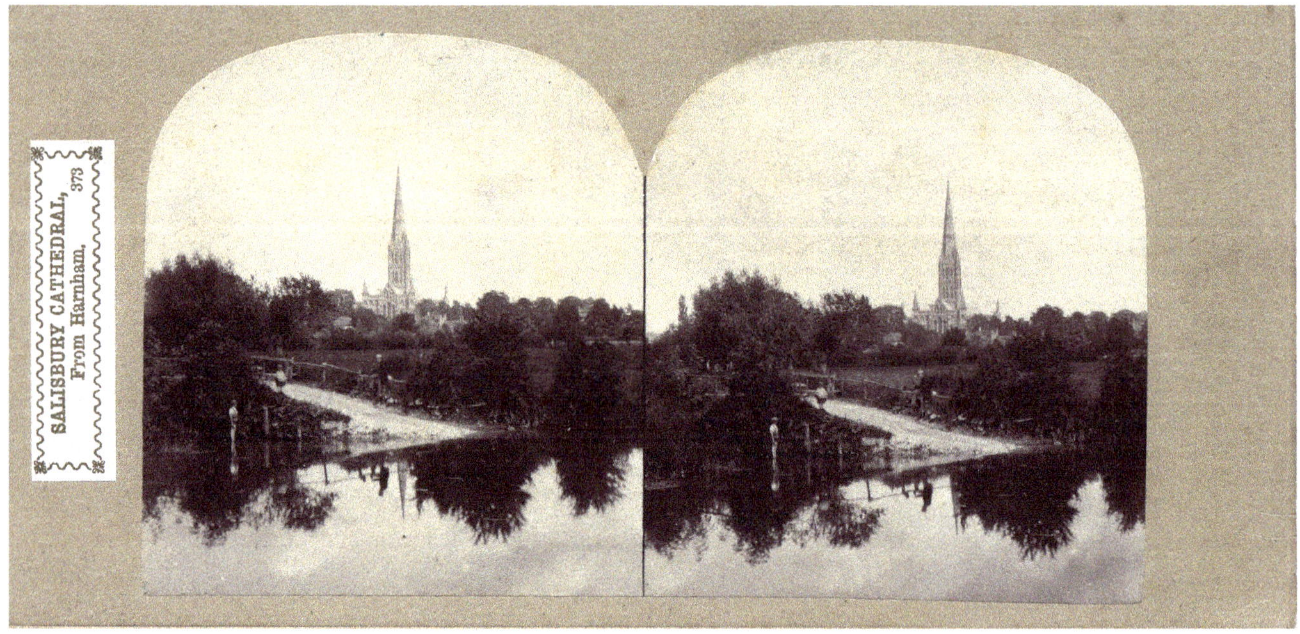

William Russell Sedgfield. *Salisbury Cathedral from Harnham. 373.* Stereoscopic view. Albumen print. Anthony Hamber collection.

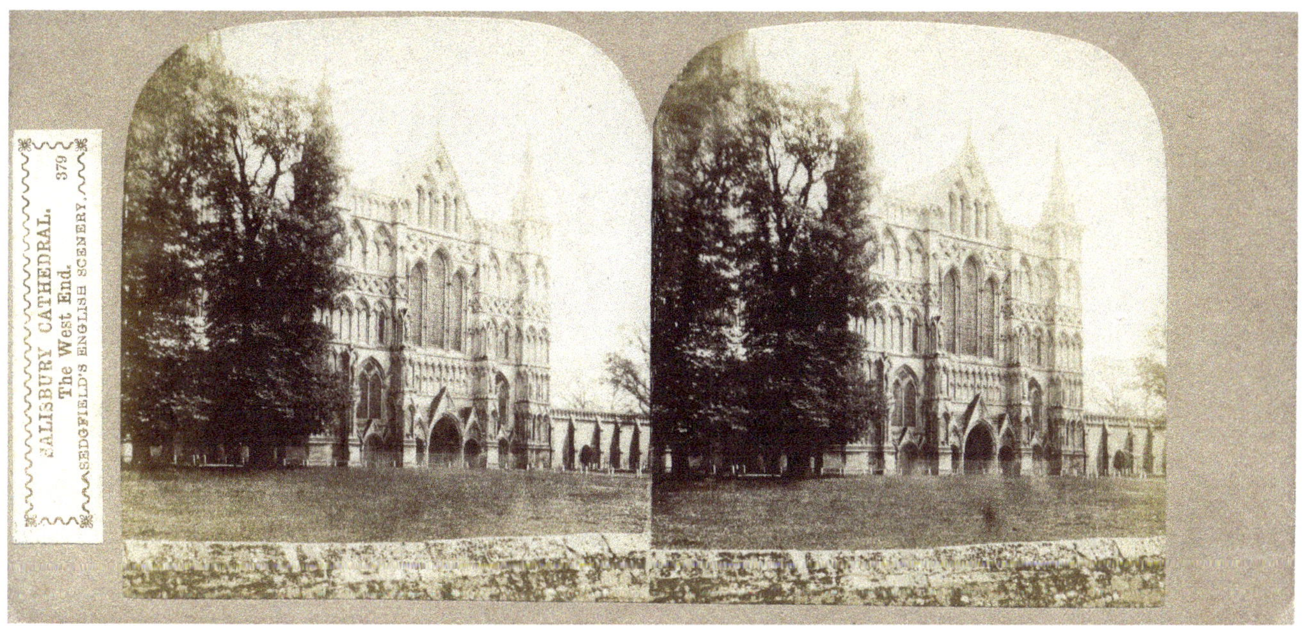

William Russell Sedgfield. *Salisbury Cathedral. The West End. 379.* Stereoscopic view. Albumen print. Anthony Hamber collection.

advertised during the 1860s and 1870s by Thomas Edwards, of St Ann Street, on the verso of his carte de visites. It 1875 he was offering this service at a cost from 2 guineas. These were probably produced by a solar enlarger, the origins of which dated back to the mid-1850s but which became popular a decade later. Some very large photographs were made up using a mosaic system of smaller paper prints enlarged from the same negatives, there being no paper large enough to produce a single print.

Three photographic formats were particularly popular during the second half of the nineteenth century; the stereoscopic view, the carte de visite and the cabinet card.

The stereoscopic view first appeared commercially in the late 1840s though its rise in popularity was significantly enhance by the royal patronage of Queen Victoria at the Great Exhibition of 1851. The format consisted of two images within a mount measuring approximately 8 x 17.5 cm and primarily used the daguerreotype process until the second half of the 1850s, when the albumen paper print process became popular. Millions of albumen print stereo views were produced from the late 1850s until the end of the century. The format was used occasionally for portraiture, but architecture and sculpture became particularly popular subject matter. William Russell Sedgfield created a large set of stereoscopic views of the cathedral.

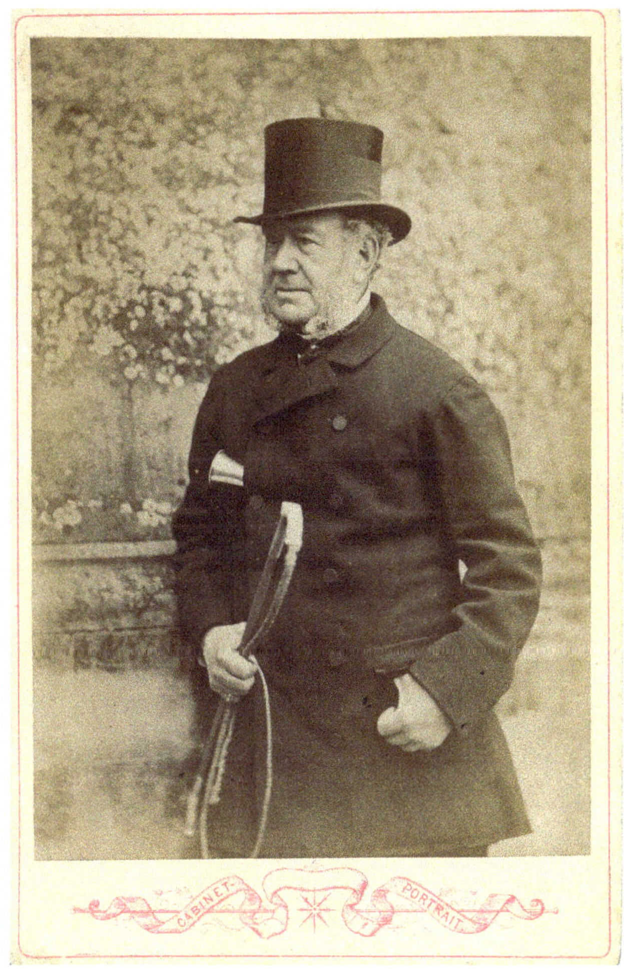

Henry Brooks. Portrait of Jacob Pleydell-Bouverie, 4th Earl of Radnor. Early 1880s. Cabinet Card. Albumen print. Anthony Hamber collection.

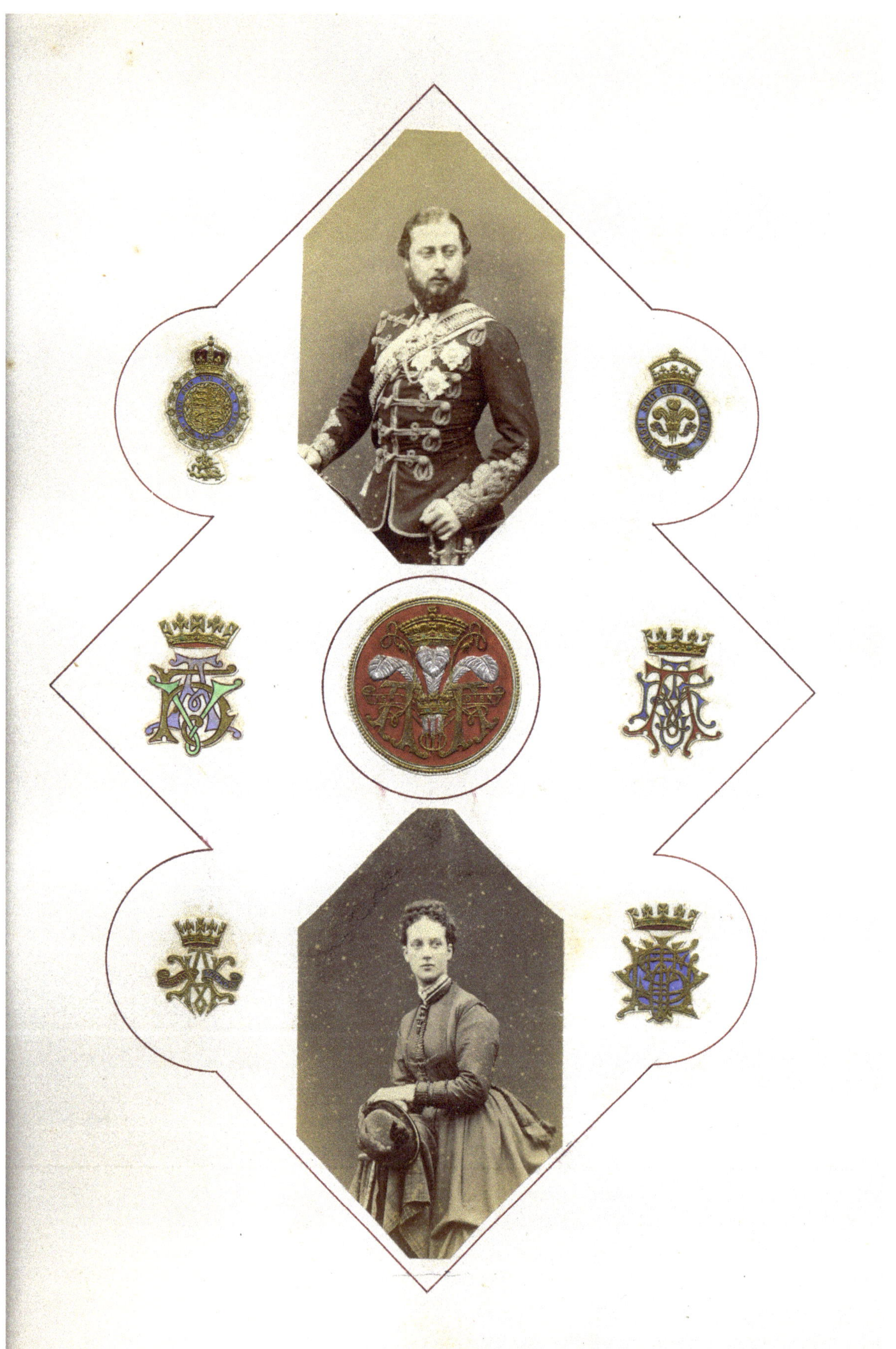

Unidentified photographer. Portraits of Edward, Prince of Wales (later King Edward VII) and Alexandra, Princess of Wales. c. 1867. Carte de visites. From *Monogram Book. Mary Cadogan.* Anthony Hamber collection.

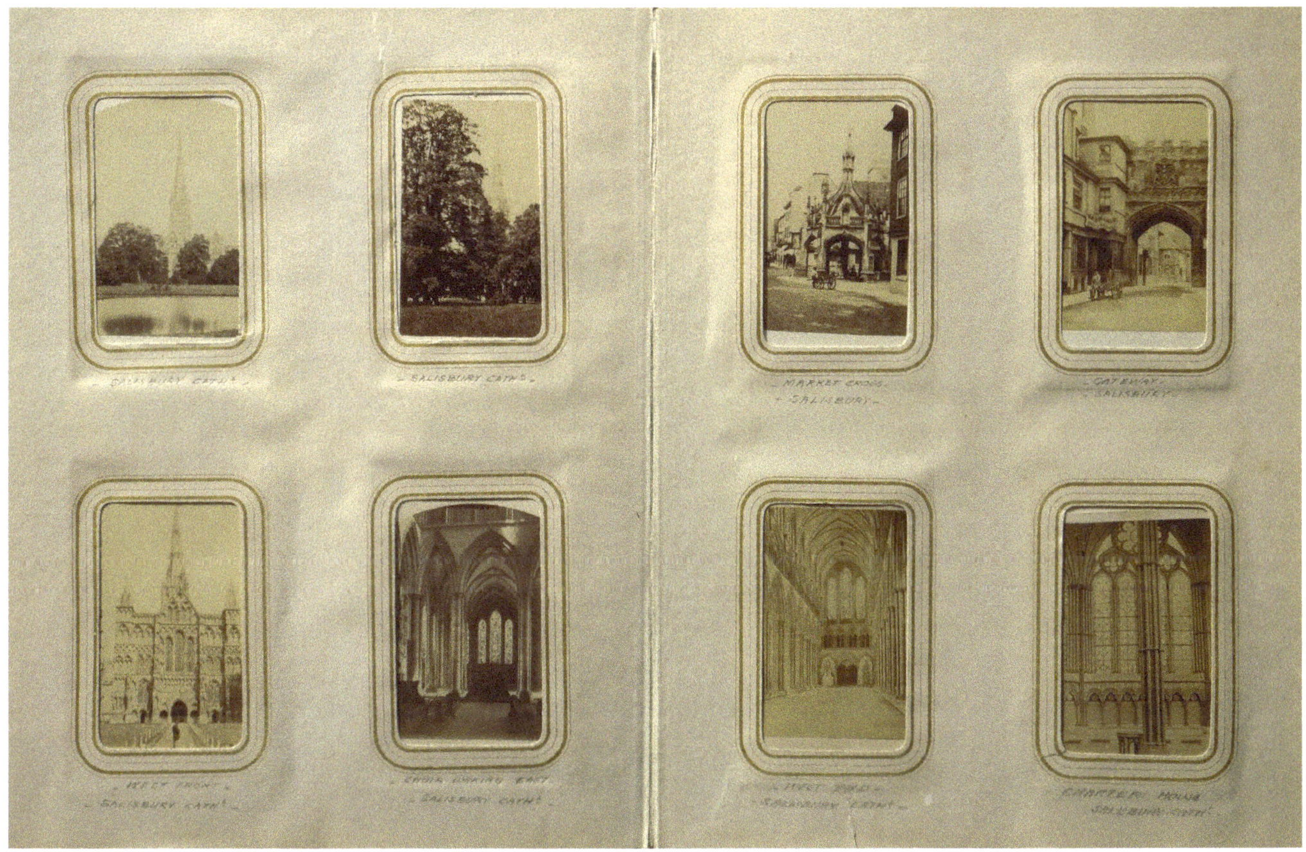

View of two pages of a carte de visite album showing views of Salisbury. Anthony Hamber collection.

The carte de visite (approx. 10 x 6 cm) format of a small photograph was patented in Paris by photographer André Adolphe Eugène Disdéri(1819–1889) in 1854. It was slow to gain widespread use until 1859, when Disdéri published portraits of Emperor Napoleon III (1808–1873) in this format. The format then had a meteroric rise in popularity, particularly for portrait photography. John Jabez Edwin Mayall (1813–1901) sold hundreds of thousands of his carte de visite portraits of the British royal family from 1860 onwards. Following the sudden death of Prince Albert in December 1861, 70,000 of Mayall's carte de visite portraits of Albert, stocked by Marion and Co. of Soho Square in London, reportedly sold out in one week.[31] Other carte de visite subject matter included architecture, sculpture, landscapes and advertising.

The cabinet card format (approx. 16.5 x 10.7 cm) was introduced in 1866 by London photographer Frederick Richard Window (1824–1875). It became popular for architectural and topographical views in the early 1870s, and then a commercially successful portrait format from the mid-1870s until the early 20th century.

Photographic accessories to house the carte de visite and cabinet card were produced in primarily two forms. One was the album, into which loose, unmounted photographic prints could be pasted in a sequence determined by the owner. The other was the specially manufactured carte de visite, and later cabinet format, albums. These had pre-cut windows in the pages that were made from two layers of stiff card separated with a piece of board. Each window had a slot at its base through which carte de visite cards could be inserted.

Early instances of photography in Salisbury

Photographic studios began to appear in Wiltshire in increasing numbers after the Great Exhibition closed. In April 1852, Marks of Devizes began advertising his daguerreotype photographic portrait studio, in Long Street, specimens being available from Bull, bookseller.[32] This may have been George Marks, who had previously operated a studio in Marland Place, Southampton. Marks appears to have very quickly identified that there

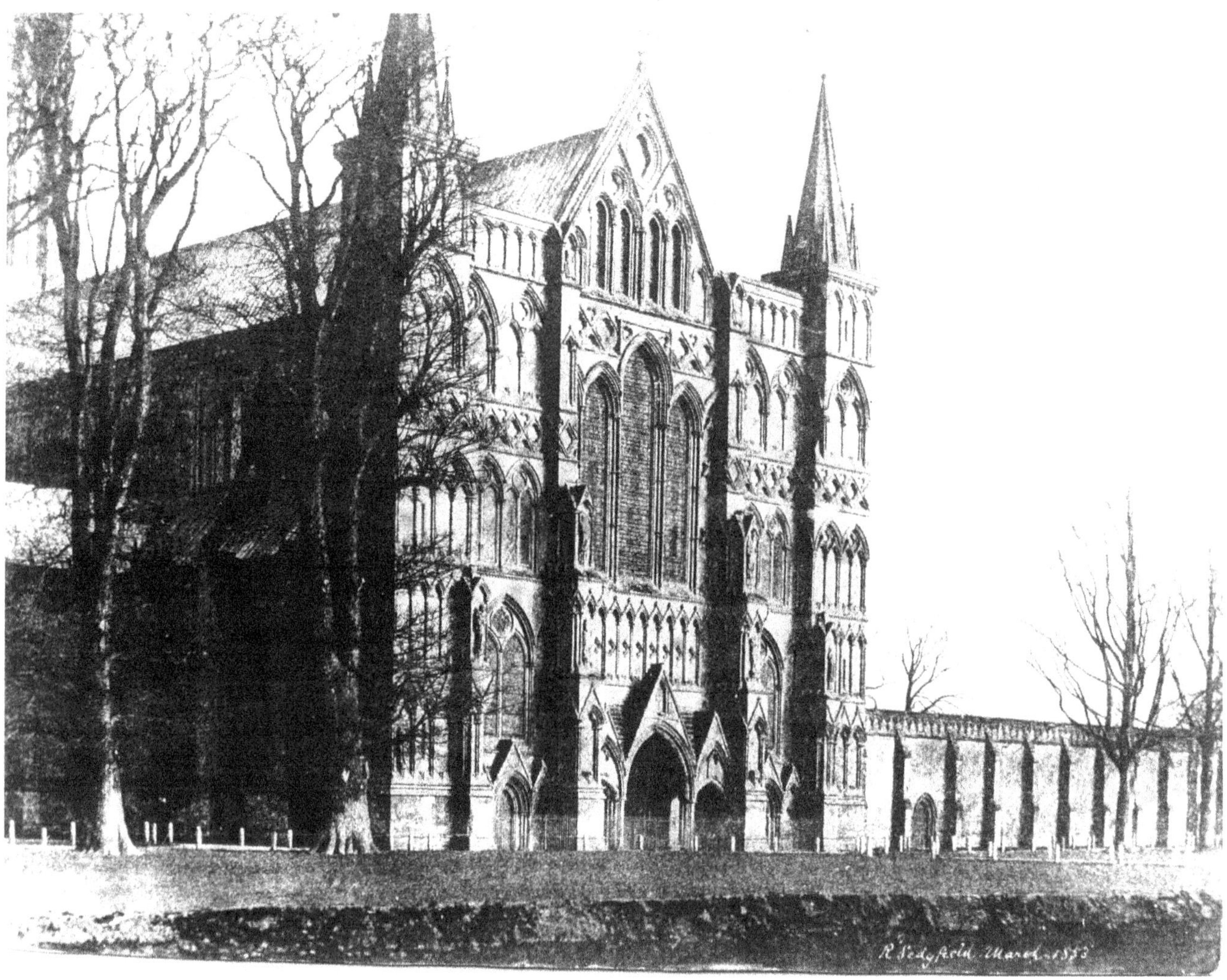

William Russell Sedgfield. View of West front of Salisbury Cathedral from the North-West. March 1853. Albumen print. Private collection.

was little market for his services in Devizes since he advertised that his studio would 'finally close' on the 1st May 1852, only weeks after it had opened.[33]

Quite how many daguerreotype or calotype photographs were taken in and around Salisbury by either itinerant photographers or local amateurs during the first half of the 1850s remains unclear. The paucity of extant daguerreotypes taken in Salisbury belies their mid-19th century popularity. In terms of the calotype, this remained subservient to the daguerreotype. However, gauging the scale of either process taken in and around Salisbury during the 1840s and 1850s remains, at the time of writing, extremely difficult to determine. It may be that while photographers advertised that they would take daguerreotypes and calotypes, their popularity was already in decline and few citizens of Salisbury availed themselves of this service, preferring the wet collodion glass negative process.

One of the earliest commercial photographers to visit and record Salisbury was William Russell Sedgfield (1826–1902). A native of Devizes, Sedgfield trained as an engraver and may have begun to experiment with photography as early as 1842, when he contacted Henry Talbot regarding use of Talbot's calotype process. Having received a demand for £20 from Talbot's solicitor for a licence, Sedgfield decided to continue to take calotype photographs without a licence. He appears to have taken photographic portraits of a number of people in Wiltshire, though it is not clear whether any were living in Salisbury or its surroundings. Sedgfield was also in correspondence with the influential writer on photography, Robert Hunt (1807–1887). Having experimented with photography during the second half of the 1840s, Sedgfield appears to have changed career and soon after 1851 became a fully-fledged professional photographer.

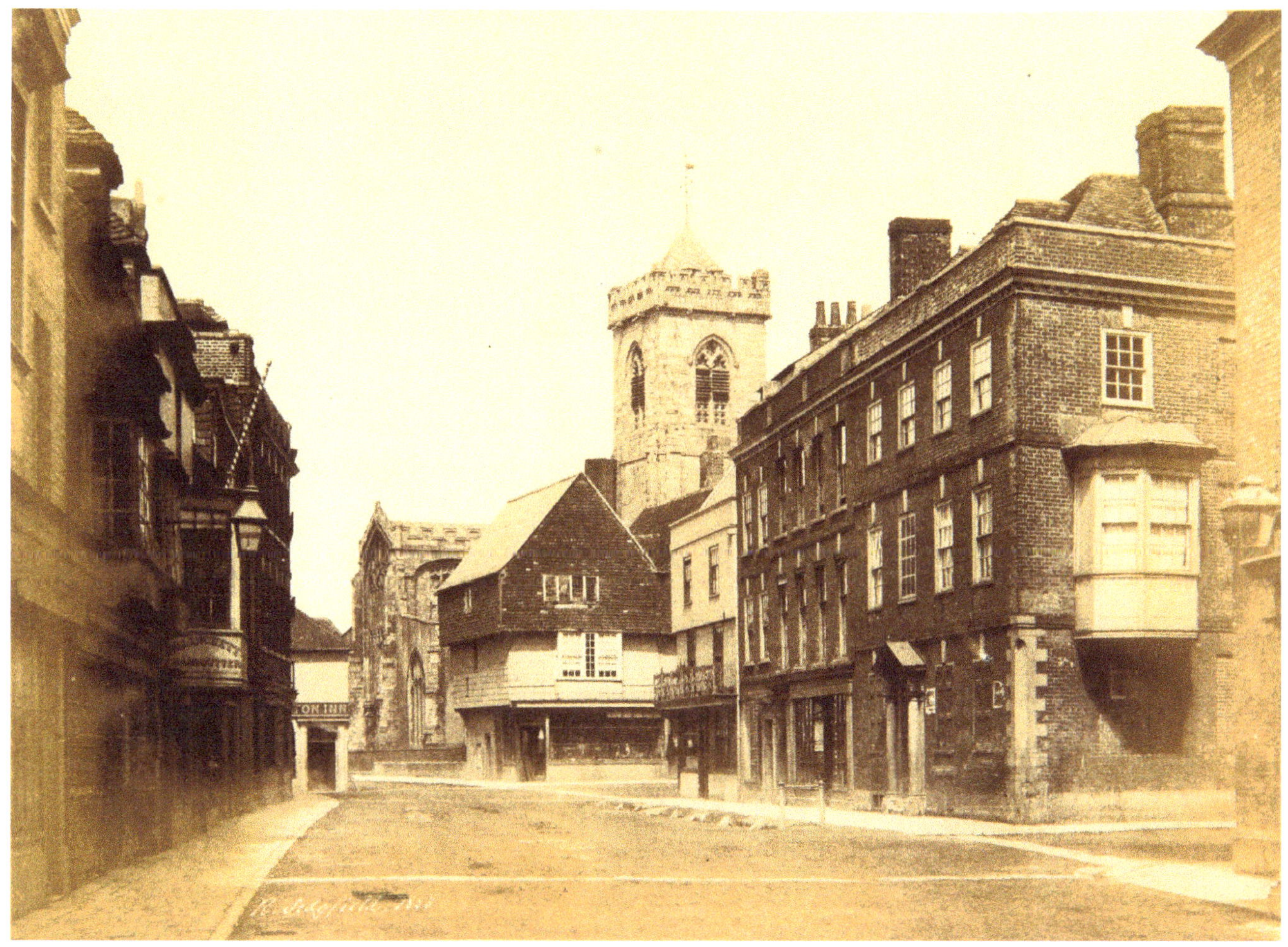

William Russell Sedgfield. View of the High Street towards St Thomas's Church. 1853. Albumen print. Private collection.

In March 1853 Sedgfield visited Salisbury and took a number of calotype views of the cathedral and the city. The following September a set of ten photographs by Sedgfield was available through commercial outlets in Salisbury. The set was advertised at 25s., 'in a neat cover'. Individual photographs from the set could be had for 3s. However, it is significant that the advert stated that 'specimens' might be seen at Brown's in the Canal and Frederick Blake in the Market Place, where subscribers' names would be received. This suggests Sedgfield was unclear as to the size of the market for his photographs, which included the cathedral, parish churches, the Poultry Cross and the High Street.[34] The rarity of these photographs suggests that Sedgfield did not sell many of them.

At the same time, a view of Salisbury Cathedral by Sedgfield appeared in Part V of *The Photographic Album*, published by Joseph Cundall in November 1853. A review in *Notes and Queries* stated:

> To this beautiful specimen of the art we may certainly refer as a proof that it is quite possible to obtain upon paper the greatest nicety of detail; in short, every minuteness that can be desired or ought to be attempted.[35]

Sedgfield returned to photograph in Salisbury on a number of occasions. In 1856 he recorded the 'Dinner in the Market Place, Salisbury, to celebrate the Peace of 1856', a photograph he exhibited at the photographic exhibition held by the Norwich and Norfolk Fine Arts Association between 17th November 1856 and 14th February 1857. (Cat. No. 89.) In 1857 Sedgfield placed a full-page advertisement in the 1858 edition of *Brown's Stranger's Handbook and Illustrated Guide to Salisbury Cathedral.* Sedgfield returned to photograph in the city in the late 1850s and 1860s when he took two cameras, one 9¼ x 7¼ inches and the other 11½ x 7½ inches. He used the larger plate camera in 'portrait' format for interior views of the cathedral

ADVERTISEMENTS. 21

LIST OF PHOTOGRAPHS

OF

Salisbury & the Neighbourhood

BY

W. R. SEDGFIELD,

WHICH MAY BE OBTAINED OF

MESSRS. BROWN & CO., NEW CANAL,

Price 4s. each, mounted.

Cathedral from Harnham
General View of ditto from South
Spire, from Bishop's Garden
West Door
Cloisters—interior
Two Arches of Cloisters
Saint Ann's-street
Old Sarum Stonehenge
Beeches in the New Forest
Road in ditto

Also, a large selection of Views in Derbyshire, Yorkshire, and Warwickshire; amongst the Views in Warwickshire are—

Cæsar's Tower and Part of Kenilworth
Lunn's Tower and Gate House, Kenilworth
Great Hall, Kenilworth
Doorway near the White Hall
Warwick Castle and Bridge
Beauchamp Chapel, Warwick
Shakespeare's House, Stratford-upon-Avon
The Parade, Leamington
&c. &c. &c.

W. R. S. also begs to call attention to a great variety of

Stereographs of the Cathedral, Cloisters, Old Sarum, Stonehenge, &c. &c.,

Price 1s. 6d. each.

Universal Exhibition of Photography at Brussels.—Mr. Sedgfield's Calotypes do honour to English Photography, as well as his pretty landscapes and studies of hedges and bushes. A portrait (probably from a picture of Sir Joshua Reynolds's) forms a very remarkable specimen of a copy from an oil painting. Salisbury Cathedral, Warwick Castle, and a perspective view under the arch of a tunnel, by Mr. Sedgfield, of London, are without doubt very fine pictures.—*From the Journal of the Photographic Society.*

Advertisement of William Russell Sedgfield. *Brown's Stranger's Handbook and Illustrated Guide to Salisbury Cathedral*, Brown and Co; Simpkin and Co., Salisbury; London, 1858.

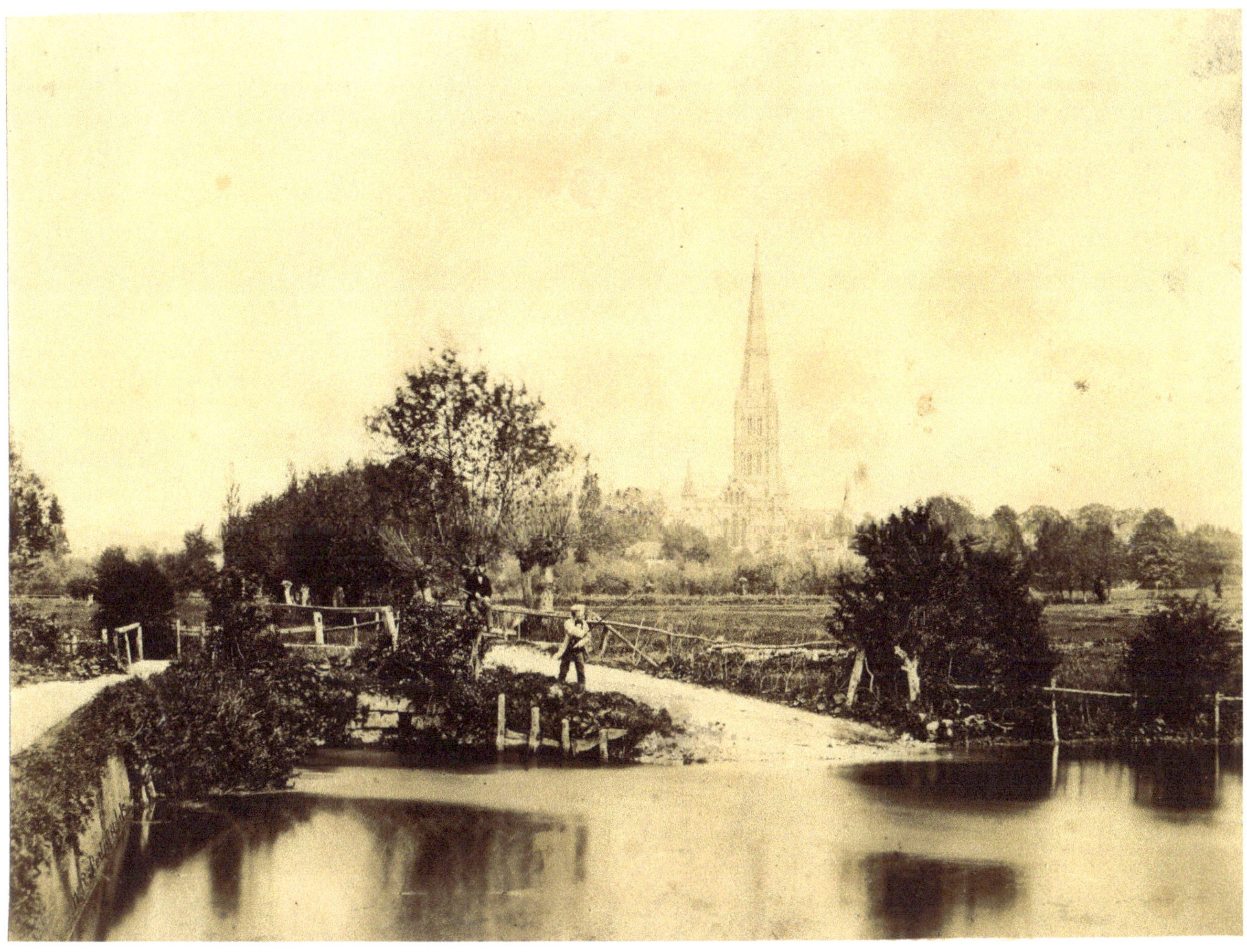

William Russell Sedgfield. View of Salisbury Cathedral from Harnham Mill. c. 1858. Albumen print. Anthony Hamber collection.

and the smaller camera in 'landscape' format for the general view of the building that he took from the Mill at Harnham. Sedgfield took a large number of stereo views of the cathedral around 1858 as well as views at Harnham Mill and from Harnham Bridge looking North towards the Close.

One of the earliest photographers to offer professional services in Salisbury was an itinerant by the name of John Clarke (1829–1879). Clarke had originally been a miniature painter and then actor at the Strand Theatre in London in 1852, and chief comedian there between 1852 and 1855, and again between 1858 and 1862. He operated a photographic studio at 89 Strand, Westminster between 1852 and 1853, and again between 1857 and 1862. Quite how Clarke juggled his two careers has yet to be established, as has why he headed out into the provinces to ply a trade as an itinerant photographer.

The first advertisement in the *SJ* for Clarke's daguerreotype portrait studio was in the issue of the *SJ* for 24th June 1854, though he appears to have opened for business earlier that summer. Significantly, Clarke advertised his services as a 'Miniature Painter and Photographist' thereby maximising his potential earnings. In early July he advertised that he would prolong his stay for another fortnight. Subsequent advertisements stated 'that Business in London will compel him to leave for a few days; but that he will return to complete his engagements on Monday 24th July, at Mr. Webb's, Gunmaker, 38 Catherine-Street Salisbury, where specimens may be seen. Portraits cost 5s. and would be retaken, free of charge, 'if not entirely approved of'.

Clarke, who also noted that he would visit Shaftesbury 'by desire', prolonged his stay in Salisbury until at least 5th September 1854,

DAGUERREOTYPE PORTRAITS.
MR. JOHN CLARKE, Miniature Painter and Photographist, of 89, Strand, London, having met with considerable patronage during the past week, is induced to prolong his stay for ANOTHER FORTNIGHT.
PORTRAITS taken in the above beautiful Art, with all the latest Improvements, for 5s.—MINIATURES on Ivory, Card, &c., at Mr. Webb's, Gunmaker, 38, Catherine-street, Salisbury, where Specimens may be seen.
Portraits retaken, free of Charge, if not entirely approved of. [1957

Advertisement of John Clarke. *Salisbury Journal*, Saturday 1st July 1854 p. 3.

according to the advertisements he placed in the *SJ*. In an advertisement on the 29th July he stated he had stereoscopes and 'Views' on display, though their subject matter remains to be established, as does whether these 'views' were his own photographs or by others.

Another photographer – a Mr Shoosmith – began to place advertisements in the *SJ* in the summer of 1855. This may have Decimus Shoosmith (1832–1922), who may have worked in a London studio as an operator before setting off as an independent. In his advert he referred to six years of experience as a photographer and advertised that specimens of his photographs were on display at 'Mr Roe's, Printer, Queens Street'. A framed daguerreotype portrait cost 2s. 6d. and Shoosmith set up his studio next to the 'Roman Catholic Chapel' (St. Osmund) in Exeter Street where he stated he took portraits 'by his celebrated coloured photographic process', which were described as 'coloured collodion.' Shoosmith advertised at the end of October that this was 'positively the last week'[36] He was in Frome from December 1855 until the end of March 1856, as advertised in the *Somerset & Wilts Journal* in December 1855.

GREAT REDUCTION IN THE PRICE OF PHOTOGRAPHY.
MR. SHOOSMITH returns thanks to the Inhabitants of Salisbury and its Vicinity for their kind and very liberal support, and begs to inform them that he is now taking the
FINEST DAGUERREOTYPE PORTRAITS IN FRAME COMPLETE FOR 2s. 6d.
Six years' experience enables him to compete with any operator in this process.
Mr. S. also calls particular attention to his UNRIVALLED, INSTANTANEOUS,
COLOURED COLLODION PORTRAITS,
for which he has received such universal renown. These Portraits being Coloured (equal to Ivory Miniatures) by an entire New Process of Mr. Shoosmith's own discovery, are far preferable to the Daguerreotype or any other process yet invented. They are warranted not to Fade, and can be seen in any Light.
Parties are respectfully solicited to compare Mr. Shoosmith's Portraits with any others taken, as they are warranted not to be equalled for their bright and distinct appearance.
Portraits taken at the party's own Residence in Town or Country.
☞ Observe—Mr. Shoosmith, Exeter Street, near the Roman Catholic Chapel.
Specimens may be seen at Mr. Roe's, Printer, &c., Queen Street; or at the above address. [6906

Advertisement of Mr. Shoosmith. *Salisbury Journal*, Saturday 4th August 1855 p. 2.

PHOTOGRAPHIC PORTRAITS.
POSITIVELY THE LAST WEEK.
MR. SHOOSMITH begs to inform his Friends and the Inhabitants of Salisbury and its vicinity, that in consequence of the unfavourable weather of last week, he is induced to remain in this City until THE END OF THE PRESENT WEEK, when his Engagement must POSITIVELY TERMINATE.
☞ All Parties wishing Portraits taken by his celebrated
COLOURED PHOTOGRAPHIC PROCESS,
are requested to apply immediately to Mr. SHOOSMITH, near the Roman Catholic Chapel.
Salisbury, Oct. 27, 1855. [7928

Advertisement of Mr. Shoosmith. *Salisbury Journal*, Saturday 27th October 1855 p. 2.

While Clarke and Shoosmith did not settle in Salisbury, 1855 also saw the arrival of one of the first generation of resident commercial photographers, William Thomas Pitcher (1828–1909). His advertisements in the *SJ* stated that he had previously been for 'many years' a camera operator in the studio of Richard Beard and a 'Photographist' in London at the Royal Polytechnic Institution. Pitcher's advertisement for his 'Photographic and Daguerreotype Miniatures' in the *SJ* for Saturday 21st July 1855 stated that he intended 'practising … the Beautiful Art in this city for a short time' and that 'specimens of various styles' were on view at F.A. Blake's, booksellers, on Blue Boar Row on the Market Place. It is not clear where Pitcher had his first photographic studio and he gave a Winchester Street address at the bottom of this advertisement. By August 1855 Pitcher was advertising his studio in the Market Place, next to the Council Chamber.

In his advertisement in the *SJ* for 8th September 1855, Pitcher included, for the first time, a line which read 'Paintings, Prints, Models,

PHOTOGRAPHIC AND DAGUERREOTYPE MINIATURES.

MR. W. T. PITCHER, many years Operator with Mr. BEARD (the Patentee of the Daguerreotype process), and late Photographist at the Royal Polytechnic Institution, LONDON, begs to announce to the Inhabitants of SALISBURY and its Vicinity, that he intends practising the above BEAUTIFUL ART in this City for a short period, and respectfully solicits their Patronage.

Deep has been the regret of hundreds of families, when distance or death has separated them, that they have lost the valuable opportunity of retaining of each other a faithful Portrait, painted by Nature's own pencil. The strongest inducement is now held out to possess these life-like Pictures, by the cheapness and rapidity with which they are executed.

Specimens of the various Styles are on view at F. A. BLAKE's, Bookseller, Market Place. An early inspection will be esteemed. [6800

Winchester Street, Salisbury, July 21, 1855.

Advertisement of William Pitcher. *Salisbury Journal*, Saturday 21st July 1855 p. 2.

Articles of Virtu etc. etc. copied' This reflected the wide range of subject matter that mid-nineteenth century commercial photographers were willing to document, and presumably was aimed to meet contemporary demand.

At the end of the first year that he operated in Salisbury Pitcher claimed to have taken '1,000 very accurate portraits during his residence in Salisbury for a period of four months.'[37] He announced, in an advertisement placed in the *SJ* on the 8th December that he was closing his studio for the season on 22nd December 1855. He reopened for business in March the following year.[38] By the end of 1857, in an editorial piece, it was stated that Pitcher had taken in total some 5,000 portraits during his residency in Salisbury and his studio would be open during the Christmas period.[39] By 1859 Pitcher was claiming in his advertisements in the *SJ* that he had taken nearly 9,000 portraits in Salisbury, the equivalent of three-quarters of the population. Surprisingly, to date, the author has been unable to locate any surviving photographs by Pitcher. While this probably points to the hyperbole of his advertisements, it is hoped that this study may lead to the identification of some of his extant photographs.

Like many early professional photographers, Pitcher also offered to teach photography and supply photographic apparatus. He also set up temporary studios in neighbouring towns. In November 1856 it was noted that Pitcher had been taking portraits in Fordingbridge, but that it was his last week and

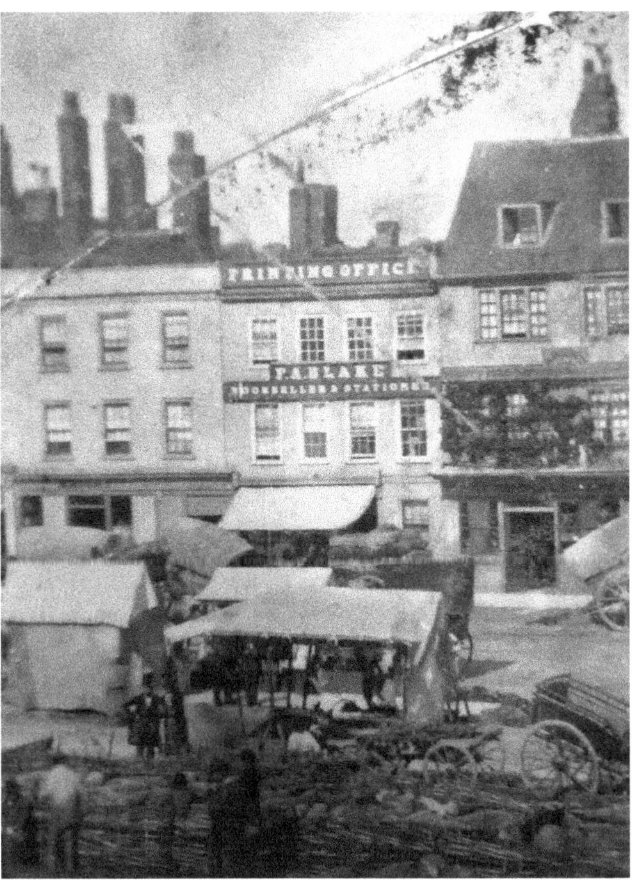

View of shop of F. A. Blake on Blue Boar Row. Mid 1850s. Detail of glass plate negative. The Salisbury Museum.

IMPORTANT NOTICE.

PHOTOGRAPHIC AND DAGUERREOTYPE MINIATURES.

MR. W. T. PITCHER many years Operator with Mr. BEARD (the Patentee of the Daguerreotype process), and late Photographist at the Royal Polytechnic Institution, LONDON, begs to announce to the Inhabitants of SALISBURY and its Vicinity, that he HAS OPENED an ESTABLISHMENT for PHOTOGRAPHIC PURPOSES in the MARKET PLACE, where he has every facility for the production of the most delicate specimens in the above beautiful Art.

Deep has been the regret of hundreds of families, when distance or death has separated them, that they have lost the valuable opportunity of retaining of each other a faithful Portrait, painted by Nature's own pencil. The strongest inducement is now held out to possess these life-like Pictures, by the cheapness and rapidity with which they are executed.

PAINTINGS, PRINTS, MODELS, ARTICLES OF VERTU, &c. &c., COPIED.

Specimens of the various Styles are on view at F. A. BLAKE'S Bookseller, Market Place. An early inspection will be esteemed.

*** THE ART TAUGHT AND APPARATUS SUPPLIED.

Attendance at the Establishment from Nine till Dusk.

Market Place, Salisbury, September 8th, 1855. [7318

Advertisement of William Pitcher. *Salisbury Journal*, Saturday 27th October 1855 p. 2.

it was recommended by the *SJ*'s editor 'that those who have not yet availed themselves of his services to do so at once.'[40] He continued to set up temporary studios in neighbouring towns and in May 1858 it was noted that he intended to set up a portrait studio in Warminster.[41] Whether this would be a permanent subsidiary to his Salisbury studio is unclear.

However, Pitcher's fortunes began to collapse at the end of the 1850s, though the background to his demise remains unclear. He moved his studio to a private house in St Ann Street in 1859. This move away from the busy Market Place indicated the beginning of the rapid decline of his photographic business and in March 1861 his household furniture and effects were auctioned by J. Sutton, without reserve, perhaps an indication that his business had finally failed.[42] The 1861 census – taken on the 7th and 8th April – found Pitcher as a 'photographic artist' lodging in the Morepack Inn at 26 Endless Street. The 1871 found him as a commercial traveller living in Vauxhall in Lambeth, London.

While there were a handful of other commercial photographers in Salisbury at the time, Pitcher was the most prominent Salisbury photographer operating in the second half of the 1850s. His photographic career in the city reflected the rising competition amongst the burgeoning market for commercial photography. Salisbury in the 1860s was to experience a step change in the number of commercial photographers and the products and services they offered.

1860s in Salisbury

During the early 1860s commercial photography underwent a rapid expansion across Great Britain and this study examines how this was reflected in Salisbury. As commercial photography took off, a number of distinguished amateurs gave up photography, dissatisfied with the direction the medium had taken. One of these was Roger Fenton (1819–1869). In 1862, the decision by the organising committee of that year's London International Exhibition not to include photography in the Fine Arts section pointed to the medium's diminished status, and the pioneers such as Fenton became disenchanted and drifted away. In 1863 he sold his equipment and returned to the law as a barrister on the Northern Circuit. Whether amateur photographers in and around Salisbury took similar decisions remains obscure.

Having built the foundations of commercial photography during the 1850s, Salisbury became a relative hot-spot for the profession within Wiltshire during the 1860s. Some twelve photographers, half of whom were to have long-term survival, had studios in the city, far more than any other town in the county. These began to cluster in Catherine Street and the High Street, though there were outliers in Milford Street, Crane Street, St Ann Street, De Vaux Place, and Harnham Bridge. All appear to have offered very similar products and services, primarily centring on portraiture, which had enormous popularity during the 1860s. The insatiable appetite for portraits, including those of royalty, the nobility and contemporary celebrities, was to underpin commercial photography in Salisbury during the 1860s and beyond.

The change in the demographic of the city was reflected in March 1868 when a new newspaper began publication. The stated aim of the *Salisbury Times* (*ST*) was to follow a national trend and provide cheap, authoritative news and information. It cost 1d. (one penny or 0.4p) and was considerably less expensive than the *SJ* which cost 4d (unstamped) or 5d. (stamped).[43] The rise in disposable income opened up opportunities for commercial photographers and widened the client base. A number of Salisbury photographers advertised in the *ST* from its earliest issues, including Thomas Edwards, Samuel Parker, and C. J. Witcomb. Since the *ST* was clearly targeting a less affluent reader, it may be conjectured that Edwards, Parker and Witcomb were specifically targeting this emerging market, perhaps due to the competition amongst commercial photographic studios in Salisbury. Edwards, with his studio located slightly outside the city centre, may have been attempting to drive trade away from the cluster of photographers in the High Street and Catherine Street to his St Ann Street studio. Short biographies of these photographers may be found in Appendix 2.

1870s in Salisbury

While the number of commercial photographers in Salisbury plateaued by the end of the 1860s, establishing how the commercial photographic trade in Salisbury fared during the economic downturns of the 1870s remains problematic. The Panic of 1873 was a financial crisis that triggered a depression in Europe and North America that lasted from 1873 until 1879. In England this depression was to last for some two decades and resulted in bankruptcies, escalating unemployment, a halt in public works, and a major trade slump. Nevertheless, between 1870 and 1900 economic output per head of population in Britain and Ireland rose by 500 percent, generating a significant rise in living standards.

The majority of commercial photographers who had set up in business in Salisbury during the late 1850s and 1860s survived into the 1870s. A few additional commercial photographers opened for business during the 1870s. Some reflected urban development, such as Alfred Dunmore on the Wilton Road and Edward Sanger on Devizes Road. Others started business slightly outside the old city centre. James Owen opened his studio on Crane Street, Edwin Targett on Winchester Street and Thomas Jarratt on Fisherton Street.

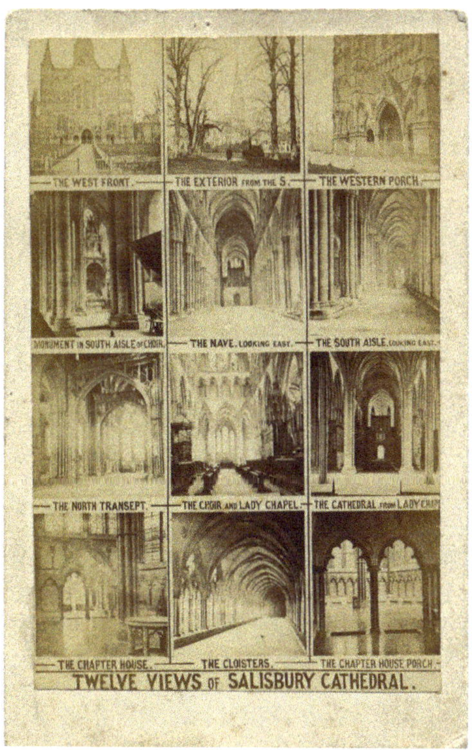

Unidentified photographer. *Twelve views of Salisbury Cathedral.* Early 1860s. Carte de visite. Albumen print. With the stamp of Westley's Library, Cheltenham on the verso. Anthony Hamber collection.

One approach to examining the economic impact on commercial photographers in Salisbury of the depression following 1873 might be to examine changes in the levels of advertisements in local newspapers. In the first three decades of photography, photographers used a variety of channels to target the emerging commercial market. Advertising in the local Salisbury press seems to have been popular in the 1850s and 1860s. Changing the window displays of photographic studios was another form. On special occasions, such as annual fairs or new-year gift giving, fliers might be distributed. Using photographic formats for advertising purposes was also a tactic. For instance, the carte de visite format was used, perhaps as a free sample of photographs on offer.

While advertisements by local photographers in the *SJ* declined in the 1870s, perhaps indicating that photographers were tightening their financial belts, mention of the medium and its application continued to be regularly found in news columns. Although there was incremental progress in terms of photographic equipment and materials, the photographic products and services offered during the 1870s differed little from those of the previous decade. One characteristic of the photographic advertisements was the promotion of new print processes, such as the carbon print and collotype, licensed under brand names such as the Chromotype, or companies such as the Autotype Company. The arrival of the *ST* provided another newspaper for the city and, as mentioned above, a number of local photographers regularly advertised in its columns.

Owen's professional history might point to commercial photography in Salisbury being not only comparatively resistant to the financial depression, but that trade increased. While there was no mass collapse of photographic businesses, Owen, who had only set up his photographic studio in 1878, prospered to such an extent that by 1880 he moved to a new studio in Catherine Street. His advertisement in the *ST* provided the context:

> In returning thanks to the Nobility, Gentry and the Public of Salisbury and neighbourhood for the support he has received during the past two years, begs to inform them that in consequence of increasing business he has had erected an entirely

MR. JAMES OWEN,
PORTRAIT PAINTER & PHOTOGRAPHER,
29, CATHERINE STREET, SALISBURY,

In returning thanks to the Nobility, Gentry and the Public of Salisbury and neighbourhood for the support he has received during the past two years, begs to inform them that in consequence of increasing business he has had erected an entirely

NEW STUDIO,
with all the latest improvements for the production of
HIGH-CLASS PHOTOGRAPHS.

The Studio is also especially adapted for photographing Family Groups, Children, and all subjects requiring instantaneous exposures.

Mr. OWEN PERSONALLY gives Sittings for Photographs from Nine until Dusk Daily.

PRICE LIST ON APPLICATION. [1503

Advertisement of James Owen. *Salisbury Times*, Saturday 7th February 1880 p. 1.

> New Studio with all the latest improvements for the production of High-Class Photographs.[44]

Owen's studio continued to thrive at 28 Catherine Street into the early 20th century.

This chapter has provided an overview of the rise of commercial photography in Salisbury. The subject matter to which photography was applied to record Salisbury and its citizens is described in more detail in the next chapters and in the biographies of Salisbury photographers found in Appendix 2.

In summary, Salisbury was typical in that its size could not support a commercial photographer during the 1840s. Following the arrival of a few itinerant photographers, from the mid-1850s a number of commercial photographers set up in business in the city. During the 1860s the number of commercial photographers plateaued and remained reasonably constant during the 1870s and beyond. However, the scale, scope and role of amateur photography in Salisbury during these decades remains unclear. Their story deserves to be unearthed and told since – during the 1850s in particular – they worked on an even footing with the emerging class of commercial photographers.

1 *Reports by the Juries on the Subjects in the Thirty Classes into which the Exhibition was Divided*, vol. 1, Spicer Bros.; W. Clowes, London, 1852, p. 520. Citation from the two-volume edition of the *Reports*.
2 *The Times*, 13th August 1852, p. 4.
3 See Anthony Hamber, *Photography and the 1851 Great Exhibition*, Oak Knoll Press and V&A Publications, London, 2018.
4 See Anthony Hamber and Jane Howells. 'Salisbury and the 1851 Great Exhibition', *Sarum Chronicle*, No. 14, 2014, pp. 112–128.
5 *First Report of The Commissioners for the Exhibition of 1851*, W. Clowes and Sons, London, 1852. Appendix XVIII. Return of Schools reported to the Executive Committee as having entered the Building, p. 96.
6 See http://digital.nls.uk/pencilsoflight/history.htm.
7 'Fine Arts: The Calotype Society', in *Athenæum*, 18th December 1847 p. 1304.
8 See Michael Pritchard, 'Who were the amateur photographers?' at http://eitherand.org/reconsidering-amateur-photography/who-were-amateur-photographers/ for an overview of amateur photography during the period 1839 to 1914 and Michael Pritchard, *The development and growth of British photographic manufacturing and retailing 1839–1914*, Ph.D., De Montfort University, 2010.
9 This figure has been established through the correlation of a number of online and printed sources, including ancestry.co.uk, FindMyPast.co.uk, Photolondon.org.uk and Bernard & Pauline Heathcote, *A Faithful Likeness: The First Photographic*

Portrait Studios in the British Isles, 1841–1855 (Lowdham, 2002). The actual figure may be higher due to some individuals not stating their profession as professional photographers (rather calling themselves 'artists'), illegible handwriting on the census forms, and transcription errors made to create the digital data sets used by online genealogical resources.

10 There were 28 shire counties in England; 13 counties in Wales; 34 counties in Scotland; and 32 counties in Ireland. This is a total of 107. An average of ten photographers per county would be conservatively realistic. As Schaaf has pointed out, many of the earliest photographers are ones that historians have failed to identify and are only to be found in private diaries. See Larry J. Schaaf, "Splendid Calotypes' and 'Hideous Men': Photography in the Diaries of Lady Pauline Trevelyan', *History of Photography*, Volume 34, Number 4, November 2010, pp. 326–341.

11 I thank Michael Pritchard for supplying these figures.

12 See Grace Seiberling, (with Carolyn Bloore), *Amateurs, photography, and the mid-Victorian imagination*, University of Chicago Press, Chicago, 1986.

13 *SJ*, Saturday 30th October 1858 p. 2, an article entitled 'A Lion Story'; *SJ*, Saturday 7th January 1860 p. 5 referring to an article entitled 'Vegetation on the Moon's Surface.'

14 *Photographic Notes*, 1st September 1860 p. 230.

15 See Audrey Linkman, *Analysing Victorian Family Portrait Photographs – A Checklist of Procedures* and Audrey Linkman, *The Victorians: Photographic Portraits*, Tauris Parke Books, London & New York, 1993.

16 A discussion on the use of blue glass in photographic studios can be found in the *Photographic News*, 15th June 1877 p. 288.

17 *The Mechanic's Magazine, Register, Journal and Gazette*, Saturday 21st August 1852 pp. 153–154.

18 See R. Derek Wood, *The Calotype Patent Lawsuit of Talbot v. Laroche 1854*, Privately published by R. D. Wood, Bromley, 1975.,https://web.archive.org/web/20100323063132/http://www.midley.co.uk/laroche/TalbotvLaroche.htm

19 Frederick Scott Archer, 'On the Use of Collodion in Photography', *The Chemist*, March 1851, pp. 257–258; John Werge, *The Evolution of Photography*, Piper & Carter; John Werge, London, 1890 p. 42.

20 *SJ*, Saturday 15th March 1856 p. 2 and Saturday 20th December 1856 p. 2.

21 *SJ*, Saturday 15th July 1876 p. 5.

22 *op. cit*, p. 8.

23 *British Journal of Photography*, 1st December 1876 p. 570 and p. 576.

24 *SJ*, Saturday 20th December 1856 p. 2.

25 *SJ*, Saturday 30th January 1858 p. 4.

26 *SJ*, Saturday 1st October 1859 p. 4.

27 *SJ*, Saturday 1st October 1859 p. 4.

28 Advertisement in *The Photographic Journal*, 16th January 1860 [n.p.] An Atkins & Son, of 37 Blue Boar Row, was listed as a dealer in photographic materials in *Kelly's Directory of the Chemical Industries*, Kelly's Directories Ltd., London, 1921 p. 256. It is assumed this is the same family.

29 *SJ*, Saturday 5th November 1864 p. 5.

30 *SJ*, Saturday 24th April 1875 p. 1.

31 'Miscellenea', *Photographic Journal*, 15th March 1862 p. 21.

32 *Wiltshire Independent*, Thursday 15thApril 1852 p. 2.

33 *Wiltshire Independent*, Thursday 22nd April 1852 p. 1

34 Advert in *SJ*, Saturday 18th June 1853.

35 *Notes and Queries*, 13th August, 1853 p. 157.

36 *SJ*, Saturday 27th October 1855 p. 2.

37 *SJ*, Saturday 8th December 1855 p. 3.

38 *SJ*, Saturday 8th March 1856 p. 3.

39 *SJ*, Saturday 26 December 1857 p. 5.

40 *SJ*, Saturday 1st November 1856 p. 3.

41 *SJ*, Saturday 22nd May 1858 p. 8.

42 *SJ*, Saturday 9thMarch 1861 p. 4.

43 Stamp Duty was a tax imposed on British newspapers first introduced as early as 1712. However, this was repealed in 1855 so it is unclear why the *SJ* continued to mention unstamped and stamped prices.

44 *ST*, Saturday 7th February 1880 p. 1.

4 SALISBURY CATHEDRAL – A CASE STUDY

THE CATHEDRAL IN Salisbury has represented a magnet for a variety of travellers and pilgrims for centuries. The advent of the railway network from the 1840s promoted new forms of affordable tourism and led to an increase in those travelling to or passing through the city.

Quite when the first photographs of the cathedral were taken has yet to be established, though this is likely to have taken place in the 1840s, perhaps by amateurs rather than visiting professionals.

One photographer who one might consider should have documented the cathedral was none other than one of the inventors of photography, a native of Wiltshire, living at Lacock Abbey some 30 miles north-west of Salisbury. In 1840 Henry Talbot was appointed High Sheriff of the County of Wiltshire and had to travel to Salisbury to sit in the Assizes courts that were held there on a quarterly basis each year. However, he appears never to have taken the opportunity to photograph the cathedral or any other part of the city. This is curious not only because it would seem to have offered eminently suitable subject matter, but also because Talbot's uncle, William Thomas Horner Fox Strangways, 4th Earl Ilchester (1795–1865), career diplomat, botanist and art collector, twice suggested in letters to his nephew that Talbot should do so. On 7th March 1840 Strangways wrote a letter to Talbot providing detailed consideration of viewpoints and technical issues:

> How you must grudge this fine weather to the Assizes [in Salisbury] – I wish you could photogenize the Courts – At least if tomorrow is a fine Sunday can you not photogenize the Cathedral? [He continued] If you do take off the Cathedral Let me recommend to take nearly a front view – of whatever side you copy – so as to give the lights & shade of the ornaments rather than the masses – I say this, because there is a famous point of view in which the church is usually drawn, some half way along the diagonal path across the Close – which gives the masses, seen in perspective, at the most picturesque angle – but I am afraid in that case that the architectural details would not come out in the shady corners & that our reflected lights would not be strong or clear enough to produce the required effects, By the way that will be the dark side of the Church this time of year. I would rather take the West end nearly full, when the sun has come round enough to give light & shade to the details & to detach the lines On a South front you might vary your position a little more – on the West the light being weaker I should think you must take your view near & opposite.'

On 2nd November 1841 Strangways wrote from Frankfurt, thanking Talbot for 'your beautiful Calotypes' and suggesting 'I wish some fine day you would take the cathedral of Salisbury'.[1] Talbot seems to have ignored his uncle's suggestions.

The earliest extant photographs of the Cathedral are particularly significant for they predate a major restoration campaign on one of the most distinctive parts of the building, that of the West front. Between 1855 and 1861 the Chapter House was restored by public subscription, a project directed by Henry Clutton (1819–1893), and William Burges (1827–1881).[2] At the outset there was a suggestion to exploit photography. In a letter from 'A Dilletante' of Devizes, to the *Wiltshire Independent*, the writer hoped the organisers of the proposed restoration 'will see the necessity of making immediate application to the Dean and Chapter, for permission to take 'Photographs,' 'Casts,' and 'Squeezings,' from the various parts, and cause the same to be deposited in some appropriate building, as a step towards the formation of a museum of our local antiquities'.[3] However, while such a formal photographic campaign does not appear to have taken place, some photographs of the Chapter House are recorded as early as 1854. George C. Warren exhibited 'Interior of Chapter House, Salisbury' together with 'Salisbury

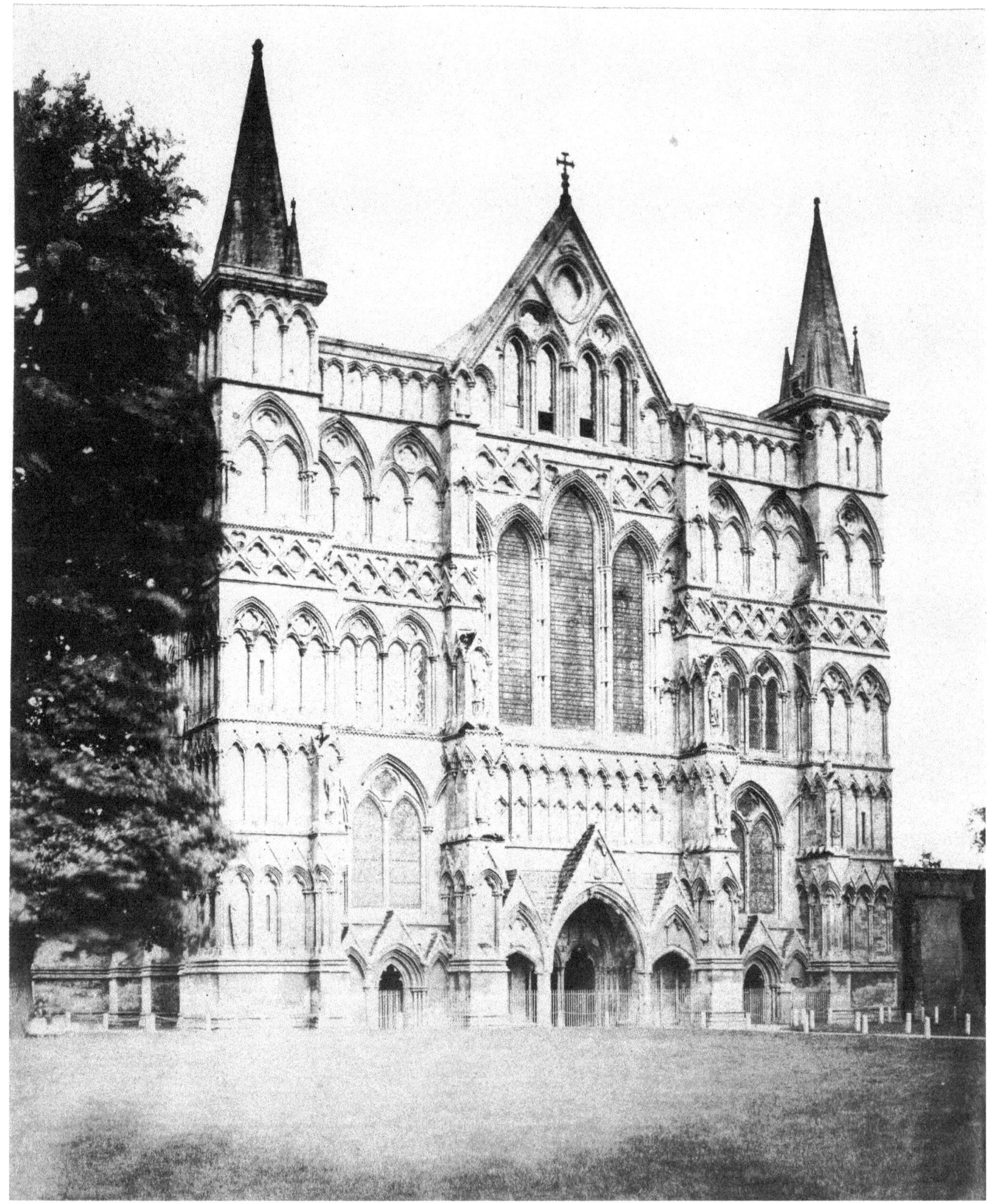

Henry Brooks. West front of Salisbury Cathedral. Early 1860s. Albumen print.
Anthony Hamber collection.

Cathedral', 'Architectural View of West Front, Salisbury Cathedral' and 'Architectural Details from Winchester and Salisbury Cathedrals' at the exhibition of the Photographic Society held in the Gallery of the Society of British Artists, Suffolk Street, Pall Mall, London between 4th January and end of

February 1854. These were catalogue numbers 451, 579, 835 and 457. The dates of the exhibition confirm that Warren must have taken these photographs in 1853. George Charles Warren (1828–1901) was a London photographer who exhibited a number of photographs at the exhibitions of the Photographic Society in the mid-1850s.

In 1862 the eminent and prolific English Gothic Revival architect Sir George Gilbert Scott (1811–1878) produced a report for the Cathedral Chapter on the repairs most urgently needed and the following year the Ecclesiastical Commissioners allowed the Dean and Chapter the sum of £10,782 to spend on the fabric in lieu of the transfer of the Cathedral estates to them in 1840 and again in 1861. Gilbert Scott was then formally appointed and G.P. White of Pimlico in London, who had earlier worked on the project to restore the Chapter House, was contracted as the builder. However, it was soon calculated that £10,000 would be far from sufficient to cover the restoration that the Cathedral required, and, on the 6th April 1864, a public meeting was held in Salisbury at which the Dean outlined that a sum of £40,000 was actually needed. Subscriptions were entered into and together with public donations the restoration work was commenced.[4]

One of the main issues concerning the West façade remains identification of how many contemporaneous medieval statues originally filled the niches. When in 1865 James Frank Redfern (1838–1876) commenced work to 'refill' the 150 niches of the West front with life-size statues, only nine badly weathered statues dating to the 14th century remained in place.[5] Over the centuries a number of prints of the façade had been made but the number of statues depicted varies. Until the late 1990s no architectural historian had made a serious attempt to analyse photographs of the state of the West façade before the Scott restoration campaign of the 1860s. This is curious since of the significant number of photographs of the cathedral taken before the restoration work commenced in 1863, several were by local photographers of the West façade. The work on the West front during the second half of the 1860s and early 1870s was also, perhaps inadvertently, captured by a photographer.

One of the photographers to document the West front, William Russell Sedgfield (1826–1902), had extensively photographed, published and exhibited views of the cathedral prior to the restoration of the West front and the Choir Screen. In the early 1850s Sedgfield undertook a photographic campaign in Wiltshire using at least three different cameras and documented Stonehenge and Salisbury. Although Sedgfield moved to Canonbury in north London in 1854 and in 1864 settled in Kingston-upon-Thames, Surrey, he returned to photograph Salisbury on a number of occasions.[6]

From around 1853 Sedgfield's photographs of the cathedral and city began to be collected and exhibited. On the 12th October 1853, as part of the inaugural meeting of the Wiltshire Archaeological and Natural History Society, a 'Temporary Museum'

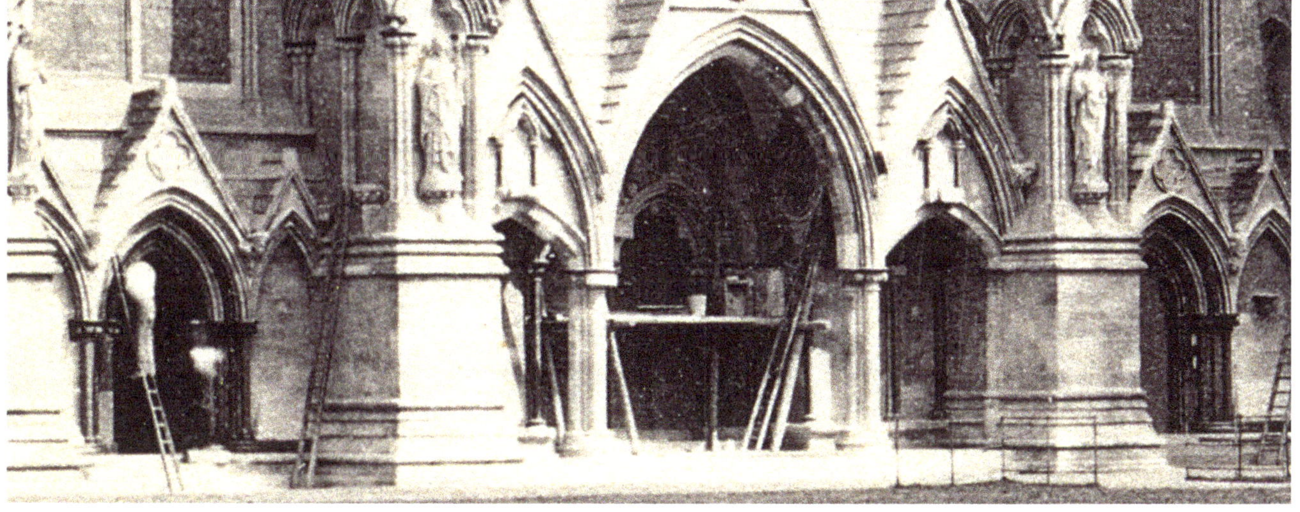

Unidentified photographer. Men working on restoration of the porches of the West front of Salisbury Cathedral. 1871. Detail of a stereoscopic view. Albumen print. Anthony Hamber collection.

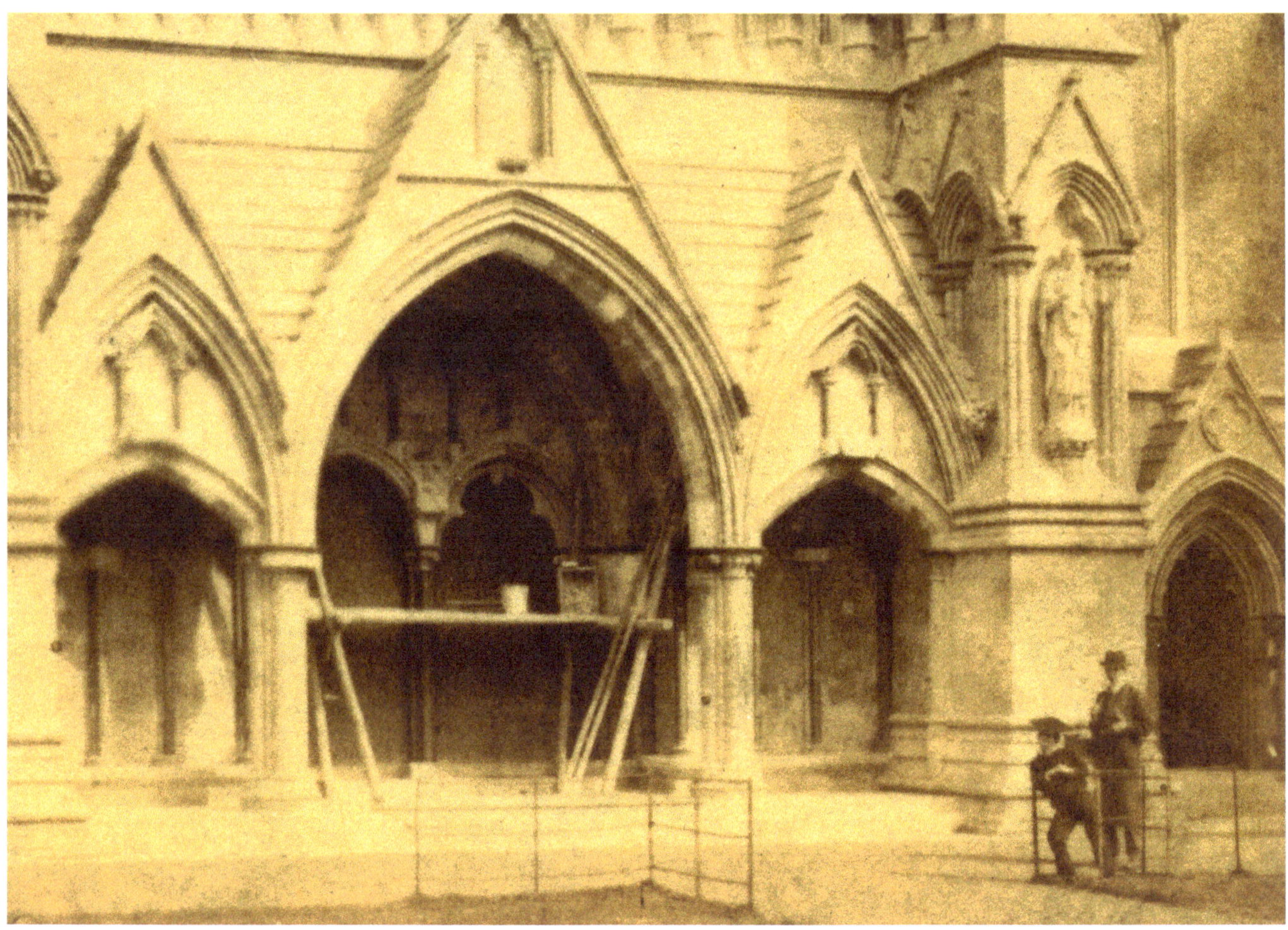

Unidentified photographer. Restoration of the central porch of the West front of Salisbury Cathedral. 1871. Detail of a stereoscopic view. Albumen print. Anthony Hamber collection

was assembled in the Town Hall of Devizes. Nathaniel Bakewell Randle, a bookseller and printer of the Market Place, Devizes, exhibited 'a large number of photographs' by Sedgfield including four of Salisbury:

Salisbury Cathedral
St. Thomas's Church, Salisbury
St. Edmund's Church, Salisbury
Poultry Cross, Salisbury

These images had probably formed part of a number of photographic views of the buildings of Devizes and Salisbury on display in Randle's shop in early August 1853.[7]

An oblique view of the West front of the Cathedral, taken from the north-west, was taken by Sedgfield in March 1853, and signed 'R. Sedgefield. March 1853' in the paper negative, and by September 1853 Sedgfield was advertising in the *SJ* that a set of ten albumen print photographs could be obtained in Salisbury from Frederick Blake or Messrs Brown and Co.

Sedgfield consistently used his views of Salisbury to market his photographs and regularly exhibited them himself, or probably influenced others to do so. A view of Salisbury Cathedral by Sedgfield formed one of the four plates in Part V of the *Photographic Album*, published in November 1853 by Joseph Cundall.[8] Sedgfield exhibited four views of Salisbury Cathedral at the 1854 exhibition of the Photographic Society. ('Salisbury Cathedral' (cat. 533), 'Salisbury Cathedral, West end' (cat.

VIEWS OF SALISBURY.

THE Public are respectfully informed, that the PHOTOGRAPHIC VIEWS of SALISBURY, taken by Mr. SEDGEFIELD, of London, may now be obtained SINGLY of Mr. BLAKE, Market Place, or of Messrs. BROWN and Co., New Canal, Salisbury.
Price 3s. each, or 25s. the Set of Ten. [6995

Advertisement of "Photographic Views of Salisbury" by William Russell Sedgfield. *Salisbury Journal*, Saturday 17th September 1853 p. 2.

no. 534), 'Spire of Salisbury Cathedral' (cat. no. 536), 'Salisbury Cathedral' (cat. no. 645)). These may have been those exhibited the previous year in Devizes. In 1856 Sedgfield exhibited four views of Salisbury Cathedral at the exhibition held in Brussels, including a general view, a view from the South, a view from the mill at Harnham, and view of the cloisters.[9] In 1857 Sedgfield exhibited two views of the cloisters of Salisbury Cathedral at the Architectural Exhibition in London.[10] His *Photographic Delineations of the Scenery, Architecture, and Antiquities of Great Britain and Ireland,* was intended to be made up of six parts and published by Samuel Highley of London between 1854 and 1855, and containing five or six albumen prints. Only four parts were published, and no views of Salisbury Cathedral were included in any of the parts.

Sedgfield returned to photograph in Salisbury in the late 1850s and 1860s when he took two cameras, one 9¼ x 7¼ inches and the other 11½ x 7½ inches. He used the larger plate camera in 'portrait' format for the interior views and the smaller camera in 'landscape' format for the general view of the building that he took from the Mill at Harnham. Sedgfield created the largest set of stereoscopic views of the cathedral in the late 1850s. These formed part of *Sedgfield's English Scenery* and were marketed through the London Stereoscopic Company. Other than general exterior and interior views of the building, Sedgfield also recorded at least one of the tombs in the cathedral, that of Giles de Bridport (d. 1262), Bishop of Salisbury from 1257 until his death. Quite why Sedgfield selected this tomb is unclear. It may have been due to the architectural nature of the tomb that made it easier to photograph than other tombs that had no canopies and only recumbent effigies.

Amateur photographers remained a hallmark of the 1850s and they gathered together within special interest groups such as the Photographic Exchange Club and Photographic Society Club.[11] One amateur was Robert William Skeffington Lutwidge, (1802–1873), an English barrister and Commissioner in Lunacy and he visited Salisbury to inspect the Fisherton House Asylum. He was also the uncle of Charles Lutwidge Dodgson, better known as Lewis Carroll, the author of *Alice in Wonderland,* and who introduced his nephew to photography.

The Photographic Album for the Year 1855. Being Contributions from the Members of The Photographic Club included a salted paper print from a paper negative of *Salisbury Cathedral, from the Bishop's grounds* by Lutwidge. It was accompanied by details of the process used, the light, exposure time, camera lens, and lens diaphragm used. The photograph is dated to October 1855. Unfortunately, Lutwidge met a

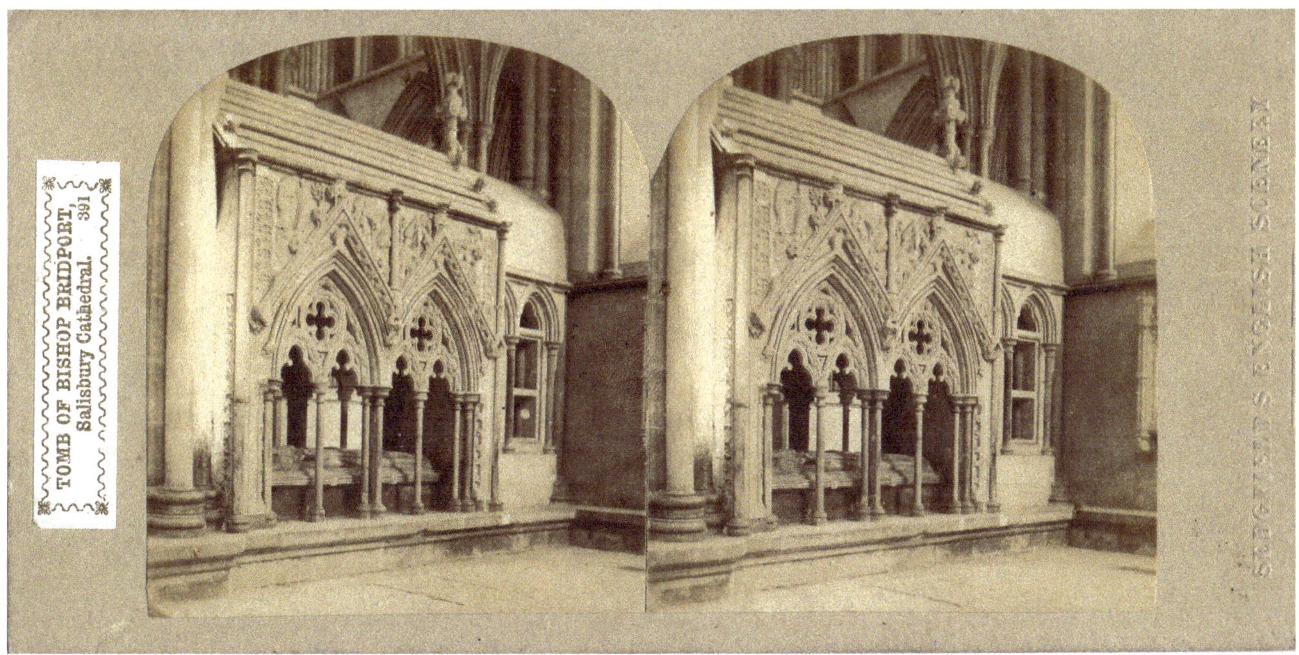

William Russell Sedgfield. *Tomb of Bishop Bridport, Salisbury Cathedral. 391.* c. 1858. Stereoscopic view. Albumen print. Anthony Hamber collection

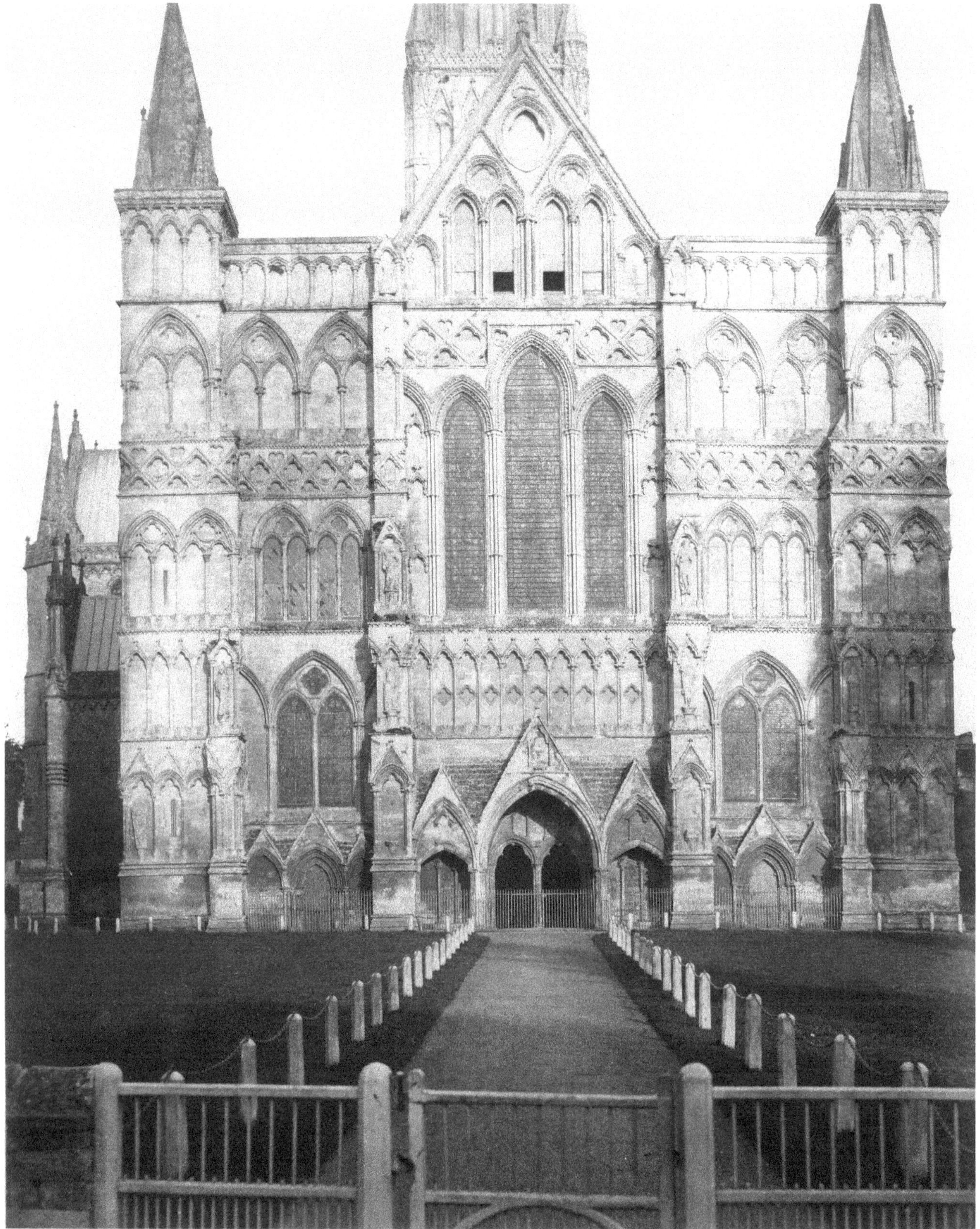

Roger Fenton. General view of the West Front of Salisbury Cathedral. 1857. Albumen print. Courtesy of Sotheby's.

gruesome end in Salisbury. During an inspection of the Fisherton House Asylum on Wednesday 21st May 1873 he was murdered by William M. Kave, a patient in the asylum.

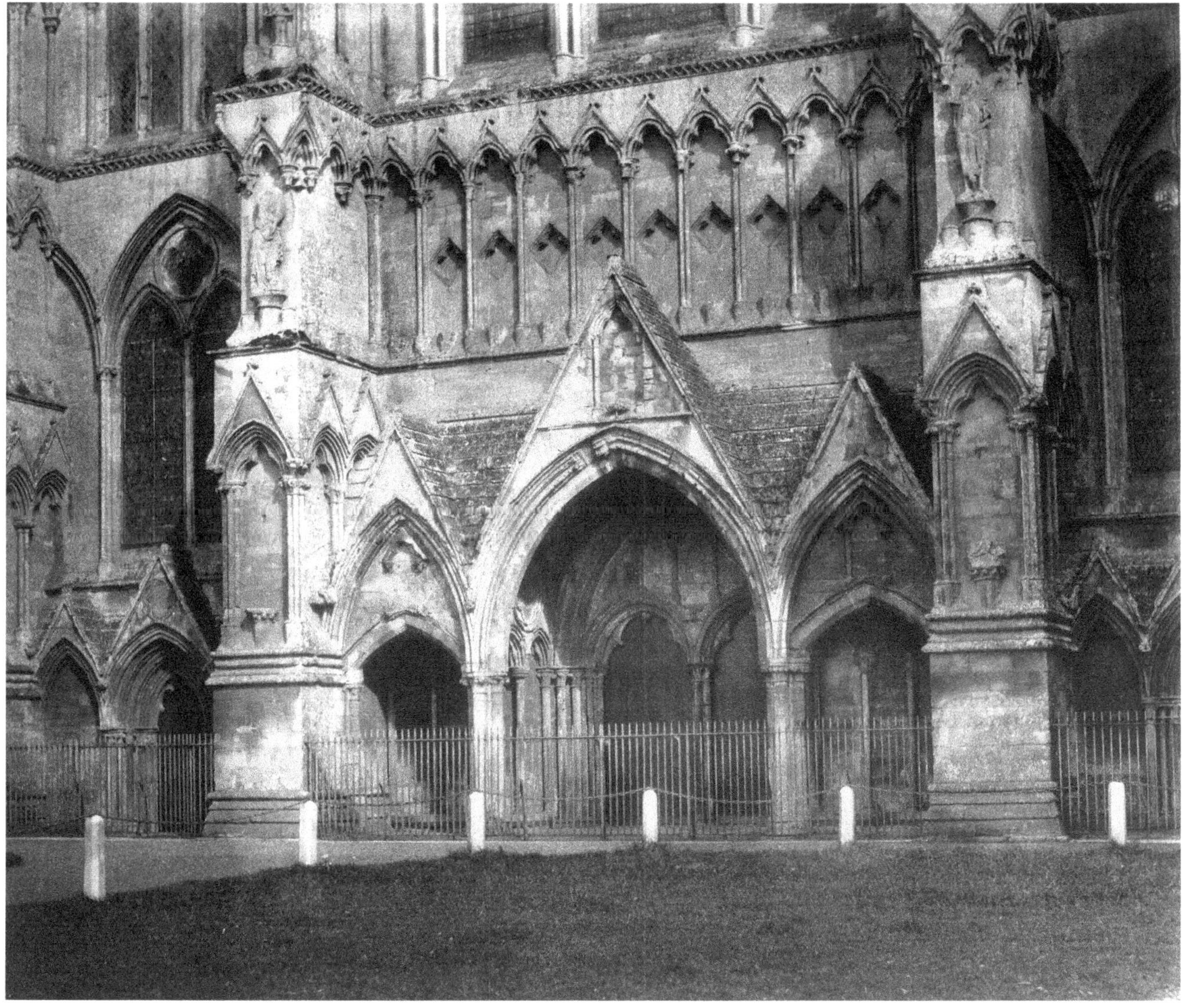

Roger Fenton. View of the West porch of the West Front of Salisbury Cathedral. 1857. Albumen print. Courtesy of Sotheby's

Roger Fenton (1819–1869), has been generally acknowledged as one of the most pre-eminent photographers of medieval architecture of the 1850s. He had been instrumental in the founding of the Photographic Society in London and in 1857 travelled to Salisbury where he made a number of views of the exterior and interior of the cathedral. More significantly, several of these images were exhibited at two major photographic exhibitions during the late 1850s.

1859 Glasgow Photographic Society

Salisbury Cathedral, South Aisle (looking east) (cat. no. 302)

Salisbury Cathedral, the Nave, from the South Transept (cat. no. 310)

Salisbury Cathedral, the Nave, from the West Gallery (cat. no. 311)

1859 London, Photographic Society

Salisbury Cathedral, the Chapter House (cat. no. 45)

Salisbury Cathedral, the West Porch (cat. no. 49)

Salisbury Cathedral, the South Aisle, looking East (cat. no. 63)

Salisbury Cathedral, the Nave, from the South Transept (cat. no. 76)

Salisbury Cathedral, interior of South Transept (cat. no. 572)

Salisbury Cathedral, the Nave, from the West Gallery (cat. no. 582)

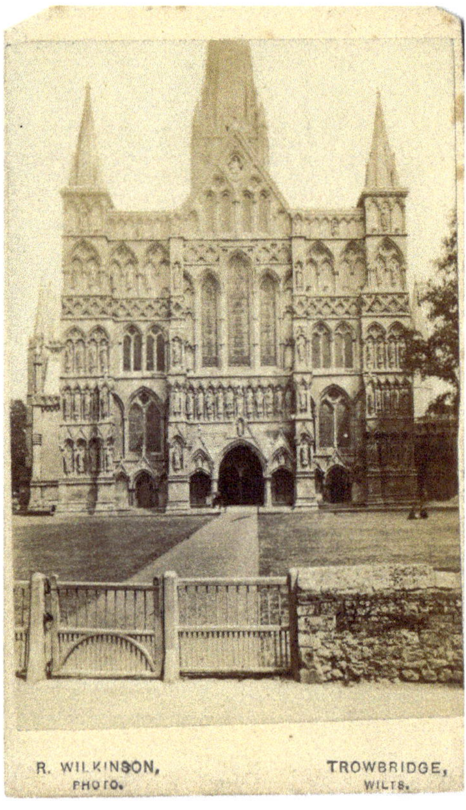

Richard Wilkinson. View of the West front of Salisbury Cathedral. Late 1860s. Carte de visite. Albumen print. Anthony Hamber collection.

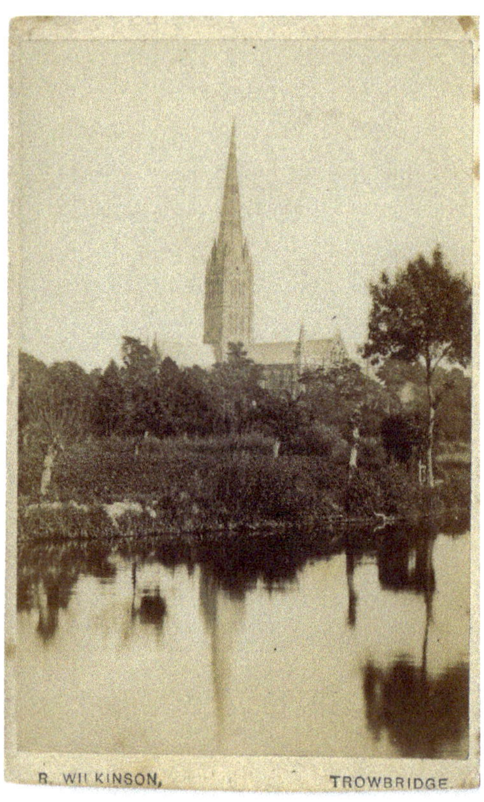

Richard Wilkinson. View of Salisbury Cathedral from across the Avon river. Late 1860s. Carte de visite. Albumen print. Anthony Hamber collection.

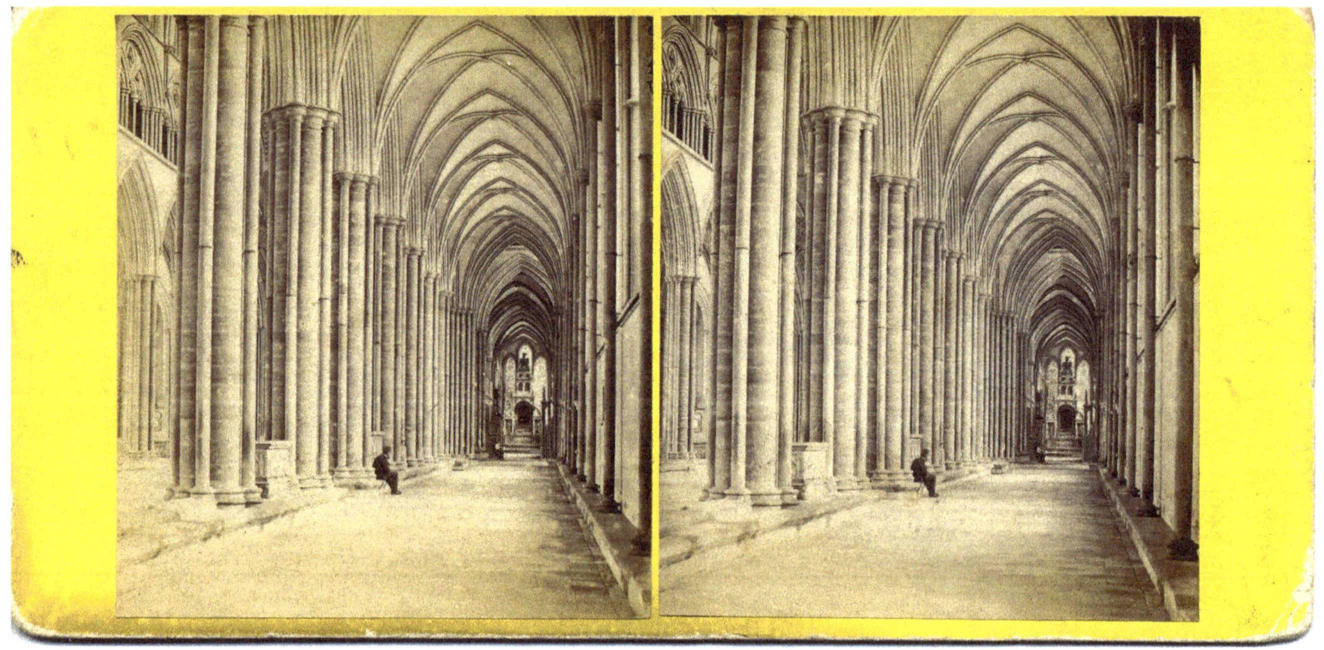

George Washington Wilson. *Salisbury Cathedral – South Aisle. No. 214.* 1860. Stereoscopic view. Albumen print. Anthony Hamber collection

A full set of the photographs of the views of the cathedral by Fenton has yet to be located but two of the most significant for architectural and sculpture historians are of the West front of Salisbury Cathedral.

While how many photographs were taken of the cathedral in the early 1850s must be left to conjecture, by the 1860s leading and lesser-known

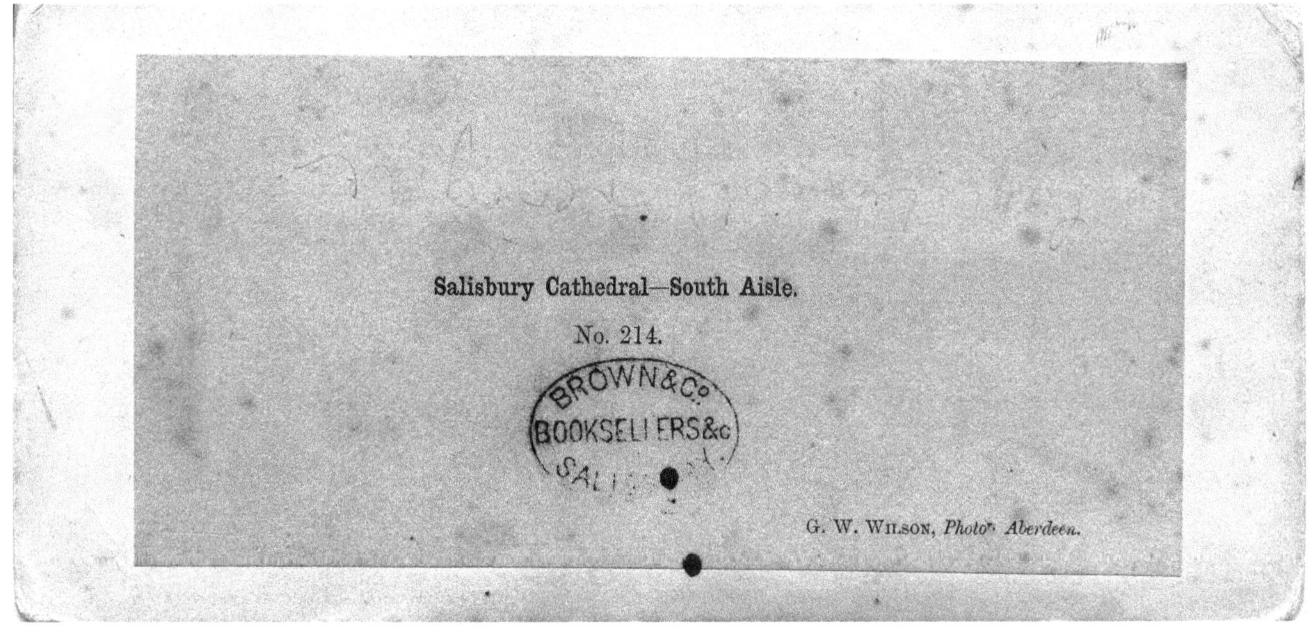

George Washington Wilson. Verso of *Salisbury Cathedral – South Aisle. No. 214.* With stamp of Brown & Co. 1860. Stereoscopic view. Albumen print. Anthony Hamber collection.

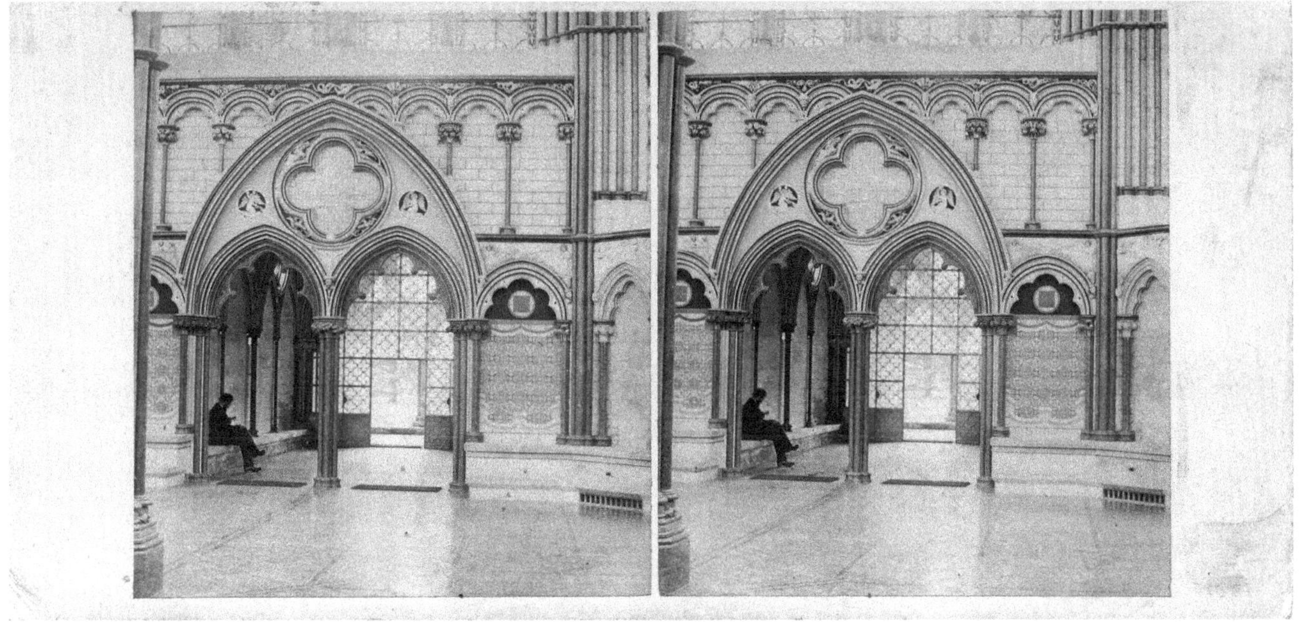

George Washington Wilson. *Salisbury Cathedral – Chapter House Entrance. No. 216.* 1860. Stereoscopic view. Albumen print. Anthony Hamber collection.

photographic companies were documenting and selling multiple views of the cathedral using a variety of print formats, ranging from carte-de-visites, through stereoscopic views to large mounted and unmounted prints.

Wiltshire photographers also began to exploit the rapidly emerging market. One was Richard Wilkinson, who had set up a studio in Church Street, Trowbridge (five doors from the Post Office) around 1863. He published a set of carte de visites of the cathedral in the late 1860s.

One of the great topographic photographers of the 19th-century, George Washington Wilson (1823–1893), visited Salisbury in 1860 and took a number of views of the cathedral as part of his first photographic foray into England from his base in Aberdeen, Scotland. He issued six stereo views including a view of the South Aisle (his catalogue

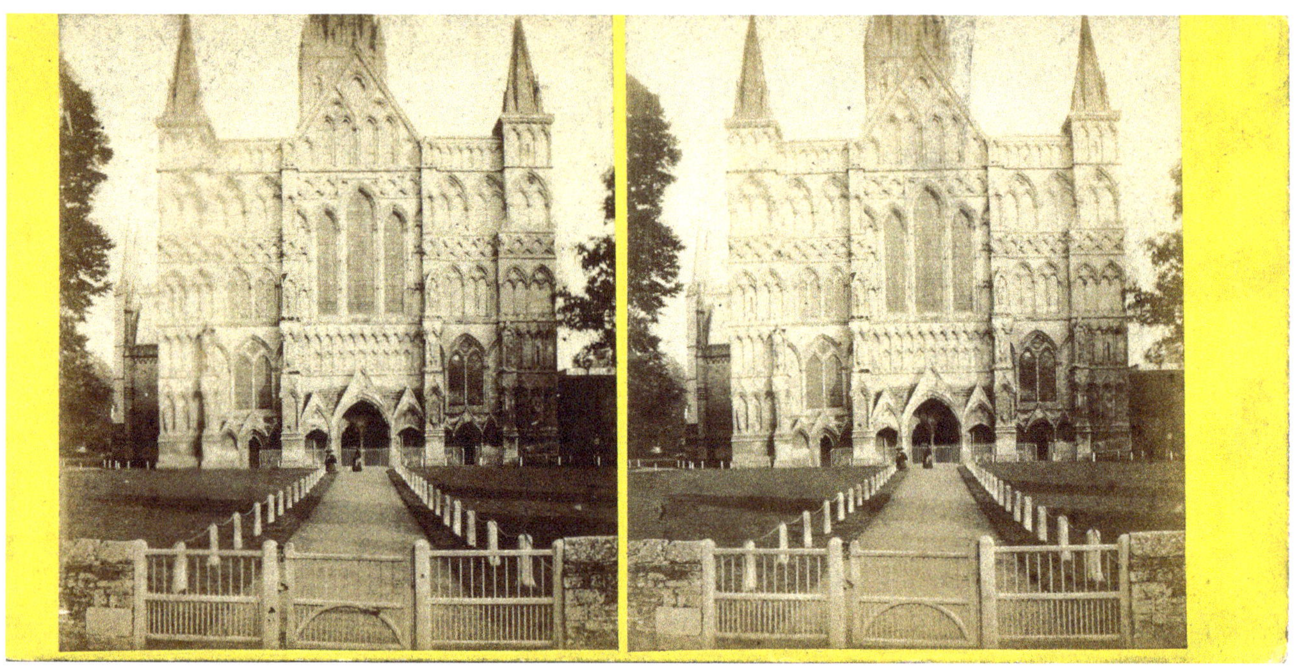

Horatio Nelson King. *Salisbury Cathedral. West End. No. 142.* Early 1860s. Stereoscopic view. Albumen print. Anthony Hamber collection.

SALISBURY CATHEDRAL.
WEST END.
(King's English Landscape and Architectural Series.)
No. 142.

Horatio Nelson King. Label on verso of *Salisbury Cathedral. West End. No. 142.* Early 1860s. Stereoscopic view. Albumen print. Anthony Hamber collection.

No. 214) the Transept (No. 215), the entrance to the Chapter House (No. 216) and a view of the Cloisters (No. 217). These received positive reviews, including one in the *British Journal of Photography* describing the set of six stereos as of 'all first rate character.'[12] During the summers of 1861 to 1863 Wilson photographed Durham, Exeter, Gloucester, Peterborough and Winchester cathedrals together with York Minster.

Horatio Nelson King (*c.*1830–1905) was another photographer to visit the city in the early 1860s. King had set up his studio on Milsom Street in Bath in 1858 and produced a number of stereoscopic views of Salisbury cathedral which formed part of his 'King's English Landscape and Architectural Series.'

Another significant modification to the cathedral was the removal of James Wyatt's reconstructed choir screen and organ loft (completed by 1792 and built from the stonework of the Hungerford and Beauchamp chantry chapels that Wyatt had removed) and its subsequent replacement by a new ironwork screen of Francis Alfred Skidmore (1817–1896) installed in 1870. This was in turn removed in 1959.

In 1870 Henry Brooks issued a set of photographs of drawings by Gilbert Scott 'prepared to illustrate his report of the works suggested for the restoration of our Cathedral.'[13]

In February 1876 George Gilbert Scott gave a paper at the Society of Antiquaries of London on the ancient position of the altar in Salisbury Cathedral.

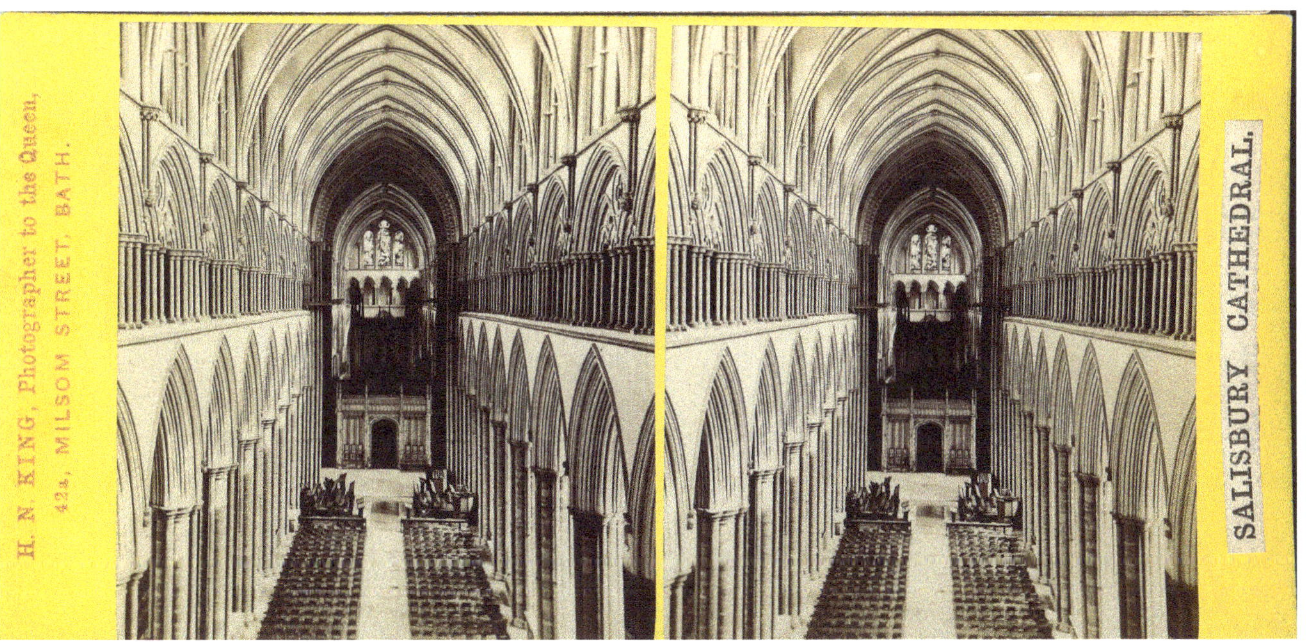

Horatio Nelson King. Salisbury Cathedral nave interior to East. Early 1860s. Stereoscopic view. Albumen print. Anthony Hamber collection.

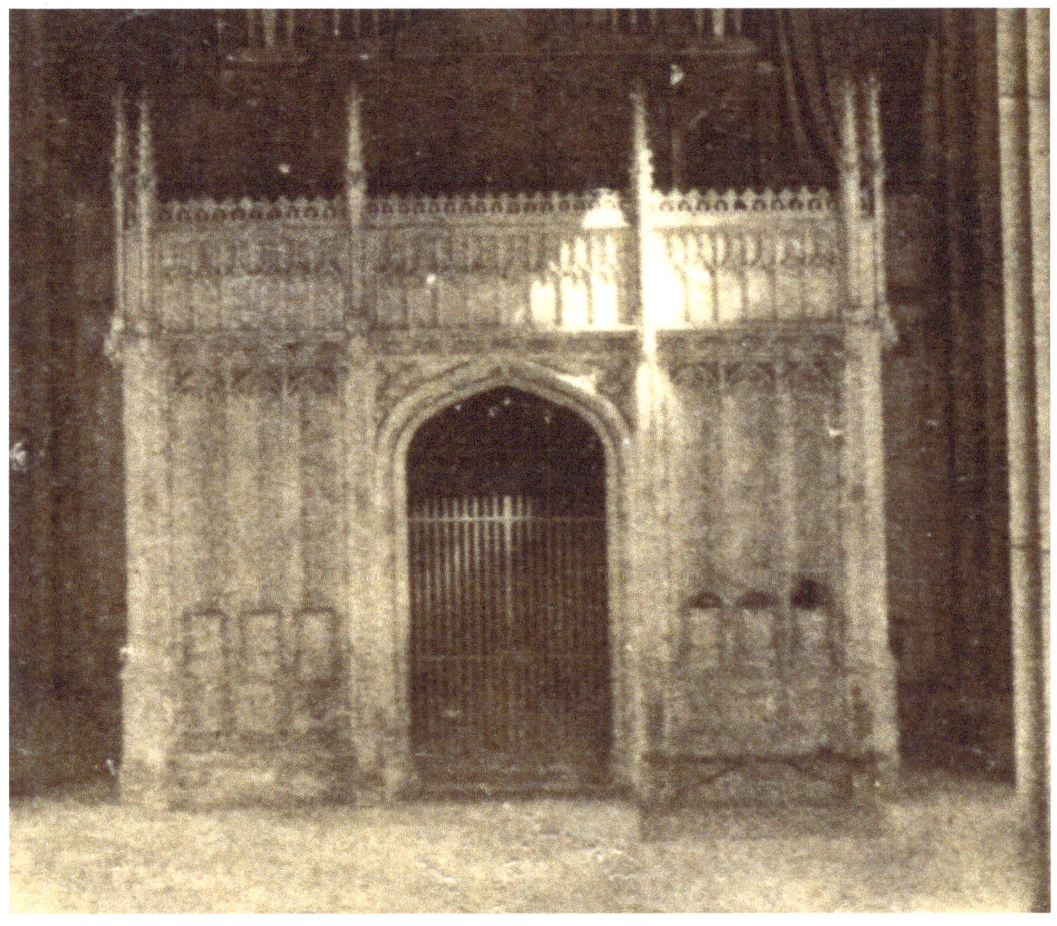

James Wyatt's choir screen. Detail of an anonymous stereoscopic view. Mid-1860s. Albumen print. Anthony Hamber collection.

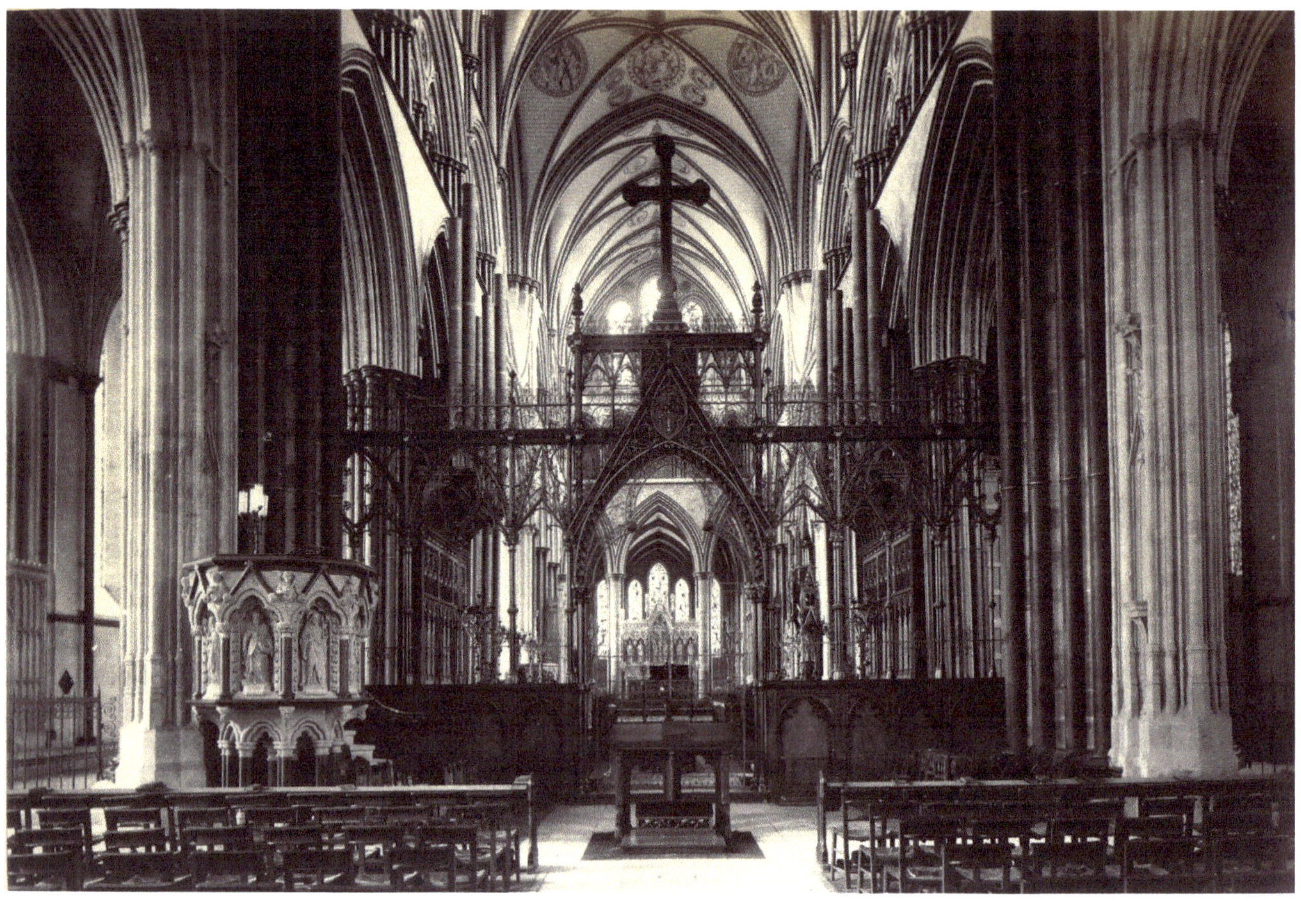

Unidentified photographer. Ironwork choir screen by Francis Skidmore. c. 1870. Albumen print. Anthony Hamber collection.

Scott noted that in the 13th century the altar was placed beneath the secular paintings of the month on the vaulting of the east end of the building. It was agreed that tracings of the paintings should be made and photographed since there was no other known record of the ancient paintings.[14] Copies of these photographs have yet to be located. In the same year, *Salisbury Cathedral: report upon the position of the high altar by Sir Geo. Gilbert Scott* was published by Bennett Bros. of Salisbury and contained one photolithograph illustration of 'part of plan from Gough's *Sepulchral monuments.*'[15]

Photographs of Salisbury Cathedral were not restricted to views taken actually of the buildings, decorations and its monuments. The Royal Architectural Museum was established in London in 1851 to educate architects and workers on architectural art. Its initial collections included plaster casts of European gothic architectural ornamentations, decorative ironwork, tiles, woodcarving, sculptural stonework and stained glass, plus architectural models, plans and drawings. In November 1872 the firm of Bedford Lemere & Co., leading London architectural photographers, published *A Series of Photographs from Selected Casts, &c., in the Royal Architectural Museum.* The first set with thirty photographs would appear to have been published in December 1872. A printed advertisement states that the set cost £3 3s. Unmounted; or mounted in Album, or bound for libraries, £4 4s. Art Workmen and Students would be supplied with single copies at 2s. 6d, unmounted. Three of the thirty photographs included details from Salisbury Cathedral; '6. Caps from Salisbury', '10. Caps in Purbeck Marble from Chertsey Abbey, the three Top Caps from Salisbury' and '15. Caps. Heads, &c. in Stone, Salisbury Cathedral.' Further photographs were published by Bedford Lemere & Co., the total eventually numbering an estimated 200. A number of these additional images included casts from Salisbury Cathedral. In 1904 the Royal Architectural Museum was wound up, with the

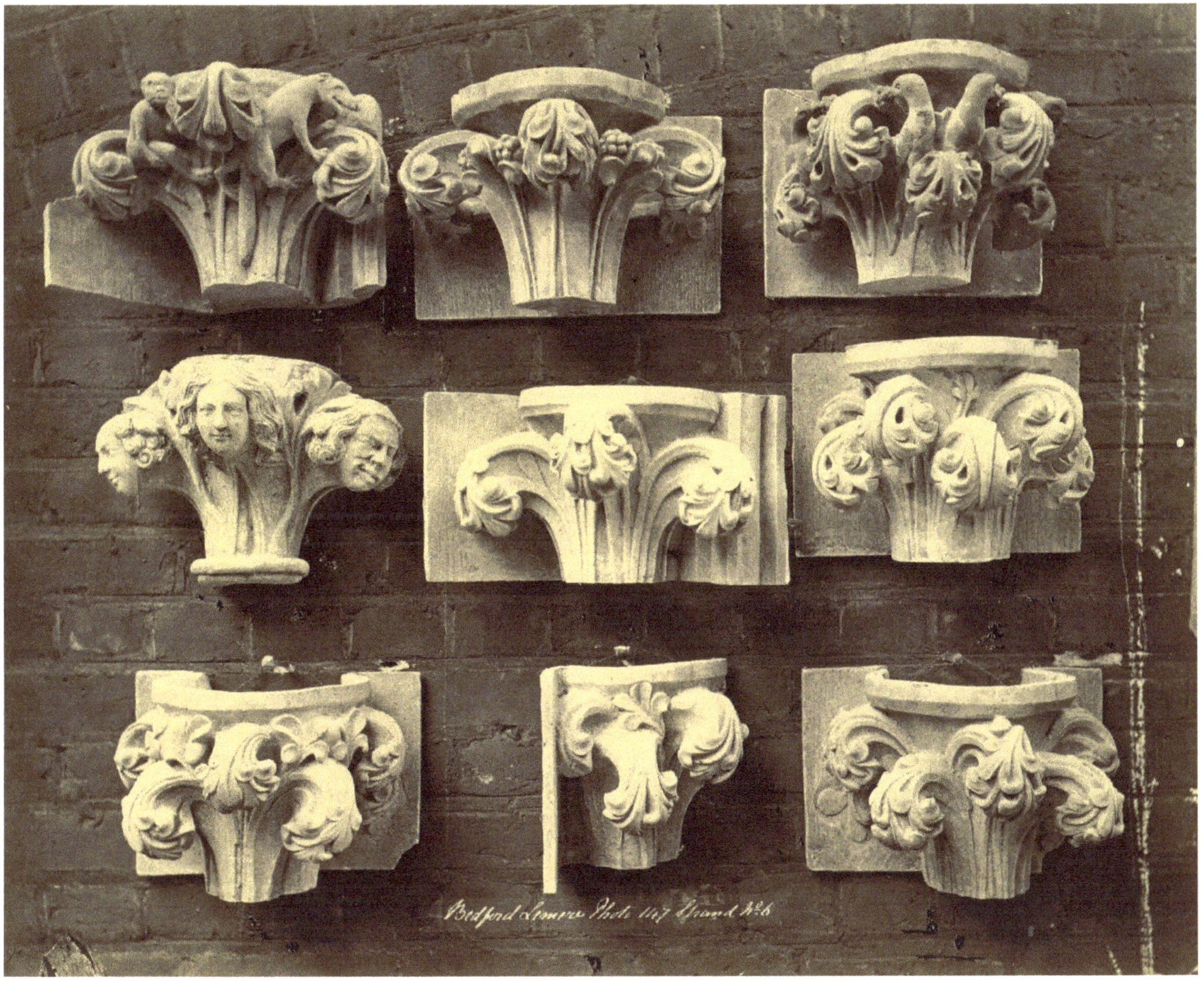

Bedford Lemere. Plaster Casts of capitals from Salisbury Cathedral Chapter House. No. 6. 1872. From *A Series of Photographs from Selected Casts, &c., in the Royal Architectural Museum.* Cornell University Library.

building and contents gifted to the Architectural Association. It closed during World War I, the building was sold and then demolished and most of the cast collections are now held in the Victoria and Albert Museum.

During the period covered by this study, thousands of photographs of the cathedral were taken, purchased and found their way across the globe. As a result, Salisbury Cathedral became appreciated as the best example of Early English Gothic architecture. One question that deserves further research is the channels that enabled global distribution. Where, prior to 1880, could photographs of the cathedral be bought outside Great Britain; in Paris, Berlin, Madrid, Vienna, Rome, New York etc.?

1 The letters are in the Fox Talbot Museum in Lacock. Schaaf No. 04056 and No. 04353.

2 The sculptors John Birnie Philip (died 1875) and the Belgian Theodore Phyffers (fl.1840–1872) worked on restoration of the Chapter House.

3 *Wiltshire Independent*, Thursday 13th September 1855 p. 3.

4 *Brown's Stranger's Handbook and Illustrated Guide to Salisbury Cathedral*, Brown & Co.; Simpkin and Co., Salisbury; London, 1884 'The Work of Restoration' p. 88. In fact the total sum expended was some £60,000.

5 A photograph of Redfern's effigy of Our Lord in Majesty, intended for the West gable of the Cathedral, was exhibited at the meeting of the Ecclesiological Society on 2nd April 1867. *The Ecclesiologist*, Volume XXVIII, 1867 p. 183. See Tim Ayres (ed.), *Salisbury Cathedral: The West Front - A History and Study in Conservation*, Phillimore Press, Chichester, 2000.

6 Hardwicke Knight, 'Russell Sedgfield, the complete

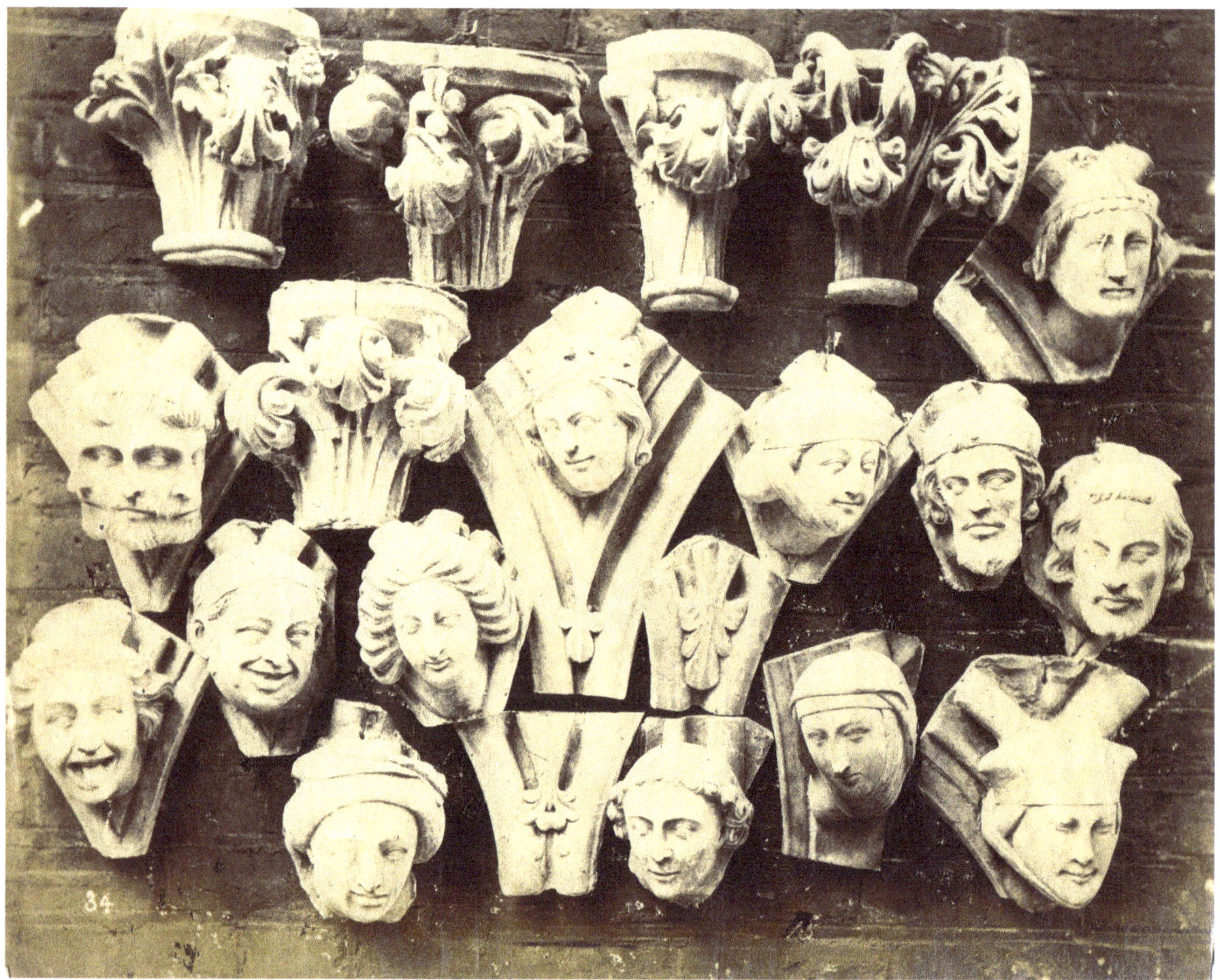

Bedford Lemere. Plaster Casts of heads and capitals from Salisbury Cathedral Chapter House. No. 34. 1872. From *A Series of Photographs from Selected Casts, &c., in the Royal Architectural Museum.* Anthony Hamber collection.

photographer', *History of Photography*, Volume 1, Number 4, October 1977 pp. 301–312.

7 *Wiltshire Independent*, Thursday 11th August 1853 p. 3.

8 An advertisement by Joseph Cundall in *Notes and Queries*, 19th November 1853 p. 506.

9 *Catalogue de l'exposition instituée par l'Association pour l'encouragement de development des Arts Industriels en Belgique*, Brussels, 1856 cat. no. 195. Sedgfield's exhibits were mentioned in *Journal of the Photographic Society*, 21st October 1856 p. 149.

10 Catalogue number 389.

11 See Grace Seiberling and Carolyn Bloore, *Amateurs, Photography and the Mid-Victorian Imagination*, University of Chicago Press, London, 1986, and Roger Taylor and Larry Schaaf, *Impressed by Light: British Photographs from Paper Negatives, 1840–1860*, Yale University Press, London, 2007.

12 *British Journal of Photography*, 1st January 1862 p. 11.

13 *SJ*, Saturday 30th April 1870 p. 5.

14 *SJ*, Saturday 5th February 1876 p. 8.

15 Richard Gough, *Sepulchral monuments in Great Britain applied to illustrate the history of families, manners, habits and arts...from the Norman Conquest to the seventeenth century...* Richard Gough, London, 1796.

5 COMMERCIAL PHOTOGRAPHY AND ITS APPLICATIONS

FROM THE 1850S an astonishing range of applications of photography is to be found across Great Britain. This chapter aims to provide evidence of the scale and scope of photography in Salisbury during the period 1839 to 1880. The details have been gleaned primarily from local newspapers, and while this source may appear somewhat limited, it serves its purpose in highlighting the manner in which the medium documented the city, its population and local events. However, this chapter remains – frustratingly – largely unillustrated. One outcome of this study is hopefully that examples of the photographs discussed below will be rediscovered.

What follows is a selected series of representative subject headings that evidences the diversity of applications to which photography was put. While these case studies examine the subject matter depicted, it is often unclear exactly why the photographs were taken and for what eventual purpose. Some may have been the result of commercial contracts, others speculative ventures aimed at subsequently selling photographic prints. Another possibility was the use of photography to produce intermediaries for printed images created through a variety of manual reprographic (and ultimately photomechanical) processes.

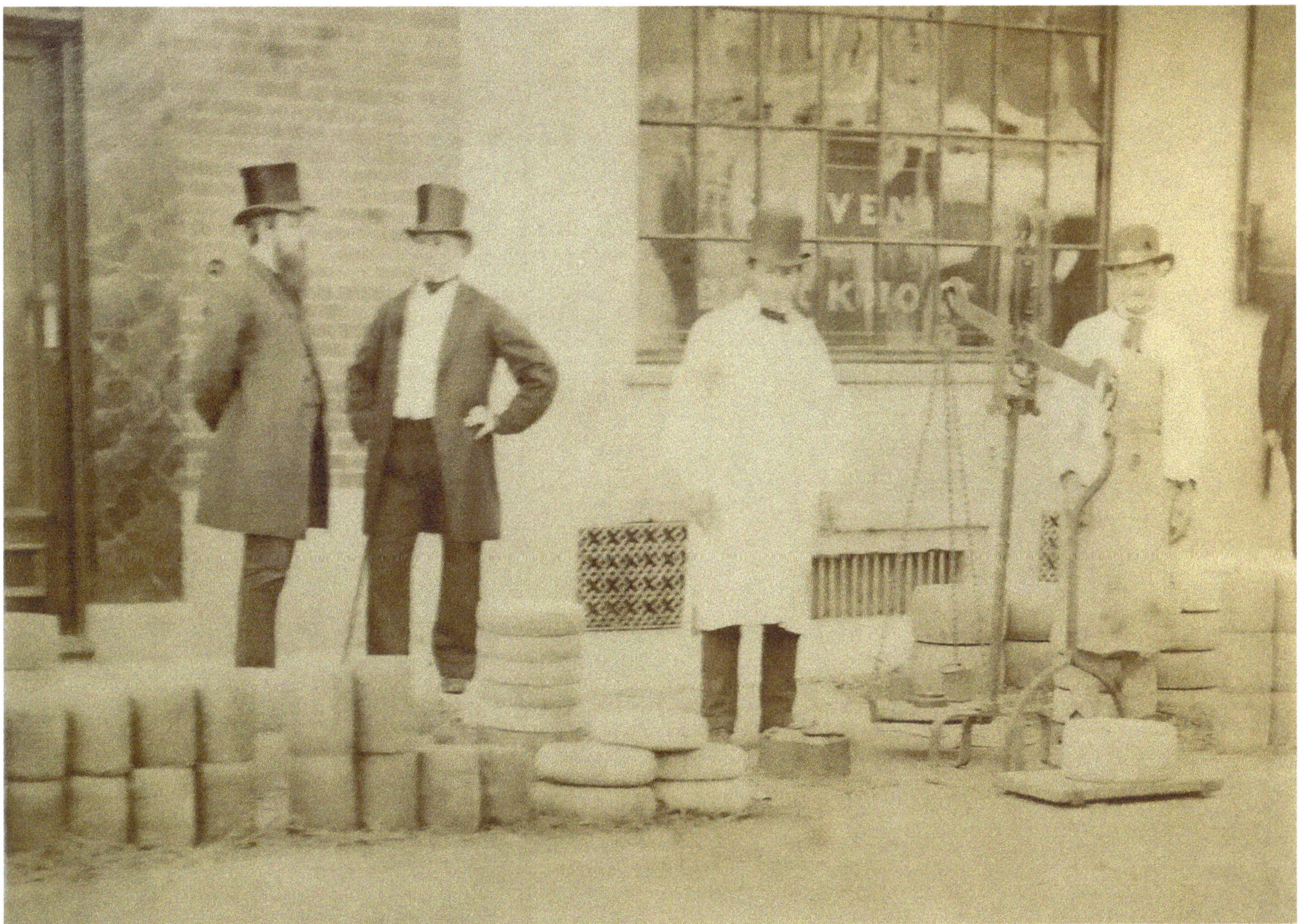

Unidentified photographer. Cheese being sold at the site of the Cheese Cross on the Market Place. c. 1858. Albumen print. The Salisbury Museum.

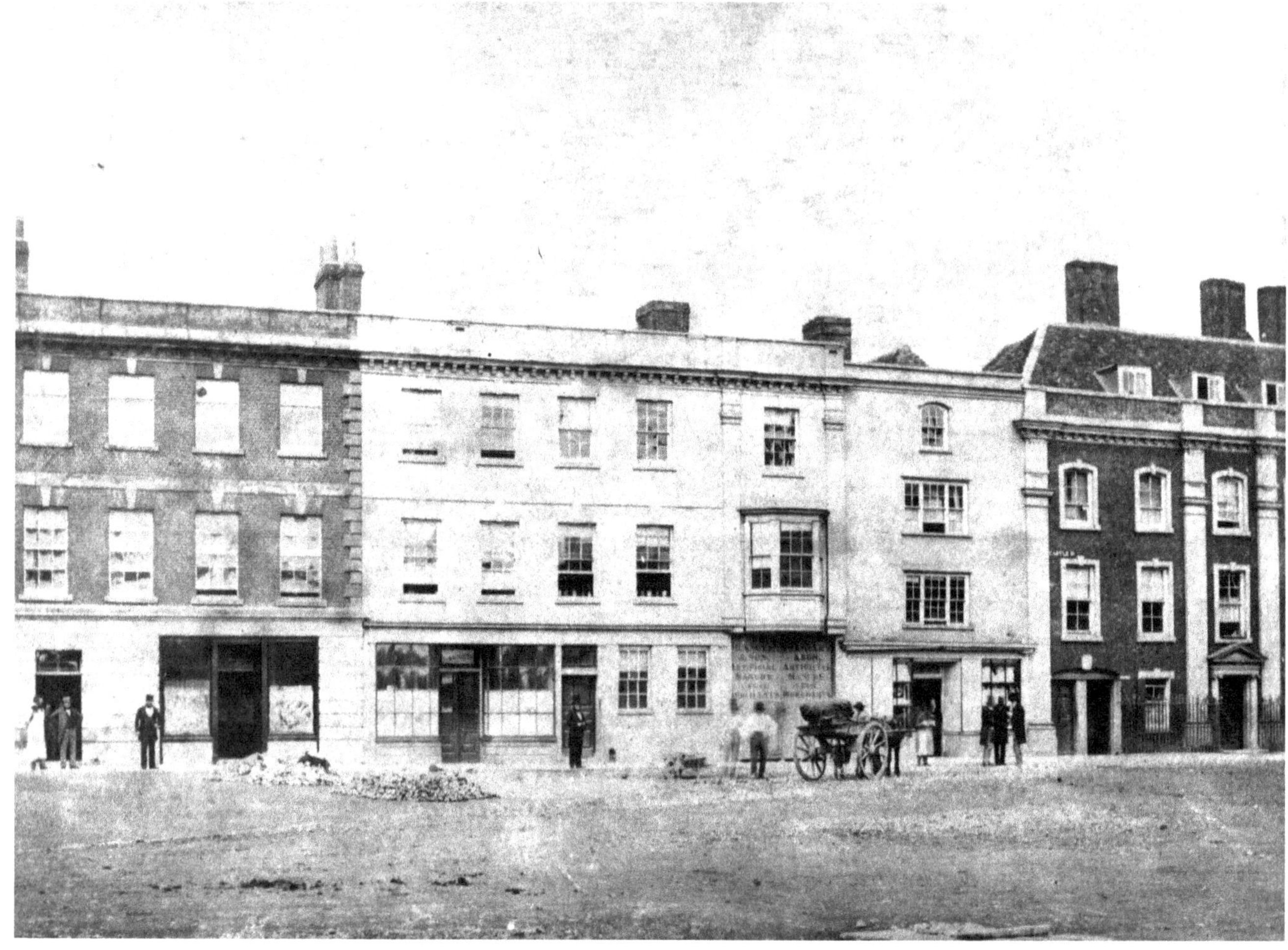

Unidentified photographer. View of the Maidenhead Inn, by the site of the Cheese Cross on the Market Place. Pre-1858. Albumen print. The Salisbury Museum.

Urban Development

THE POPULATION OF the city did not rapidly expand during the period covered in this study. There was some ribbon development of villas along the Wilton Road and the southern end of the Devizes Road. Some expansion took place in Milford during the 1860s. There was no large-scale construction of domestic buildings in the city centre, the three ancient parishes of St. Martin, St. Thomas, and St. Edmund. The rows of mid-Victorian terraced houses so common in other cities in Great Britain were to appear primarily on the outskirts of the city in Fisherton Anger and Milford in the later part of the century. However, there was a significant amount of commercial building in central Salisbury during the 19th century and perhaps the most noticeable area redeveloped was the Market Place.[1]

The example of the construction of the building that became the site of the Salisbury Public Library, retaining only the façade of the former Market House, is a relevant case study for the multiple uses of graphic and photographic recording.

The Maidenhead Inn was situated on the west side of the Market Place opposite the Cheese Cross where milk and cheese had been traditionally sold. It had long been a place of all sorts of entertainment, including card games and in 1771 the exhibition of a three-foot woman, Maria Theresa, known as the Corsican Fairy.[2] Since the death of her husband in 1827 it had been run by Jane Hibberd.

The Salisbury Railway and Market House Company was set up by Dr. Andrew Bogle Middleton (1819–1879) who had rid the city of cholera in the mid-19th century. It was incorporated in 1856. The site selected for the new Market House was that of the Maidenhead Inn, which had to be demolished.

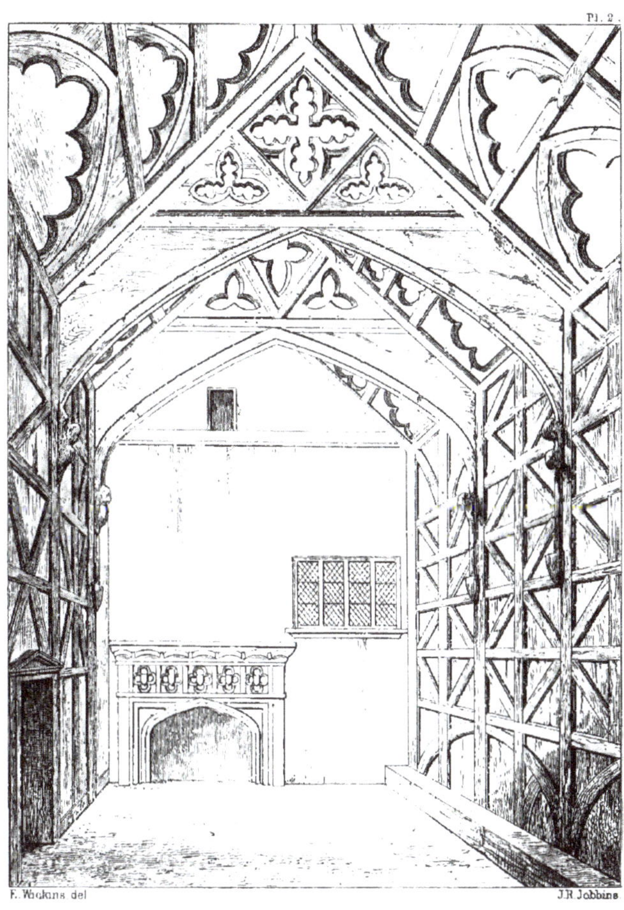

"Hall in Market Place Salisbury". Engraving by J. R. Jobbins after a drawing by Elizabeth Wickens of the medieval hall of the Maidenhead Inn prior to its removal. Illustration to an article by T. J. Pettigrew "On the Antiquities of Wiltshire", *Journal of the British Archaeological Association*, 1859.

The architect for the new building was John Strapp (1821–1900), engineer of the South-Western Railway, and the building was to house the Cheese Market and the Corn Exchange. The Salisbury Railway and Market House Company struggled after World War II and the building was used for various functions such as the Three Counties Cat Show and wrestling matches. The company was liquidated in 1968 and the site redeveloped to become the Salisbury Public Library with only the original façade surviving.

The great advantage of the location selected by Middleton was that a railway could be built directly from the Market House to link with the Great Western Railway and South Western Railway lines at the main line stations at Fisherton. Both narrow gauge and broad gauge lines were laid down to connect with the South Western Railway line, enabling cattle and merchandise to be sent by any of the four railways which at that time served the city.[3]

A photograph of the exterior of the Maidenhead Inn prior to its demolition exists and may have been specifically taken to record the building prior to its demolition.[4] However, there was local antiquarian knowledge that parts of the interior of the building were of historic significance. Elizabeth Wickens made a drawing of the medieval hall inside the Maidenhead Inn and this was reproduced as an illustration to an article by T. J. Pettigrew 'On the Antiquities of Wiltshire' that was published in the *Journal of the British Archaeological Association* in 1859. The late 15th-century roof from the former Maidenhead Inn was saved and installed in the St Edmund's School in Bedwin Street, built in 1860.

The new Market House was inaugurated on Tuesday 24th May 1859 and Henry Brooks took a photograph of the interior of the building that was reproduced as a wood engraving in the 18th June issue of the *Illustrated London News*. This was also mentioned in the *SJ* in the next month.[5]

In 1863 a photograph was taken from Queen Street looking west across the Market Place. A copy of this photograph in Salisbury Museum

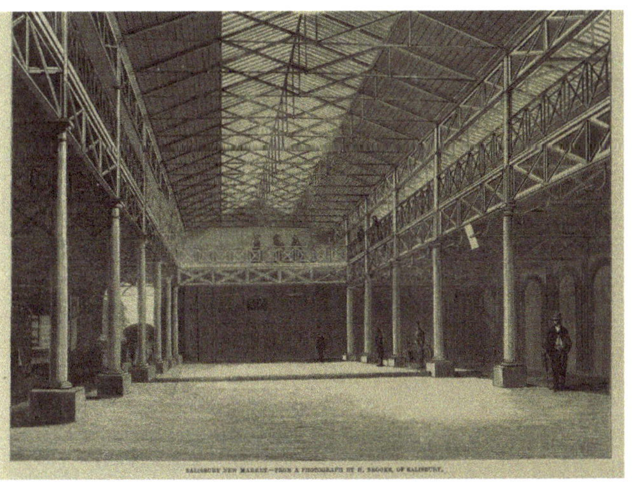

Salisbury New Market - From a photograph by Henry Brooks of Salisbury. Wood engraving. *Illustrated London News*, 18th June 1859 p. 588.

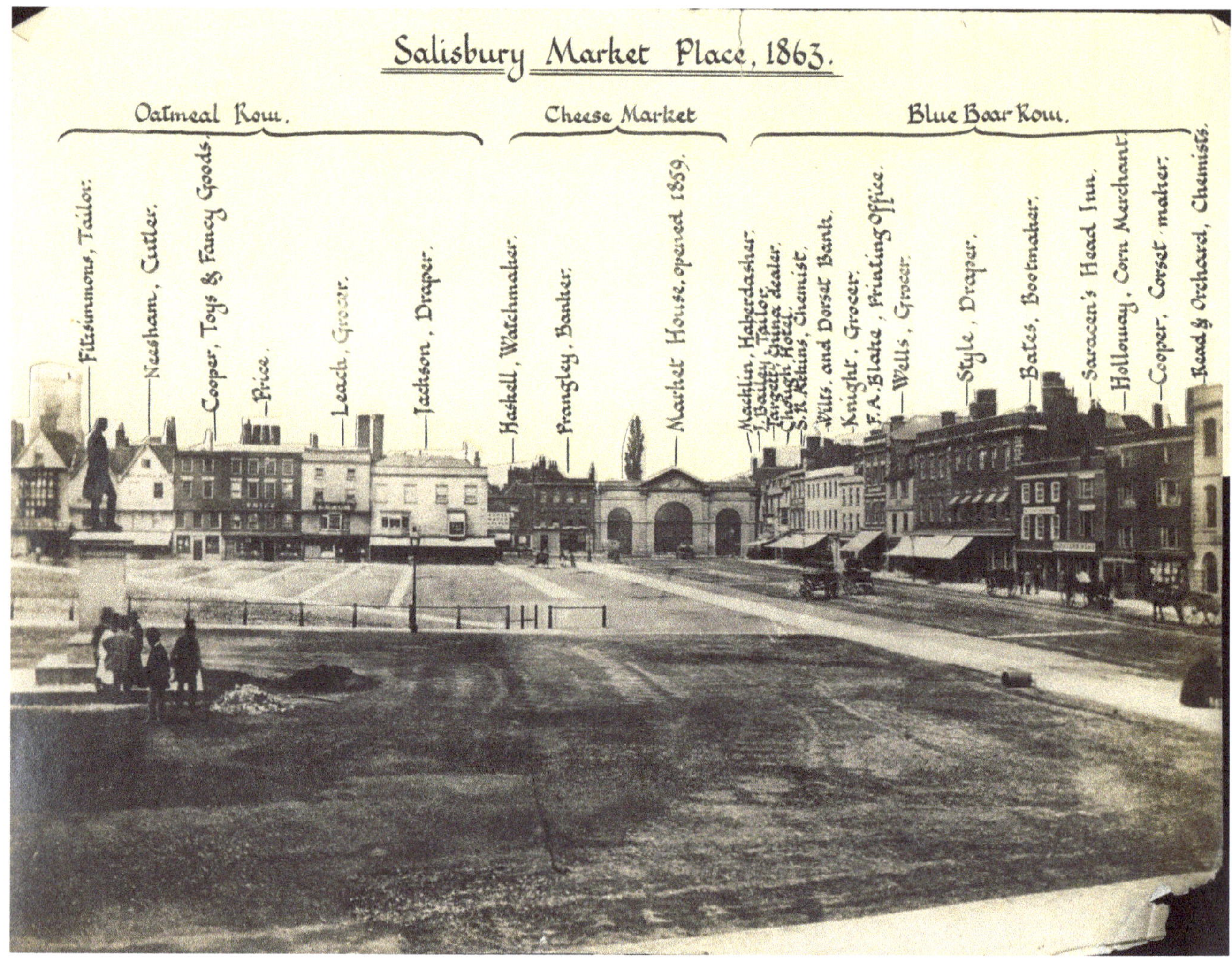

Unidentified photographer. Annotated view of the Market Place from Queen Street. 1863. Albumen print. The Salisbury Museum.

was at some point annotated, indicating which tradespeople occupied the buildings recorded. Comparing this photograph with those taken during the late 1840s and 1850s documents the evolution of the architecture of the Market Place that was to continue during the second half of the 19th century.

Another example of photographic documentation of building work can be found in the construction of the Italianate building on the corner of the High Street and Bridge Street. The site had been occupied by the chemist, Thomas Barber, until the early 1870s. A photograph of the building survives. It was probably taken around late 1872 when Barber's business left the building prior to its demolition. The new building, the premises of Richardson Bros., wine and spirit merchants, was taken during its construction, probably in 1874. The company was related to the famous London family of wine merchants and the firm occupied the building until 1929. Quite why a photograph was taken while the building remained under scaffolding is unclear. It may have been used as a contractual tool to show progress of the works, perhaps for the architect.

Documentary The Crimean War

SALISBURY'S CONNECTION WITH the British Army dated back to before the War Office first purchased land on Salisbury Plain in 1897 and the establishment of the camps at Bulford, Larkhill and Tidworth. The 62nd (Wiltshire) Regiment of Foot was raised in 1756, the Wiltshire Regiment being formed in 1881.

The 62nd (Wiltshire) Regiment of Foot participated in the Siege of Sevastopol in winter

1854. On 8th September 1855, it was among the battalions which took part in the failed assault of the Redan bastion. The regiment suffered heavy casualties, including half of its officers and senior non-commissioned officers. How many men of the 62nd (Wiltshire) Regiment of Foot were from Salisbury has yet to be established. A stained-glass window by the firm of Messrs O'Connor of London was installed as a memorial to those who fell, in the aisle of the south-east transept of Salisbury Cathedral.

Citizens of Salisbury could experience an aspect of the Crimean War since a Russian gun captured at Sevastapol during the war had been presented to the city by Lord Panmure (1801–1874), Secretary of State for War, and placed in front of the Council Chamber in January 1858. It was moved to a plinth on the Queen Street side of the Council Chamber in June 1863 when it was replaced by a statue of Sidney Herbert (1810–1861), 1st Baron Herbert of Lea and MP for South Wiltshire 1832 to 1881, by Baron Carlo Marochetti (1805–1867). In the *Illustrated London News* for the 11th July 1863, an illustration of the inauguration of the statue was credited as being 'from a photograph by J.W. Miell, of Salisbury'. This followed a note in the *SJ* for Saturday 4th July 1863:

THE HERBERT STATUE.

We have had an opportunity of inspecting some very excellent photographs of the inaugural ceremony, on Monday last, executed by Mr. James. W. Miell, of 21, Catherine-street, in this city. He has also taken a good photograph of the statue, which is a most faithful

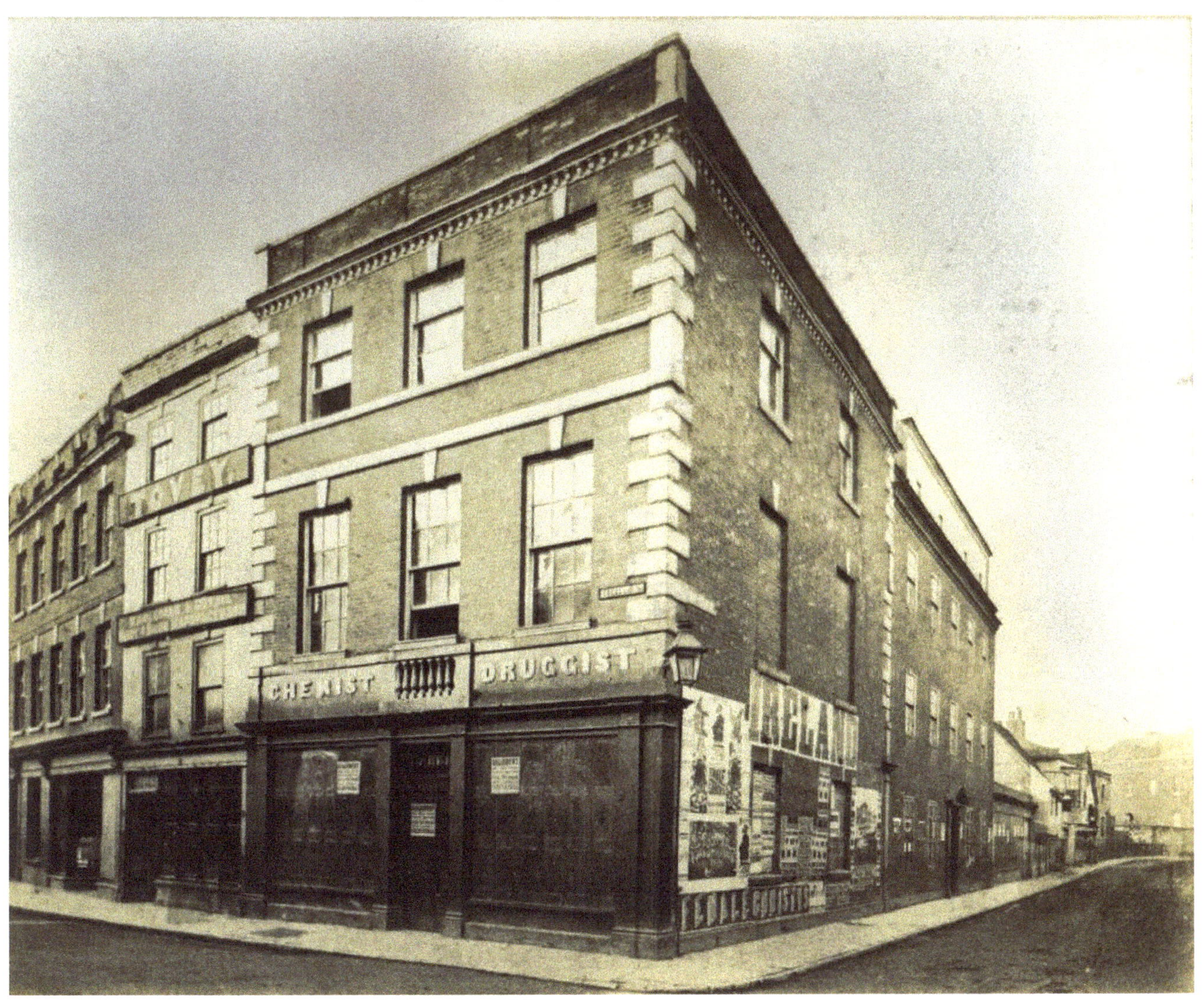

Unidentified photographer. View of the premises of the chemist Thomas Barber on the corner of the High Street and Bridge Street, prior to demolition. 1872. Albumen print. The Salisbury Museum.

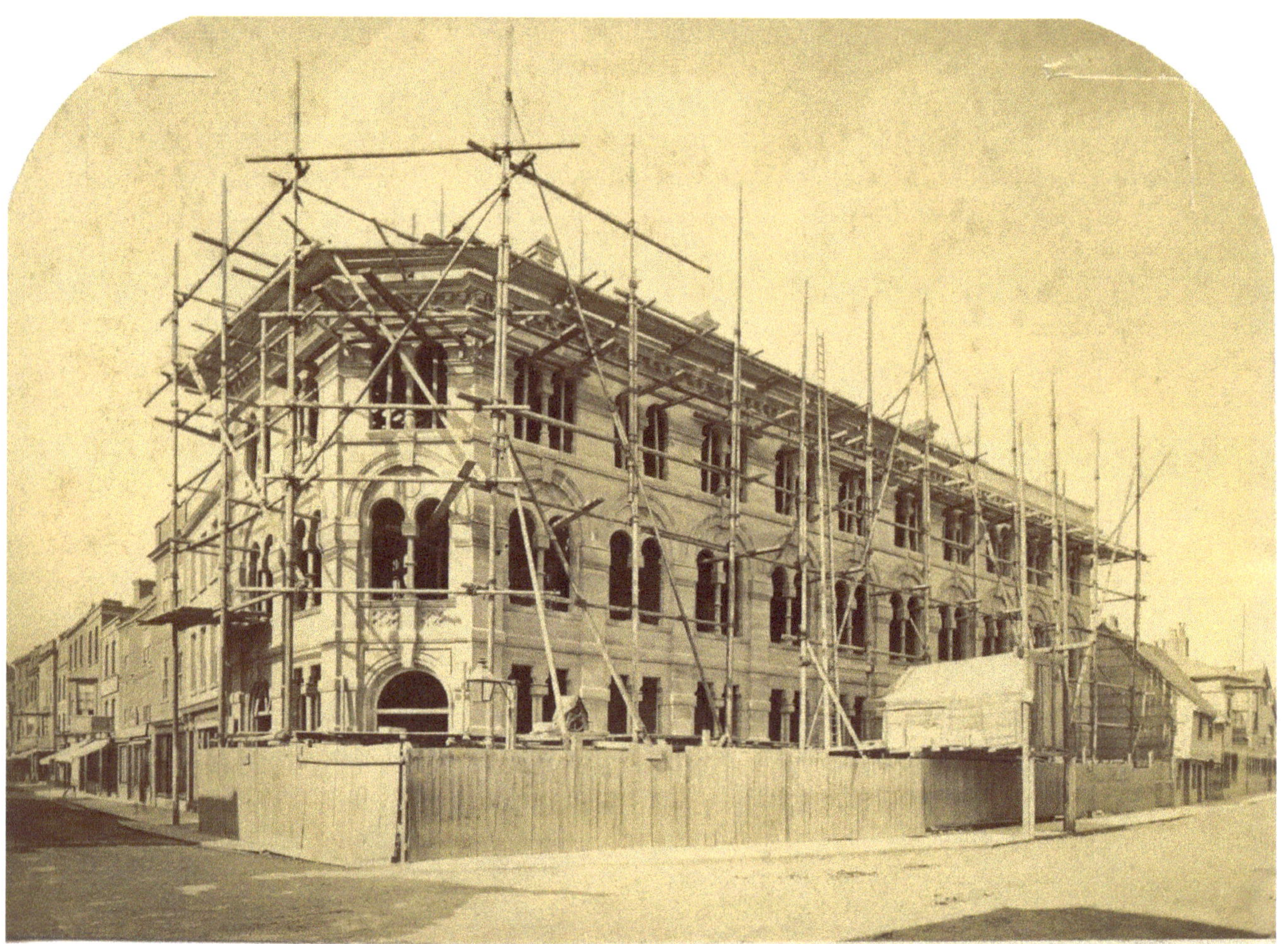

Unidentified photographer. View of the premises of Richardson Bros., wine and spirit merchants, under construction at the corner of the High Street and Bridge Street. 1874. Albumen print. The Salisbury Museum.

> representation of this integrating work of art. Mr. F. Treble, of Catherine-street, has also photographed the statue, in good style, by order of Baron Marochetti.[6]

This statue was in turn removed in 1953 to Victoria Park.

On the 29th May 1856 a festival to celebrate the conclusion of the Crimean War was held in the Market Place in Salisbury and some 3,000 citizens sat at tables to a dinner of roast beef and plum pudding. 900 gallons of beer were drunk. The visual documentation of this event included the combined use of photography and traditional reprographics processes.

At least two photographers documented the celebratory scenes in the Market Place. One was William Russell Sedgfield, who exhibited a copy of his photograph of the festivities at the exhibition held later that year by the Norfolk and Norwich Photographic Society.[7] The other photographer is only known through a credit printed on a lithograph by the local artist Walter Francis Tiffin, as mentioned previously, active in the city from around 1844, and published by the local stationer, bookseller and publisher Brown & Co. The print clearly states that the image had been created from photographs taken especially for the purpose. The photographer was named as 'E. Whitlock' – probably the local chemist Edwin Whitlock (1825–1887) of the Market Place – who in 1852 had exhibited crystals, chemicals, 'Metallic substances' and Pulvermacher's Hydro-Electric Chain Battery at the Salisbury Exhibition of Local Industry. Whitlock seems to have been an amateur photographer, as he was never listed in any trade directory as being a photographer or offering photographic services.

William Toomer (*c.*1820–1887), the Postmaster of Salisbury, exhibited in the Post Office a 'photograph on glass' – a paper print from a

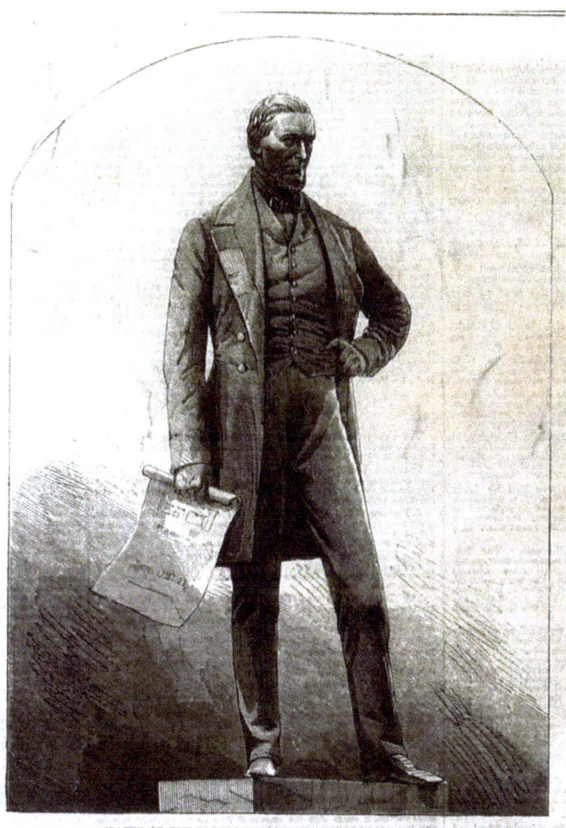

STATUE OF THE LATE LORD HERBERT OF LEA, AT SALISBURY.

collodion on glass negative – of the market place Crimean festivities of 29th May 1856.

Following the Crimean War, and with increasing concerns of an invasion by the French, on 12th May 1859 the Secretary of State for War, Jonathan Peel (1799–1879), issued a circular letter to lieutenants of counties in England, Wales and Scotland, authorising the formation of volunteer rifle corps. Salisbury enthusiastically followed the call and formed No. 1 company of the Wiltshire Rifle Volunteers. In September 1860 some eleven hundred volunteer riflemen of the Wiltshire Rifle Volunteers congregated in the Market Place

left: Statue of the late Lord Herbert of Lea, At Salisbury. Wood engraving after a photograph by James Miell. *Illustrated London News,* 1st August 1863 p. 104.

below: Unidentified photographer. View of North-east corner of the Market Place towards Castle Street during the 1856 Peace Festival. May 1856. Displayed in Salisbury Post Office by William Toomer (c.1820–1887), the Postmaster of Salisbury. Albumen print. The Salisbury Museum.

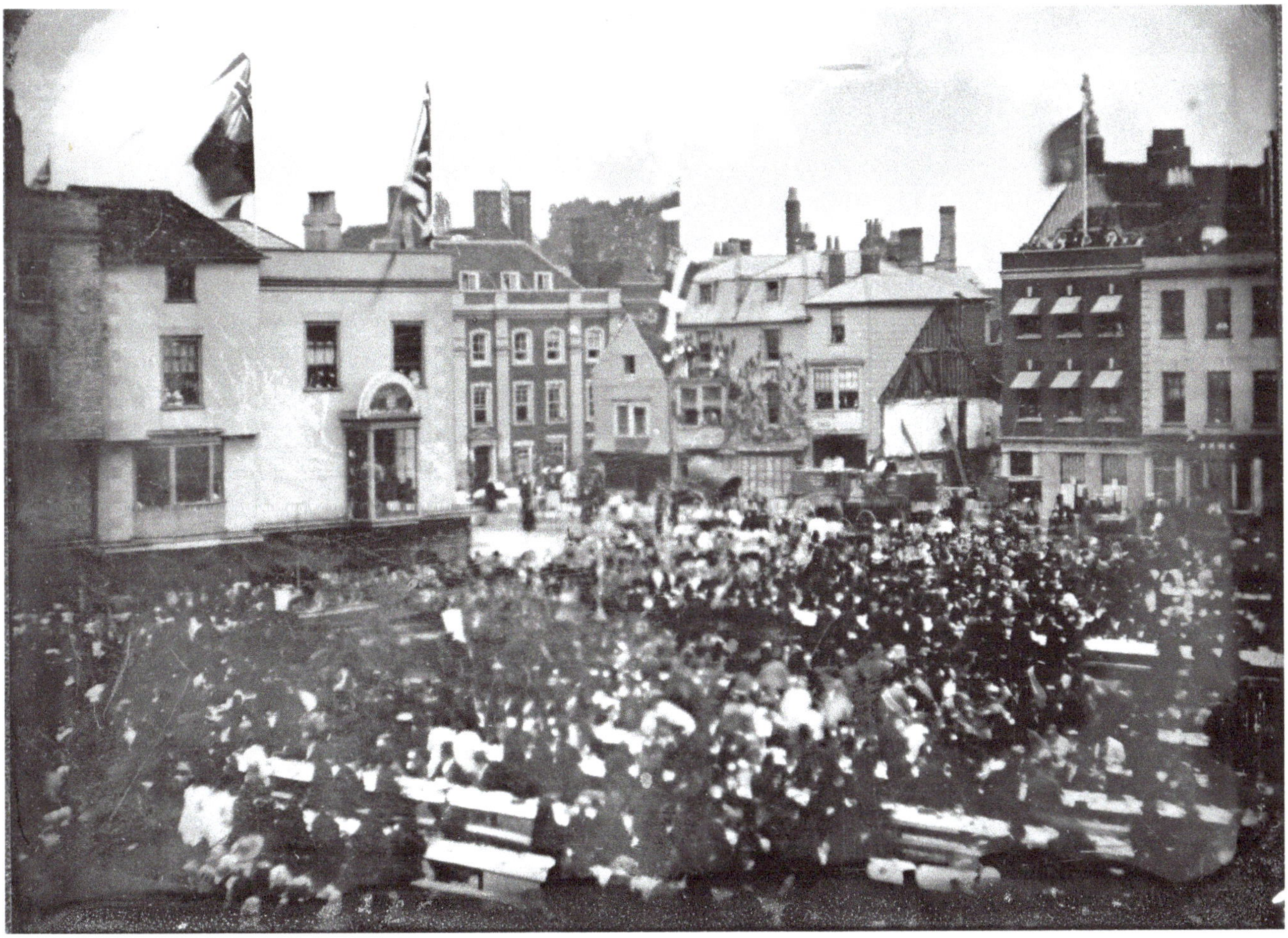

and then marched to Clarendon to undertake manoeuvres. Before it left the Market Place, the band of the 1st Wiltshire Rifles (Salisbury), numbering some 28 musicians led by William Price Aylward (1811–1890), who ran a Musical Emporium in the Canal, was photographed by two local photographers, Miell and Witcomb.[8] A little more than a decade later, James Miell photographed, 'by the special permission of Colonel Everett', the battalion officers of the First Battalion of the Wilts Rifle Volunteers on the parade ground at the encampment on Homington Down.[9]

Documentary

Salisbury has been perennially in danger of flooding, most recently in 2014. In January 1841 a flood devasted the parishes of Shrewton, Maddington, Rollestone, Orcheston St. George, Orcheston St. Mary, Tilshead and Winterbourne Stoke. At Shrewton and Maddington thirty-six houses had been destroyed, three lives lost and just under £10,000 of damage caused. A relief fund was formed to aid those impacted by this flood. Although not so badly affected by the flood, Fisherton Street was impassable by foot for two days and the south western portion of the Close had the 'appearance of a large and unbroken sheet of water.'[10]

Another flood occurred in January 1877 and the photographer Edward Wynne Sanger of Devizes Road advertised 'the only complete series of Photographs of the Floods in Fisherton Street.' A series of twenty-four views costing 10 shillings (or could be had at 6d. each) obtainable from his studio in Devizes Road or Mr. Jarratt, the Infirmary; or Mr. Hiller, News Office, Fisherton Street.[11]

Some documentary photography was comparatively ambitious by contemporary standards. In August 1875 a grand fete was held in Wilton Park in aid of the funds of the 14th Wilts Rifle Volunteers. Some 11,000 attended the event. Amongst the activities there was an ascent of the balloon of the leading aeronaut Henry Tracey Coxwell (1818–1900), which took place at Wilton Park. The balloon rose to some 2,500 feet. An 'instantaneous photograph' of the event was subsequently available free by post for seven stamps from the photographer, Henry Drew of the Market Place, Romsey.[12]

Art and Archaeology

During the 1840s interest in local history, archaeological and architectural subjects spread across Great Britain and some thirty-five societies promoting these activities were formed.

These provided opportunities for photographs to be exhibited and discussed at both formal and informal gatherings. In addition, a number of these societies began to assemble photographic collections.

The Wiltshire Archaeological and Natural History Society (WANHS) was founded in Devizes in 1853 and Salisbury was to host several of the society's annual meetings, which included a 'temporary museum' of artefacts from members' collections. The Society's use of photography has yet to be full examined. However, it did form a photographic collection. One champion for photography was the President, Horatio Nelson, 3rd Earl Nelson (1823–1913) of Trafalgar House. At the annual meeting of the WANHS held in Devizes in August 1863, Lord Nelson proposed that 'no church should be restored or old building pulled down without a photograph being taken of it.'[13] Nelson persisted in his view, and at the tenth annual meeting of the WANHS held in Devizes in August 1866, he reiterated his proposal that photography be used to retain 'the recollection of old buildings by means of photography.'[14]

The city became a regular location for a range of meetings of archaeological societies. In July 1849 the Archaeological Institute held its annual meeting at Salisbury and a temporary exhibition of a significant number of various types of artefacts was exhibited at the King's House in the Close. A detailed description of these was published in the *SJ*, though no photographs were listed.[15]

There are no records in the society's journal that any photographs were exhibited at the Temporary Museum of the WANHS's second annual meeting held in Salisbury in 1854. However at the fifth Annual meeting held in Bradford in 1857, James Edward Nightingale (1816–1892)[16] of Wilton, a prominent antiquarian, local historian and Fellow of the Society of Antiquaries, exhibited 'a series of 21 photographs, consisting chiefly of views in and near Rome.'[17] It would seem that he may also have been a photographer since he exhibited four images at the 1858 exhibition of Photographic Society of London:

Cat. No. 623 Cedars in Wilton Park
Cat. No. 646 Cedar in WiltonPark
Cat. No. 683 Houses in the Rue St.Pierre, Caen
Cat. No. 697 Palais de Justice, Rouen

All these images were listed as calotypes – prints from Talbot's paper negative process – an interesting fact given that from the mid-1850s the albumen print from the wet collodion glass negative had become the predominant combination. Nightingale continued to exhibit photographs from his collection and in January 1871 he put on display 'some large and very successful photographs of well-known buildings in Venice' at a loan exhibition held under the auspices of the Wilton Literary Institute. Nightingale also acted as one of the 'superintendents' of the exhibition.[18]

August 1858 saw Salisbury hosting the Fifteenth Annual Meeting of the British Archaeological Association, though, again, no photographs appear to have been exhibited.

In September 1859 at the WANHS annual meeting, held in Marlborough, Henry J.F. Swain, Recorder of Wilton, of Netherhampton House, exhibited a photograph from the charter granted by Henry I to the Burgesses of Wilton.[19]

In 1860 the *Wiltshire Archaeological and Natural History Magazine* noted that Elizabeth Wickens (*c.* 1788–1866), the local amateur topographical artist, had donated to the society a 'Photograph from an original drawing of an ancient painting representing the Great Doom, discovered in St. Thomas's Church.' The coat of whitewash that had been applied over the chancel in 1593, at the time of the Reformation, was removed in 1819 and the western side (of the chancel arch) was found to be covered with a painting. Miss Wickens made a pencil drawing. After being covered again with whitewash, the painting remained hidden until 1876 when it was exposed and in 1881 Clayton and Bell of London were commissioned to restore it.

The monument at Stonehenge provided subject matter for a number of photographers, frequently as a result of a scholarly meeting. By the second half of the 1850s a number of Salisbury print and book sellers were offering photographic views of Stonehenge. Local photographers including James Miell and Frederick Treble documented the monument in the mid-1860s using stereoscopic and carte de visite formats.

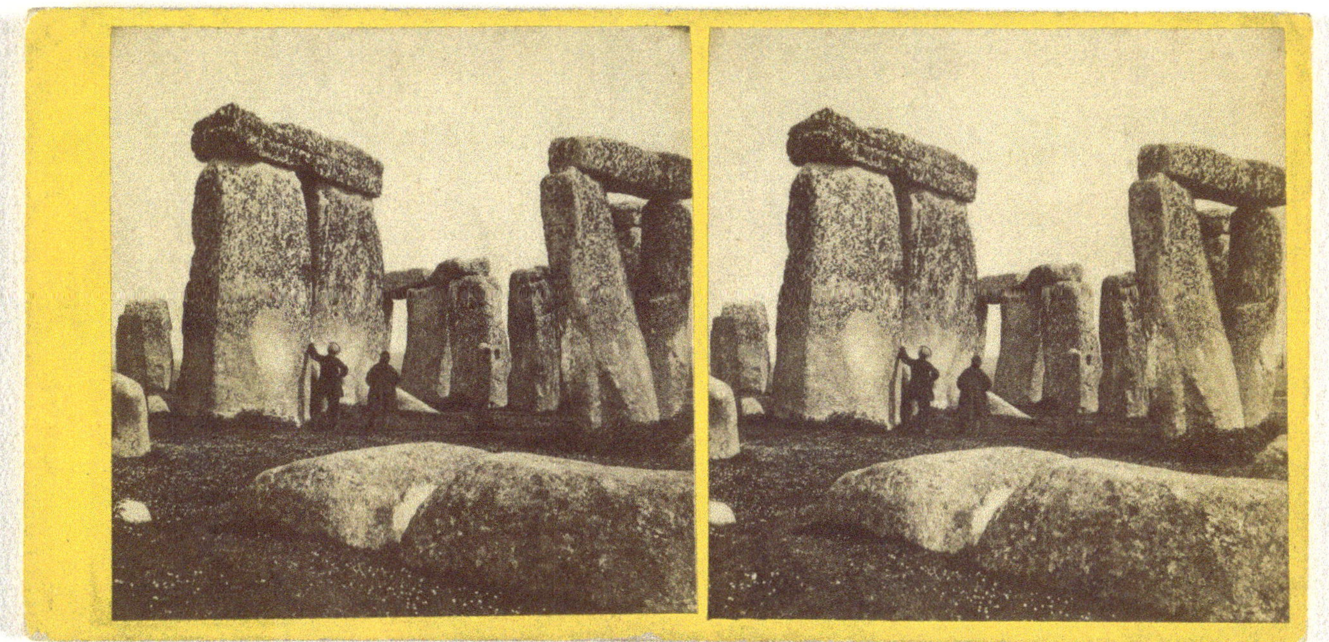

James Miell. Stonehenge - Near View from the South East. No. 37. c. 1865. Stereoscopic view. Albumen print. The J. Paul Getty Museum 84.XC.873.300.

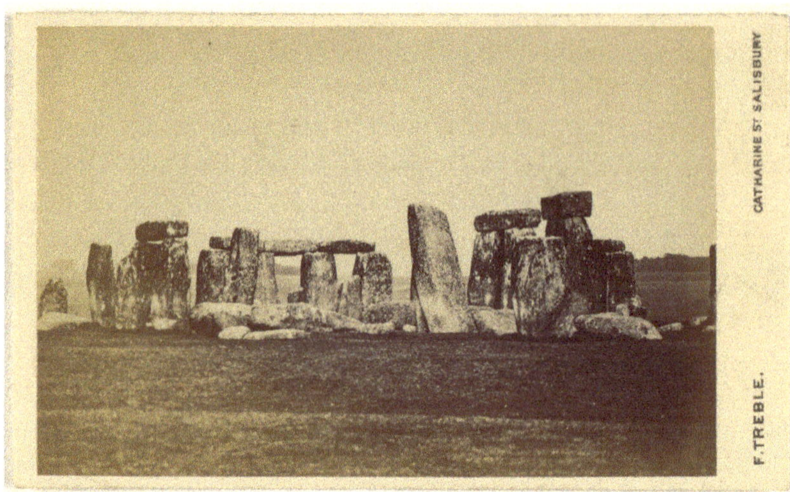

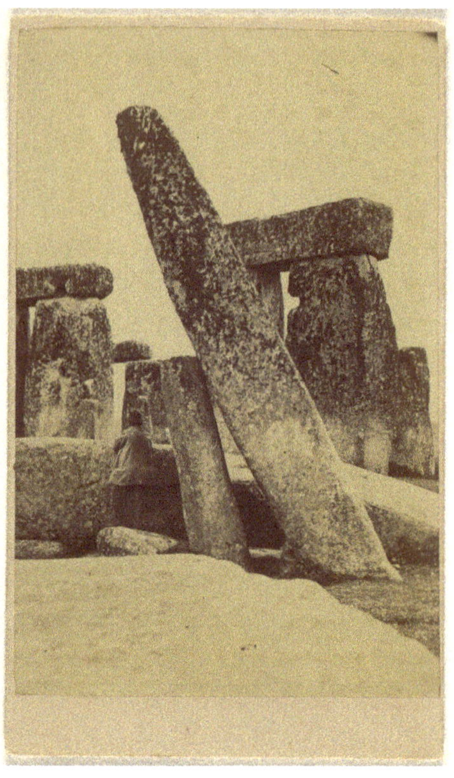

above: Frederick Treble. General view of Stonehenge. Early 1860s. Carte de visite. Albumen print. The J. Paul Getty Museum 84.XD.1157.1992.

right: Frederick Treble. Early 1860s. View of one of the blue stones and leaning inner sarsen uprights (Stone 56) of Stonehenge. Carte de visite. Albumen print. The J. Paul Getty Museum 84.XD.1157.1845.

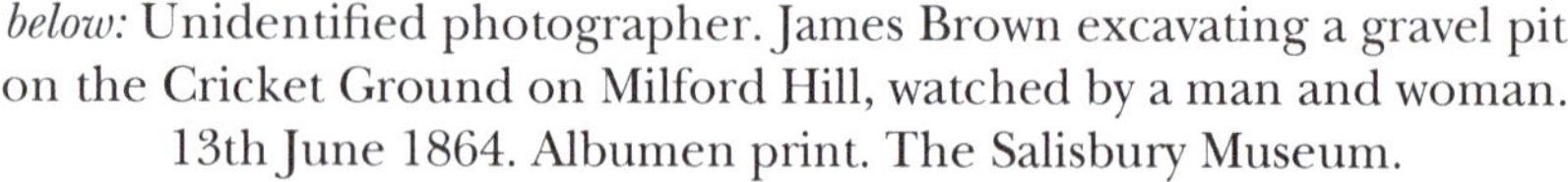

below: Unidentified photographer. James Brown excavating a gravel pit on the Cricket Ground on Milford Hill, watched by a man and woman. 13th June 1864. Albumen print. The Salisbury Museum.

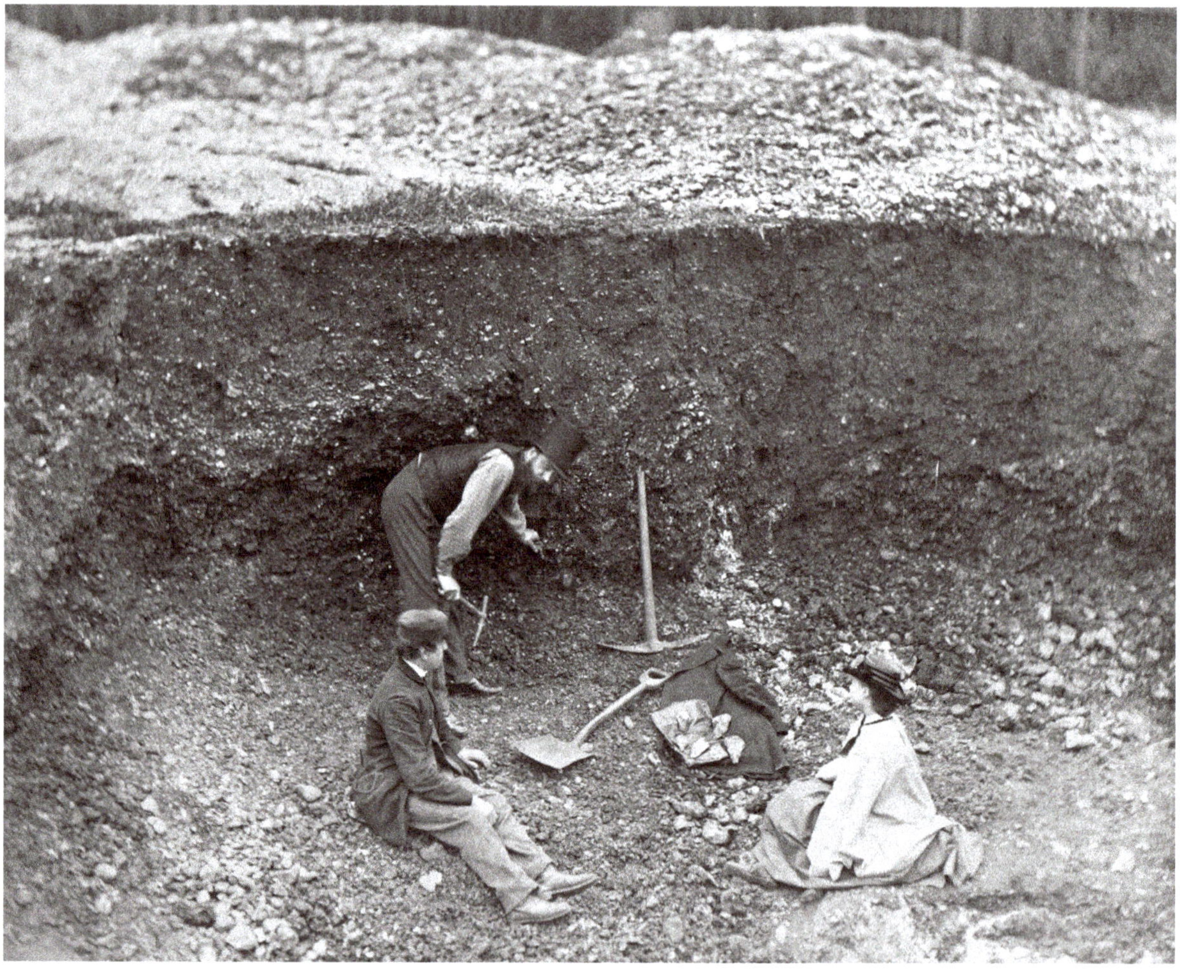

Photography was sporadically used to document archaeological excavations in and around Salisbury. The mid-Victorian archaeologists were particularly interested in the stone tools – particularly flint stone – in use from the Palaeolithic through to the Bronze Age. In 1864, Humphrey P. Blackmore, local general practitioner and curator of the Salisbury and South Wilts Museum, had begun watching the excavations for house basements and small gravel pits which were being dug for aggregates on Milford Hill. On 13th June one local antiquary, James Brown, was photographed looking for prehistoric handaxes in a gravel pit in Milford Hill. Altogether, Brown found over twenty handaxes in the gravel removed from a cellar at Elm Grove.

Church building was a hallmark of the Victorian era. The enthusiasm for building or restoring churches was galvanised by the 'High Church' Oxford Movement. The need for new churches to accommodate the rising population required the government to provide a remedy. The Church Building Act of 1818 resulted in £1 million being allocated to be spent on new churches. The 1824 Church Building Act which followed allocated another £500,000. The result was a surge in church building, particularly in the 1860s, when 1,010 were built in this decade. Between 1835 and 1875 3,765 Anglican churches were built or rebuilt.

In some instances existing churches were demolished and replaced by new buildings, predominantly in the Gothic style. In 1852 St Clement's church at Fisherton Anger was demolished and St. Paul's, located beside the current location of St Paul's roundabout, was built to replace it. The font, bell frame timbers and the six bells and various monuments from St Clement were transferred to St. Paul's which was consecrated in 1853. Carte de visite photographs of an engraving of St Clement's prior to its demolition were sold.

An interesting example of photographic documentation took place in the Bourne valley in 1867 following the decision to demolish the two existing churches at Winterbourne Earls and Winterbourne Dauntsey, and to replace them with one new parish church, St. Michael, in Winterbourne Earls. In June 1867, 14th-century wall paintings were unearthed at the old church of St. Edward at Winterbourne Dauntsey during its demolition. The church had been originally built in the 12th century. Four murals, one on a Norman wall, the others painted about c. 1553, were discovered, including one depicting Edward the Confessor as one of the Magi. Henry Brooks photographed seven or eight of the best-preserved figures and seems to have taken general views of the exterior and interior of the church. Proceeds from the sales of Brooks's photographs were given

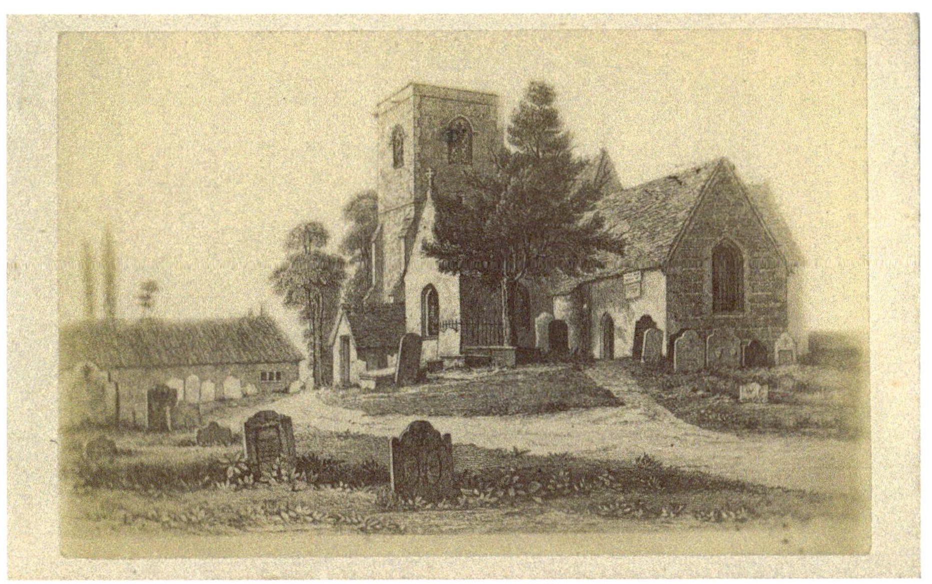

Unidentified photographer. Pre-1852 engraving of an exterior view of St. Clement Church, Fisherton Anger. Carte de visite. Albumen print. Private collection.

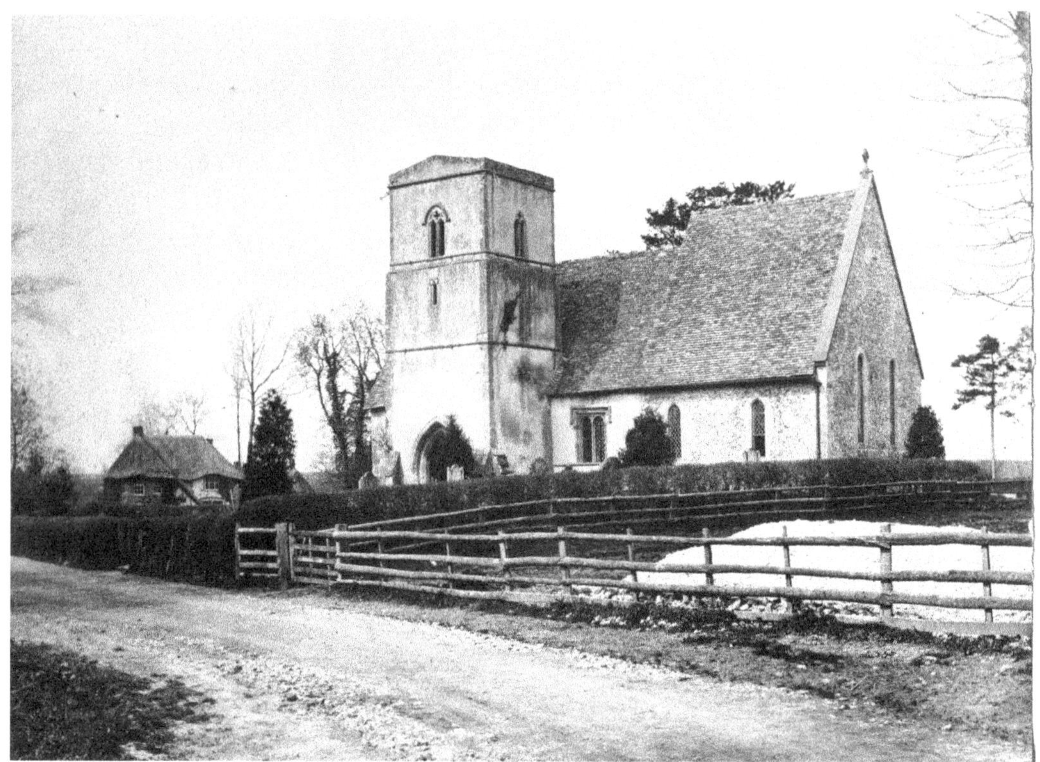

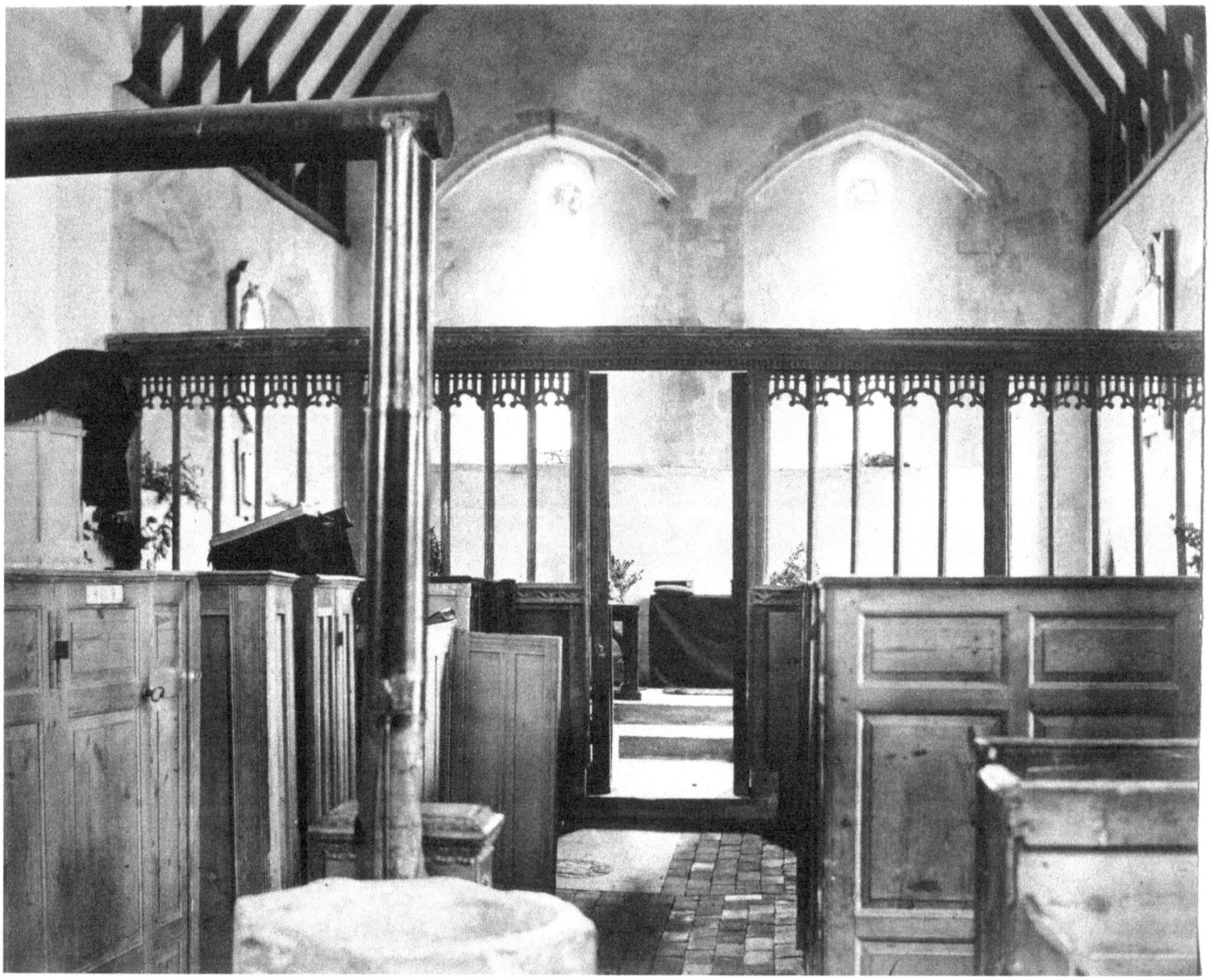

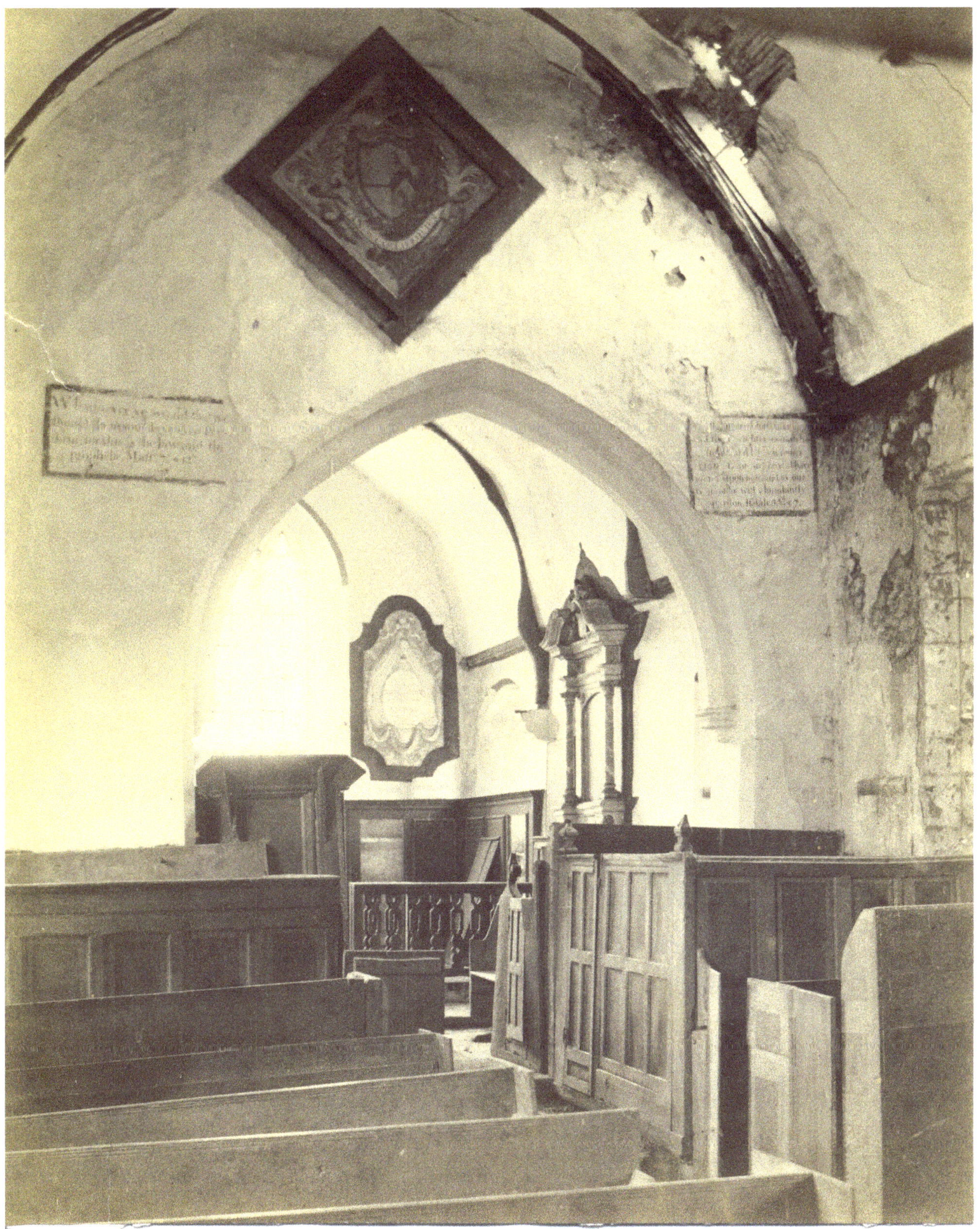

opposite top: Attributed to Henry Brooks. Exterior view of St Edward, Winterbourne Dauntsey. 1867. Albumen print. The Salisbury Museum.
opposite: Attributed to Henry Brooks. Interior view of St Edward, Winterbourne Dauntsey looking towards the altar. 1867. Albumen print. The Salisbury Museum.
above: Attributed to Henry Brooks. Interior view of St Edward, Winterbourne Dauntsey looking toward the west end. 1867. Albumen print. The Salisbury Museum.

to the funds for building St. Michael, the total cost of re-building being £3,100. The church was consecrated on 15th April 1868.[20]

Another example of photographic documentation took place in 1868 when T. G. Targett, a picture dealer of the Canal, advertised a photograph of his painting of the Church of St. Andrew, Bemerton – where George Herbert had preached – prior to its restoration. Targett copyrighted this image that could be seen at his office at Silverthorn's, cabinet maker, in the Canal.[21] In the same issue of the *SJ* Targett advertised some expensive photographs of 22 x 14 inch of the painting by Henry Leonidas Rolfe (1824–1881) of 'Freshwater Fishes of Great Britain.' These were priced at £1 1s. (Plain), £2 12s. 6d. (tinted in watercolours), £4 14s. 6d. (highly finished in water colours). An additional 10s. 6d. would apply if the photograph was framed. Significantly, Targett's advertisement stated that 'To prevent piracy, every photograph will bear the Artist's signature.'

Meetings of Professional Groups

From the 1840s the taking of group portraits of those attending meetings of professional groups and societies was undertaken by a range of amateur and professional photographers.

One of these was Henry Brooks, who on Tuesday 7th August 1860 carried his camera to the Laverstock House Asylum and took a group portrait of the attendees of visiting medical practitioners, primarily members of the Southampton Medical Society.[22]

On Thursday 22nd September 1864 James Miell took 'several good photographs… during the visit of the British Association to Stonehenge.' The *SJ* reported that 'One of these was taken during the discussion, and Dr. Thurnam [John Thurnam (1810–1873), English psychiatrist, archaeologist, and ethnologist] is seen in the act of addressing members from the impost of the great trilithon. Considering the great difficulty of obtaining pictures under such circumstances, the photographs are well executed.'[23]

School of Art

The Salisbury School of Science and Art was founded in 1865 with its inaugural meeting taking place on Thursday 19th October in the Council Chamber. In December 1866, Dr John Alfred Lush (1815–1888), the Mayor, announced that the Banqueting Room of the Council Chamber could be used by the school. Having used rooms in the Salisbury Literary and Scientific Institute (SLSI) in New Street, it took over the building following the demise of the SLSI in 1877.

At the prize giving held in December 1875, James Hussey (1808–1879), magistrate and mayor in 1843, stated that it was 'most desirable that efforts should be made to place before the students of the Salisbury School of Art, in greater number and variety, photographic, or other representations, of the works of the greatest masters, – such, for example, as the Sistine Chapel, by Michel Angelo, the set of Cartoons, now at Brompton [at the South Kensington Museum], by Raphael, and by other Masters.'[24] These photographs formed part of the Circulation Collection of South Kensington Museum/Department of Science and Art sent out on loan to the provincial schools of art. Another component of this collection was the series of photographically-illustrated titles, *Art Workmanship* volumes.

It has yet to be established to what extent the School of Art availed itself of the opportunity to borrow photographs from the Circulation Collection and whether it actually had a photographic collection of its own.

Public Lectures

Public lectures, frequently to raise funds for a new building or a charitable organisation, was another hallmark of the Victorian era and a variety of locations provided venues for such public lectures in Salisbury. Photography in two forms were increasingly used in such lectures during the 1870s.

Firstly, there were photographs. These might be pinned to display boards in the lecture theatre and examined by the audience, not necessarily during the actual lecture itself.

The magic lantern was a popular form of Victorian education and entertainment in both private and public environments. Powered by bright oxyhydrogen light, images on glass slides could be projected onto large white screens. Throughout the 19th century the graphics and images on glass slides were often painted. Photographic glass slides had first been exhibited at the 1851 Great Exhibition. These were the 'Hyalotypes' exhibited by the German-born brothers Frederick and William Langenheim of Philadelphia. From the 1860s such photographic glass slides projected by magic lanterns became popular, and increasingly used during the 1870s. By 1862 James Miell was stocking new and second-hand lantern projectors and glass lantern slides for both sale and for hire. However, these slides were not photographic.[25] By 1864 Miell was advertising lantern slide 'Views (photographic) of Egypt, the Holy Land, Rome, London, &c.' adding that 'Persons wishing to engage Lanterns &c., for Schools, Evening Parties, &c., would do well to make early application.'[26]

Knowledge of photography was comparatively limited during the 1850s. However, there were some local amateurs and collectors wishing to spread information and in October 1852 'Mr. T. Keynes, of Salisbury' gave an illustrated lecture in the Shaftesbury Town-hall, on the Daguerreotype process. This was probably Thomas Keynes, who set up a photographic studio in his auction rooms in Brown Street in September 1858. Whether the illustrations were of his own photographs, or his collection, or both, is unknown.[27]

On Tuesday 25th February 1873 George St. Clair (1836–1908), F.G.S., Baptist minister and an official lecturer of the Palestine Exploration Fund, gave a public lecture in the Council Chamber on the recent discoveries of Captain Charles Warren R.E. (1840–1927) in Jerusalem and the Holy Land. These included drawings, maps, diagrams and photographs.[28] Between 1867 and 1870 Captain Warren had carried out the first major expedition of the Palestine Exploration Fund and his work forms the basis of today's knowledge of the topography of ancient Jerusalem and the archaeology of the Temple Mount/Haram al-Sherif. In April 1874 St. Clair returned to the Council Chamber to give another photographically-illustrated lecture on the work of the Palestine Exploration Fund. Admission was free, by ticket, which could be obtained from Brown & Co. in the Canal.

Samuel Griffin (*c.*1840–1902), son of James Griffin a timber merchant of Fisherton Anger, was a regular public lecturer in Salisbury during the 1870s. He was a keen user of glass slide lantern projection, using both photographic and non-photographic glass lantern slides. On 19th January 1875 he gave a lecture on 'Italy' at the Baptist Church Mutual Improvement Society. He illustrated it with 50 magic lantern photographs of famous scenes and structures in Venice, Milan, Turin, Genoa, Pisa, Florence, Rome, Naples, Pompeii, Palermo, and other cities. The photographs were those of Ferrier & Soulier of Paris who specialised in such lantern slides that were of extremely high quality.[29] A few days before Christmas 1880, at the Maundrel Hall, Samuel Griffin used the same fifty glass slides of Italian architecture. The Rev. Edgar Nembhard Thwaites (1839–1919), rector of Fisherton, locally renowned as an evangelistic preacher and as an unusually gifted and energetic organizer, had made his parish a centre of missionary activity at home and overseas. He made some remarks as each slide was projected.[30]

The founding of the Salisbury Literary & Scientific Institute (SLSI) in 1849 provided a more formal venue for lectures on photography, or lectures illustrated with photographs. The institute met in the Assembly Rooms and during the 1850s was paying two guineas for hiring the rooms for each lecture. Across the city there were other venues including church halls and schools. The SLSI occasionally held photographically illustrated lectures. Mr Cunningham gave a lecture on Paris illustrated by photographic glass slides 'executed by French artists.'[31]

The leading architect Richard Popplewell Pullan (1825–1888) gave a lecture at the SLSI on Tuesday 21st December 1875 about the discovery of the Mausoleum of Halicarnassus and other buildings in Asia Minor. The lecture was illustrated by a number of photographs 'which were displayed by means of lime-light [projected from a magic lantern], and reflected on a white screen.'[32] The following year, it was advertised that on 12th January 1876, the Rev. Edgar Smith, vicar of All Saints, Highgate, London, would deliver a lecture in the Assembly Rooms, entitled 'Personal Reminiscences of a tour in the Holy Land.' The lecture would be illustrated by a series of paintings and photographs, which would be displayed by the magic lantern.'[33]

The theme of religious lectures using photographs of the Middle East continued. On

Thursday 9th March 1876, a fund-raising concert of sacred songs, anthems and quartets was held at the Fisherton Primitive Methodist Schoolroom and was interspersed with a selection of sacred and foreign photographs of Egypt and Palestine. The chair was taken by the Rev. J. Hill.[34]

The *SJ* also cast its news gathering net wider than the city and it included accounts of the lectures given at the Hartley Institute in Southampton. One such lecture was given in January 1873 by T. H. Thomas entitled 'An evening with the early Painters and Sculptors of Italy'; it covered the 13th, 14th and 15th centuries. Thomas's lecture was illustrated by 'a series of photographic drawings from original paintings, sculptures, etc.' projected by the magic lantern.[35]

Distinguished Visitors to Salisbury

A wide range of distinguished and celebrity visitors came to Salisbury during the mid-Victorian era. They were to experience photography from several different angles.

On 15th August 1856 Queen Victoria and Prince Albert visited the city, accompanied by four of their children, en route from Plymouth to Osborne on the Isle of Wight. The royal family lunched at the White Hart Hotel and then were given a guided tour of the cathedral. It was reported that Messrs. Brown, the book, stationery and print seller of the Canal, had supplied Her Majesty with a copy of Dodsworth's *The History and Antiquities of the Cathedral Church of Salisbury* with India proof impressions, and also several photographs of the Cathedral, &c., by William Russell Sedgfield.[36]

The temperance movement was a hallmark of the Victorian era and one particular event held in Salisbury in 1872 indicates its international dimensions. Wau-Bun-O (1815–1892) (also known as John Wampum), a Delaware Indian, was an active temperance advocate who began touring England as early as 1855 advocating abstinence from alcohol. He was a prominent official in the Good Templars' Grand Lodge of Canada. Wau-Bun-O had some form of official backing by the Canadian Government and was doing the rounds in Great Britain well into the 1880s, lecturing, opening bazaars etc.

In 1872 Wau-Bun-O was in England on a lecture tour and visited Salisbury. In June he gave a talk at the Scots Lane Schoolroom. The Rev. F. Smith first gave a lecture on Canada and Wau-Bun-O then addressed the audience,[37] probably giving the same lecture as that he gave at a meeting of the Isle of Wight Temperance Union in the first week of September 1872 (probably Thursday 5th) in which he 'descanted on the evil effects of fire-water on his tribe and deprecated on the use of tobacco.'[38]

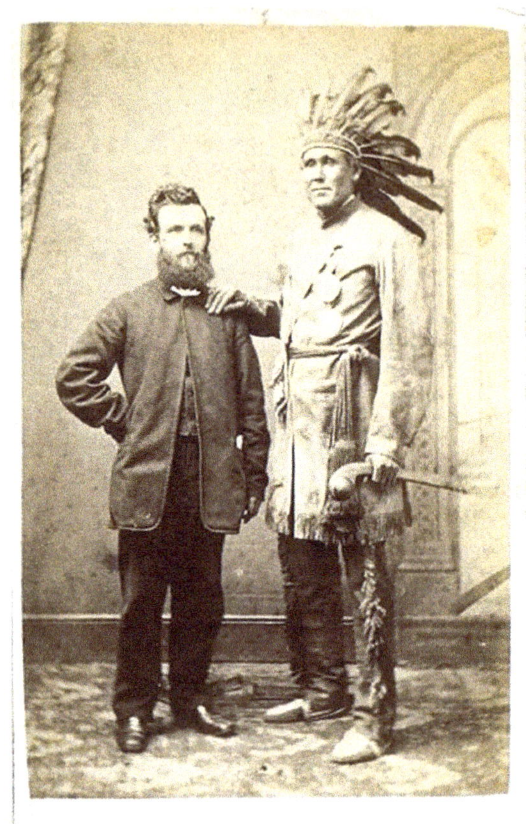

Charles James Witcomb. Portrait of Wau-Ban-O and Rev. F. Smith. June 1872. Carte de visite. Albumen print. Courtesy of Cowan's Auctions.

During his visit to Salisbury Wau-Bun-O was photographed with the Rev. Smith by Witcomb in several poses with different studio backdrops. Carte de visite photographs of these were made commercially available.

Estate Agents and Local Manufactures

One of the applications of photography was to illustrate services or the catalogues of manufacturers. These sometimes were either issued as loose photographs, or were used to provide illustrations to printed catalogues.

While today we expect details of any property for sale to be liberally illustrated, quite when estate agents availed themselves of the opportunity to photographically illustrate property details remains unclear. In January 1854 the *SJ* noted that a property auction house in London's West End, referred to as a 'Cosmoramic Auction Mart' were exhibiting 'on a large scale, photographic pictures of the property to be disposed of by auction,'[39]

Quite when properties for sale local to Salisbury were first photographically illustrated has yet to be established. Perhaps one of the earliest examples took place in 1871 when Messrs. Farebrother, Clark and Co. were instructed to sell at the Mart, Token House Yard, Lothbury in London, the Old Lodge in Nether Wallop. A series of photographs of the mansion could be examined at Messrs. Garrard and James, solicitors of Suffolk Street, Pall Mall, London, Messrs. Rawlence and Squarey of George Street, London and Salisbury, and the offices of Messrs. Farebrother, Clark and Co., Lancaster Place, Strand, London.[40] Presumably a local photographer was employed to take these photographs

In July 1874 Messrs. Waters, Son & Rawlence, auctioneers of the Canal, auctioned two properties, one known as 'Stonleigh' and the other as 'Belmont'. It was noted in the advertised sale that 'Further particulars may be obtained of the Auctioneers, Canal, Salisbury (at whose Office a photograph of the houses may be seen).'[41]

However, integrating photographs into manufactured items also took place in the city. On 9th February 1870, Arthur Foley (1831–1894/5), cabinet maker and furniture manufacturer, whose Fisherton Machine Cabinet Works was located at 39–43 Fisherton Street, had Letters Patent issued (No 383) for 'Improvements in the production of photographic pictures or designs on veneers and solid woods.' In 1873 he sent a lady's boudoir table designed by H. Dickenson to the International Exhibition being held in Vienna. The table was made of fine English woods, ornamented with inlays and incised coloured arabesques, and included panels in the casket containing photographic copies from works of art in Her Majesty's possession, 'which are printed on the natural wood.'[42] This may refer to a 'photo-on-wood' process in which the photographic emulsion was applied to the wood and the photograph printed onto this, thereby removing the need for a paper support. Foley also applied photography for other purposes. In September 1875 he placed an advertisement in the *SJ* for a 14-room detached property to be let, furnished or unfurnished, and stated that 'photographs forwarded on application.'[43]

Illustrated Publishing

THE JOURNALISTIC POTENTIAL of photography was noted in a short editorial note in the SJ in 1848. Titled 'New Mode of Counting Heads', it mentioned that a daguerreotype of the Chartists meeting held on the 10th April, 1848 in Kennington, South London, had been reproduced as a wood engraving in the *Illustrated London News* of the following Saturday and that 'the result is that the numbers present hardly amounted to 10,000.'[44] However, during the 1840s comparatively few print publishers availed themselves of this process of producing wood engravings from photographic originals.

This approach of copying original photographs and reproducing them through traditional reprographic processes is indicated by a short article in the *SJ* in January 1860. This referred to a sheet music publication by William Price Aylward (1811–1890), whose Music Warehouse was in the Canal. The publication was a 'March' composed by John Elliot Richardson, then Assistant-Organist at the cathedral. This was dedicated to the officers, non-commissioned officers, and privates of the 1st (or Salisbury) Company of the Wiltshire Rifle Volunteers, of which, as mentioned previously, Aylward was bandmaster. This sheet music was illustrated with portraits of the members of the so-called Salisbury Rifle Corps copied from photographs by Henry Brooks.[45]

Photographically-illustrated publications represent a distinct form of mid-nineteenth century publishing. Portfolios of loose photographs – perhaps with a printed title-page and list of plates – were one common format. Sedgfield's 1853 set of ten photographs 'in a neat cover' is one early and relevant example, and another of his images of Salisbury appeared in Part V of *The Photographic Album*, a part work published by Joseph Cundall. A photograph of the West Front (using prints from at least two variant negatives) by Sedgfield formed

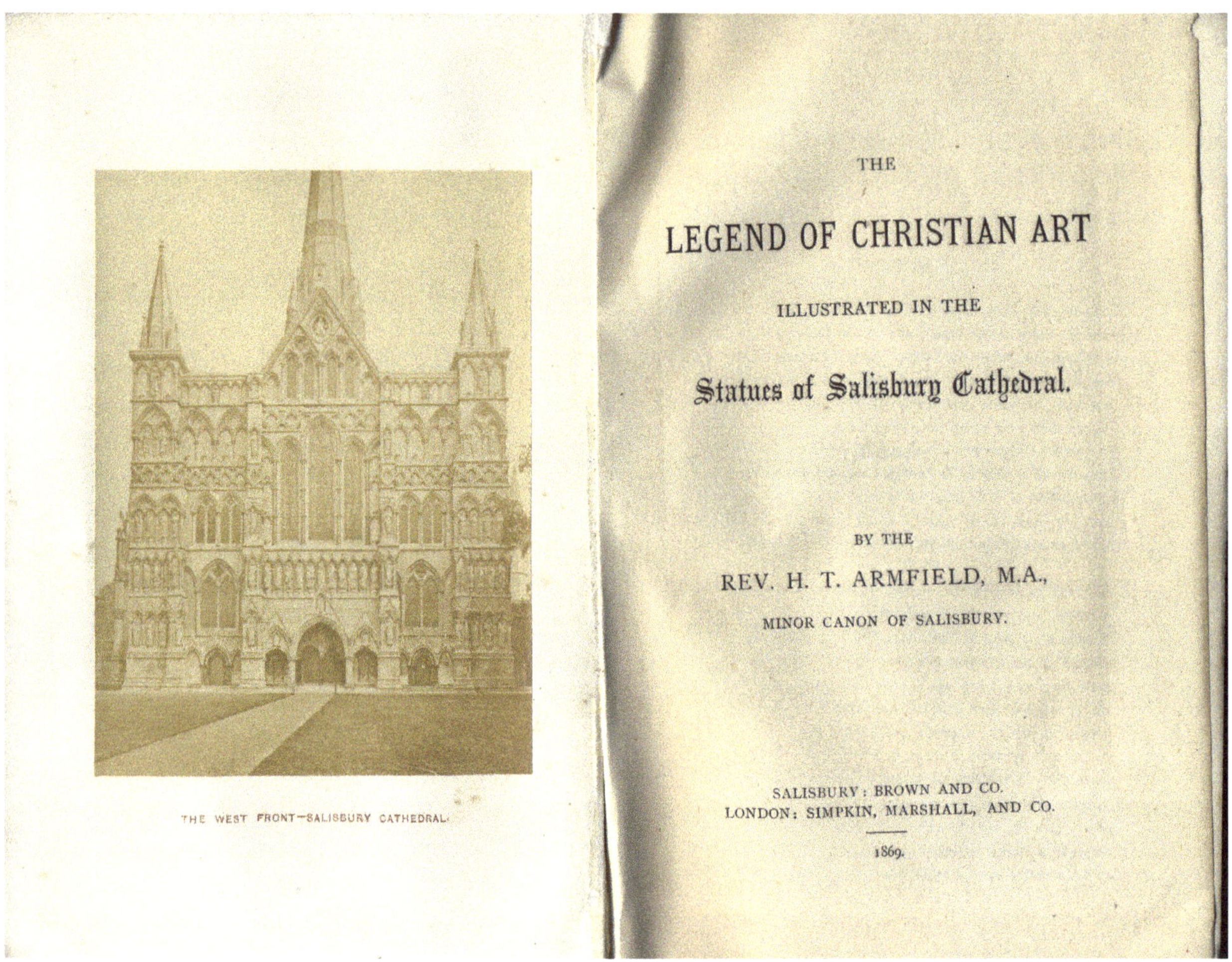
THE WEST FRONT—SALISBURY CATHEDRAL.

THE

LEGEND OF CHRISTIAN ART

ILLUSTRATED IN THE

Statues of Salisbury Cathedral.

BY THE

REV. H. T. ARMFIELD, M.A.,

MINOR CANON OF SALISBURY.

SALISBURY: BROWN AND CO.
LONDON: SIMPKIN, MARSHALL, AND CO.

1869.

William Russel Sedgfield. West front of Salisbury Cathedral. 1869. Albumen print. Frontispiece of The Rev. H. T. Armfield, *The Legend of Christian Art Illustrated in the Statues of Salisbury Cathedral*, Brown and Co.; Simpkin, Marshall, and Co., Salisbury and London, 1869. Anthony Hamber collection.

the frontispiece to The Rev. H. T. Armfield's *The Legend of Christian Art Illustrated in the Statues of Salisbury Cathedral*, published in 1869 by Brown and Co.; Simpkin, Marshall, and Co., respectively of Salisbury and London.

Photographs of the cathedral by Roger Fenton, including his view of the south aisle of the nave looking east, formed part of a portfolio of twelve photographs published as *Photographs. The Art Union of London 1859.* Two views of the West front were published as part of another portfolio, *The Works of Roger Fenton – Cathedrals*, published by Francis Frith of Reigate in 1864.

Bazaars

FUND RAISING BAZAARS took place in Salisbury, frequently to support the building or maintenance of religious buildings. On Tuesday 3rd, Wednesday 4th and Thursday 5th October 1876 a bazaar was held in the Salt Lane Schoolroom in aid of the Church Street Chapel. Over 100 photographs of the Rev. William Tranter (1778–1879), Methodist minister, in his 98th year, and a large number of photographs of the interior of the Chapel were sold, all of which had been given by the photographer Charles Witcomb.[46]

Wedding Photography

WHILE WEDDING PHOTOGRAPHY became a mainstay of 20th century professional photography, it was less common in the mid-Victorian era. A comparatively early example took place on Thursday 8th July 1875, when Robert Hawthorne Collins (1841–1908), of Boyton House,

Comptroller of the Household of his Royal Highness Prince Leopold, married in the village church of Codford St. Peter, Mary Elizabeth Wightwick, eldest daughter of the rector, the Rev. H. Wightwick. The wedding party was photographed before the wedding breakfast, though the photographer has not been identified.[47]

Trade Unionism

TRADE UNIONS HAD been legalized in Britain in 1824 and in 1871 the Trade Union Act was passed. One Salisbury resident during the second half of the 1870s, A. Smee, was the Secretary to the Salisbury District Branch of the Agricultural Labourers' Union and also the local agent for the Mutual Provident Alliance Friendly Society. Smee took a particular interest in exploiting photography to support his trade union's cause.

On Thursday 16th September 1875 a meeting was held at Stonehenge, when Mr. Joseph Arch (1826–1919), a former farm labourer and Methodist lay preacher, leader of the National Agricultural Labourers' Union (founded in May 1872) delivered a speech. It was reported that 'Photographs were taken and copies can be had of Mr. Smee, 26, Clifton Terrace, Fisherton.'[48]

In February of the following year, *The English Labourer* published an account of the scene of the eviction of Mr and Mrs Durham, their daughter and two sons from a cottage in Cherhill, near Calne, in which they had lived for 28 years. In the detailed account reprinted in the *ST* there was a mention that 'capitally executed' photographs of Mr and Mrs Durham with their daughter and two sons surrounded by their humble furniture had been taken and 'A Large number were sold.' 'The photographs large size for framing, 1s. carte de visite size, 6d., may be had of Mr. A. Smee, Fisherton, Salisbury.'[49] While the photographer has yet to be identified it would appear that Smee commissioned the photography and it is thus likely that this was undertaken by a Salisbury photographer.[50]

Poitics – Treating, Bribery and Intimidation

IN 1880, PHOTOGRAPHY became intertwined with a case of alleged election fraud that took place in Salisbury during that year's General Election.

The Conservative party sitting MPs suffered an ignominious defeat to two Liberal candidates, John Passmore Edwards (1823–1911), British journalist, newspaper owner (*The Echo*, London) and philanthropist (who vacated his seat in 1882), and William Henry Grenfell (1855–1945), British athlete, sportsman, public servant and politician. Edwards stated he had spent £679 on his campaign while Grenfell stated he had spent £742 7s. on his campaign.

Salisbury and Wilton saw two challenges to the respective results in their constituencies. In Wilton, the Liberal party lodged a complaint against the sitting MP, the Hon Sidney Herbert (1853–1913), 14th Earl of Pembroke, on the grounds of treating, bribery and intimidation. In Salisbury, the Conservatives brought a claim that Edwards and Grenfell had given 'gratuitous entertainments of music and singing at the Hamilton Hall' and 'unduly influenced voters generally by the distribution of gratuitous photographs of the respondents, and by giving of such photographs and entertainments amounted to bribery and treating.'[51] It is presumed that these photographs were carte de visite portraits, though who the photographer was and how many photographs were distributed is unknown.

A three-day investigation took place in late June in Salisbury into the case against Edwards and Grenfell. It was undertaken by Charles Edward Pollock (1823–1897), Baron of the Court of Exchequer and Sir Henry Hawkins (1817–1907), Justice of the High Court of Justice, who examined the claim under the Parliamentary Elections Act, 1868 and Parliamentary Elections and Corrupt Practices Act, 1880.

Pollock and Hawkins published their findings that were reported in the *ST* in early July. They stated that 'We report that there is no reason to believe that corrupt practices have extensively prevailed at the election to which the petition relates.'[52]

Local Collectors of Photographs

COLLECTING PHOTOGRAPHS DURING the 1840s was predominantly a metropolitan-based pastime. Opticians, chemists, print sellers etc. began to stock items from an early date as did the early daguerreotype portrait studios which began to appear in London from 1841. Richard Beard opened London's first photographic studio on 23rd March 1841. Antoine Claudet opened another in June of the same year. By 1850, however, there were only around a dozen photographic studios in London though these and a significant number of print sellers, opticians, booksellers and stationers displayed and sold photographs. Some of these photographs were by Continental photographers.

During the 1840s and 1850s there were a number of stationers, booksellers and print sellers in Salisbury from which photographs could be purchased. These included Brown & Co. in the Canal; Frederick A. Blake, booksellers, Market Place; Edward Roe, Printer, Queen Street; and some less obvious commercial premises, such as Webb's, Gunmaker, 38 Catherine-Street. Quite how many commercial establishments in Salisbury stocked photographic images, or acted as agents for photographic sales, during the 1840s is unclear. Some of the earliest photographs of Salisbury, those of William Russell Sedgfield, were advertised for sale in September 1853 through Brown in the Canal and Blake in the Market Place

Photographs were, at this time, expensive and the roles in the history of photography in Salisbury of the local aristocracy, notably the Pleydell-Bouverie family of Radnor Castle and the Herbert family of Wilton House, together with the wealthiest families in the city, has yet to be uncovered.

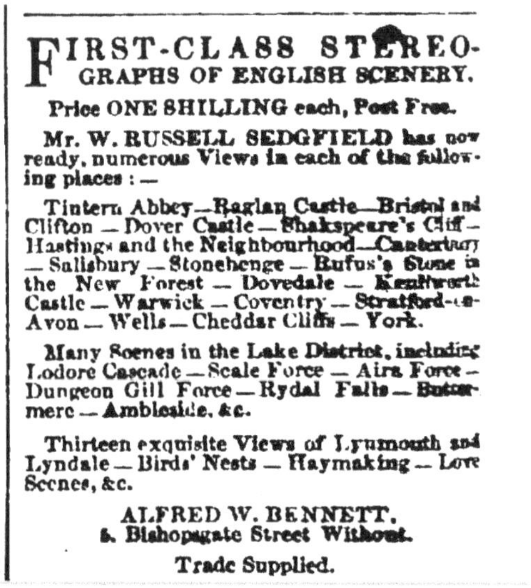

FIRST-CLASS STEREO-GRAPHS OF ENGLISH SCENERY.

Price ONE SHILLING each, Post Free.

Mr. W. RUSSELL SEDGFIELD has now ready, numerous Views in each of the following places: —

Tintern Abbey — Raglan Castle — Bristol and Clifton — Dover Castle — Shakspeare's Cliff — Hastings and the Neighbourhood — Canterbury — Salisbury — Stonehenge — Rufus's Stone in the New Forest — Dovedale — Kenilworth Castle — Warwick — Coventry — Stratford-on-Avon — Wells — Cheddar Cliffs — York.

Many Scenes in the Lake District, including Lodore Cascade — Scale Force — Aira Force — Dungeon Gill Force — Rydal Falls — Buttermere — Ambleside, &c.

Thirteen exquisite Views of Lynmouth and Lyndale — Birds' Nests — Haymaking — Love Scenes, &c.

ALFRED W. BENNETT,
5. Bishopsgate Street Without.

Trade Supplied.

Advertisement by Alfred W. Bennett for William Russell Sedgfield stereographs.
Notes and Queries, 26th June 1858.

Some local collectors acquired and exhibited somewhat exotic photographs. In early January 1874, Stephen P. Wills, partner of the Royal Wilton Carpet Factory, exhibited African beetles and insects together with a 'framed photograph of Cape diamond fields' and 'photographs of 12 natives' at the North Wilts Poultry Show at the Corn Exchange in Devizes.[53]

From 1858 the publisher Alfred William Bennett (1833–1902) of Bishopsgate, London advertised Sedgfield's various stereo views in a variety of periodicals and serials such as *The Publisher's Circular, The Bookseller,* and *Notes and Queries,* and these included reference to his Salisbury Cathedral views. The advertisement also included quotations from published reviews of the stereographs, including reviews mentioning the Salisbury images in the *Art-Journal* and *The Bookseller.* Bennett also cited other reviews including one from *Photographic Notes* which referred to the interiors of Salisbury that were 'quite remarkable.' Sedgfield also marketed interior views of Salisbury Cathedral under the title of *Sedgfield's Cathedral Interiors.* Whether this led to an increase in the numbers of photographs collected by Salisbury enthusiasts for the medium remains unclear.

One distinctive feature of commercial photography was that of photographic illustration. William Henry Fox Talbot is traditionally credited in launching this application of photography to book and other publications. His *Pencil of Nature* was published by Longman, Brown, Green and Longmans in five parts between June 1844 and April 1846. It totalled some twenty-four salted paper prints separately mounted and each accompanied by a page or so of printed text. Whether any Salisbury resident came to own a part or the whole of this publication is unknown, and it was not advertised in the *SJ.*

Photographically-illustrated books and other publications began to appear in small but increasing number from the late 1850s. The following decade is considered to be a Golden Age of the photographically illustrated book, and the advertisements of Salisbury booksellers found in the *SJ* during this period listed a number of well-known titles. Whether one could walk into Messrs. Brown & Co. and actually buy a copy of one of these photographically-illustrated books off the shelf, rather than order a copy having examined a specimen, remains unclear.

In December 1865 Messrs. Brown & Co. advertised 'Elegant Gift Books' selected from the stock of upwards of 30,000 volumes. One book that was listed was F. G. Stephens' *Flemish Relics* 'Illustrated with photographs' and costing 21s. In the summer of 1866 amongst a number of photographically-illustrated titles, Brown & Co. was advertising de-luxe books such as H. B. George's *The Oberland and its Glaciers*, illustrated with twenty-eight photographs and costing two guineas bound in elegant cloth, or three guineas bound in morocco.

This chapter has provided an overview of a range of applications to which photography was put during the 1850s, 1860s and 1870s. It is far from exhaustive and further research will hopefully reveal a fuller picture of the scale and scope of amateur and commercial photography in Salisbury during the mid-Victorian era.

1 The Ordnance Survey six inch to one-mile map of Netherhampton; New Sarum; Quidhampton; Stratford Sub Castle. (Wiltshire LXVI) published in 1887 but based on surveys undertaken between 1877 and 1879 shows the city and its immediate environs towards the end of the period covered. See https://maps.nls.uk/view/102348088
2 David Underdown, *Start of Play: Cricket and Culture in Eighteenth-Century England*, Allen Lane, London, 2000 p. 34.
3 See Alan Crooks *Andrew Bogle Middleton MRCS (1819–1879).* https://salisburymuseum.wordpress.com/2017/12/12/andrew-bogle-middleton-mrcs-1819-1879-by-volunteer-alan-crooks/
4 The late 15th-century roof from the former Maidenhead Inn was incorporated into the school built in Bedwin Street in 1860.
5 *SJ*, Saturday 18th June 1859 p. 8.
6 *SJ* , Saturday 4th July 1863 p. 5. The statue was of Sidney Herbert, Baron Herbert of Lea, born 16th September 1810, died 2nd August 1861, who was the only son of the eleventh earl of Pembroke and his second wife. He had a distinguished public career, both nationally and locally. He was elected MP for South Wiltshire in 1832 and held the seat until his ennoblement in 1861 a few months before his death. Among the offices he held were joint Secretary to the Admiralty, 1841–45 and Secretary at War 1845–6, 1852–5 and 1859–61. He was also instrumental in Florence Nightingale's expedition to provide nursing care for the Crimean War. Locally, because the twelfth earl lived abroad, it was his half-brother who lived in and maintained Wilton House. His contributions to local life and society included the building of the Italianate parish church in Wilton, charitable help for clergy families and the founding of a cottage hospital at Charmouth, Dorset. With his wife he founded the Female Emigration Fund in 1849, and in 1859 Herbert was the first president of the National Volunteer Association.

Herbert's statue, by Baron Marochetti, was unveiled by Earl de Grey and Ripon on 29th June 1863 before an audience of thousands. The statue was about 30 feet to the north of the colonnade on the front of the Guildhall, hence almost equidistant between it and the War Memorial: just how short the space was between Guildhall, statue and memorial is evident from a photograph of VE-Day celebrations published in Newman and Howells' *Salisbury past*, and that gives the clue as to why the statue came to be moved.

The City Council decided in principle in November 1952 that the statue would have to be moved in the course of preparations for Coronation celebrations. On that occasion, Alderman E.J. Case, chairman of the City Lands Committee argued that removing the statue would give more space in front of the Guildhall for civic and state occasions. An alternative to Victoria Park was a location in the grounds of the Council House. Alderman Wort argued strenuously against the removal expenditure of £110, but the decision in favour was carried by 18 votes to 7, and the statue was moved on Tuesday 12th May 1953. See http://history.wiltshire.gov.uk/community/getfaq.php?id=435
7 Cat. No. 89. The exhibition was held in the Exhibition Rooms, Broad Street, St Andrews, Norwich between 17th November 1856 and 14th February 1857.
8 *SJ*, Saturday 29th September 1860 p. 6 and 8.
9 *SJ*, Saturday 12th August 1871 p. 5.
10 *SJ*, Monday 25th January 1841 p. 4.
11 *ST*, Saturday 13th January 1877 p. 4. There was a note in the Local News section of this issue referring to this set of photographs 'obtained at a cheap rate' and Sanger's advertisement. (p. 5).
12 *ST*, Saturday 7th August 1875 p. 8 and *SJ*, Saturday 21st August 1875 p. 5.
13 *SJ*, Saturday 22nd August 1863 p. 6.
14 *Wiltshire Archæological and Natural History Magazine*, Vol. IX, 1866 p. 14.
15 *SJ*, Saturday 18th August 1849 p. 4.
16 Obituary in *The Times* (Wednesday 24th February 1892 p. 1.) states that he died at 16 Alfred Place west, South Kensington, London – the residence of his brother-in-law. His residence was The Mount, Wilton.
17 *Wiltshire Archæological and Natural History Magazine*, Volume IV, 1858 p. 250. Nightingale's name was listed in the 1858 membership list of the Architectural

Photographic Association.
18 *SJ*, Saturday 14th January 1871 p. 2. Lady Herbert and Mr. Cassey were also noted as having exhibited photographs.
19 *Wiltshire Archæological and Natural History Magazine*, Volume VI, 1860 p. 256
20 *SJ*, Saturday 1st June 1867 p. 7. See also https://history.wiltshire.gov.uk/community/getchurch.php?id=1088
21 *SJ*, Saturday 13th June 1868 p. 7.
22 *SJ*, Saturday 11th August 1860 p. 7.
23 *SJ*, Saturday 24th September 1864 p. 5.
24 *ST*, Saturday 11th December 1875 p. 8.
25 *SJ*, Saturday 1st November 1862 p. 5.
26 *SJ*, Saturday 24th December 1864 p. 5.
27 *SJ*, Saturday 23rd October 1852 p. 3
28 *SJ*, Saturday 1st March 1873 p. 6.
29 *SJ*, Saturday 23rd January 1875 p. 8.
30 *ST*, Friday 4th December 1880 p. 4. Maundrel Hall, now the Slug and Lettuce, Fisherton Street, was opened in 1880. It was named after John Maundrell, a Protestant martyr, burnt at the stake in March 1556, allegedly on the site of the hall.
31 *SJ*, Saturday 25th February 1871 p. 8. The 'French artists' were probably Ferrier & Soulier.
32 *ST*, Saturday 25thDecember 1875 p. 8.
33 *ST*, Saturday 1st January 1876 p. 5.
34 *ST*, Saturday 11th March 1876 p. 4.
35 *SJ*, Saturday 25th January 1873 p. 7. Also, the *Hampshire Advertiser*, Wednesday 22nd January 1873 p. 2.
36 *Wiltshire Independent*, Thursday 4th September 1856 p. 4.
37 *SJ*, Saturday 29th June 1872 p. 8.
38 *Hampshire Advertiser*, Saturday 7th September 1872 p. 8.
39 *SJ*, Saturday 7th January 1854 p. 4.
40 *SJ*, Saturday 1st July 1871 p. 7.
41 *SJ*, Saturday 11th July 1874 p. 4.
42 *SJ*, Saturday 19th April 1873 p. 8. See also *The British Section at the Vienna Universal Exhibition 1873. Official Catalogue, Group VIII – Wood Industry*, J. M. Johnson and Sons, London, [1873] p. 83 cat. no. 810 and Robin Jones, 'Arthur Foley: A Nineteenth Century Furniture Manufacture in Salisbury', *Regional Furniture*, Volume XI, 1997 pp. 42–49.
43 *SJ*, Saturday 11th September 1875 p. 5.
44 *SJ*, Saturday 27th May 1848 p. 2. William Edward Kilburn (1818–91) took at least two Daguerreotypes of the Chartists meeting that were subsequently purchased by Prince Albert.
45 *SJ*, 28th January 1860 p. 5.
46 ST, Saturday 7th October 1876 p .4.
47 *SJ*, Saturday 10th July, 1875 p. 8.
48 *ST*, Saturday 18th September 1875 p. 4.
49 ST, Saturday 26th February 1876 p. 8.
50 John Gorman, *To build Jerusalem: a photographic remembrance of British working class life 1875–1950*, Scorpion, 1980 p. 18.
51 *SJ*, 12th June 1880 p. 8.
52 *SJ*, 3rd July 1880 p. 8.
53 *SJ*, Saturday 10th January 1874 p. 7.

6 SELLING, BUYING AND EXHIBITING

THE ACCESS TO and availability of photographs to the inhabitants of Salisbury during the first four decades of the medium's existence were provided through a number of channels. These included photographers, book sellers, stationers, gunsmiths, music shops and print and fine art dealers. The formal exhibiting of photographs, whether for sale or simply to be viewed, formed another activity within the city.

There is limited information regarding where photographs were sold, bought and exhibited in Salisbury during the 1840s. There were few commercially available photographs – either daguerreotypes or paper prints. Those that were commercially available could be purchased primarily in London, and probably to a lesser degree in Southampton.

The *SJ* noted in September 1847 that specimen daguerreotypes by Barber, of James's Terrace in Winchester, could be seen at Brodie and Co., in the Canal, perhaps indicating that the existing booksellers and print sellers in Salisbury stocked or could source photographs during this decade. There are few references to photographs being commercially available for sale elsewhere in the city. The situation was to change significantly during the next decade and in late 1856, perhaps as a result of the lack of effective advertising by photographic printsellers, the London print dealer J. Hogarth, who also published and sold photographs, suggested that a catalogue of all photographs intended for sale should be drawn up. Many of these were reproductions of works of art.[1]

William Bird Brodie (1780–1863) was probably the leading Salisbury bookseller during the 1840s. He owned his bookselling, stationery and printing company, and in 1808 the ownership of the *SJ* passed to Brodie from his uncle Benjamin Charles Collins who had died childless.

The exact level of interest Brodie had in the emerging commercial market for photographs remains unclear. He went bankrupt in 1847 and two firms of Salisbury booksellers, stationers etc. were spawned by his demise; George Brown purchased Brodie's book business in the Canal and Frederick Blake, an employee, set up his own business on Blue Boar Row. Both were to play a significant role in the evolution of photography in Salisbury.

By 1854, booksellers were being encouraged to stock photographic images. An advertisement placed in *The Publishers' Circular* by the Photographic Institution in London stated:

> PHOTOGRAPHS.—The Proprietors of the Photographic Institution are willing to forward to Country Book- or Printsellers, a Selection of Sixty Photographs, by the best English and Continental Artists, varying in price from Three to Twelve Shillings, on condition that at least Three Pounds worth are chosen, and the rest returned within a Fortnight. The usual Printsellers' discount is allowed.—Address to Mr. Burningham, 168, New Bond Street.[2]

Brown & Co.

GEORGE BROWN AND his son William – who died in February 1867 aged only 35 – built their business in the Canal into a veritable emporium, selling books, stationery and prints.

In September 1853 William Russell Sedgfield was advertising in the *SJ* that a set of ten photographs of Salisbury could be obtained from Messrs Brown and Co. or F. A. Blake. Queen Victoria visited Salisbury on 15th August 1856 en route from Plymouth to Osborne on the Isle of Wight and it was reported that Messrs. Brown had supplied her with a copy of Dodsworth's *Salisbury Cathedral*, with India proof impressions, and also several photographs of the Cathedral, &c., by William Russell Sedgfield, one of which was a view of the High Street.

The Peace Festival of 1856 offered a commercial opportunity for Brown. In 1856 Brown

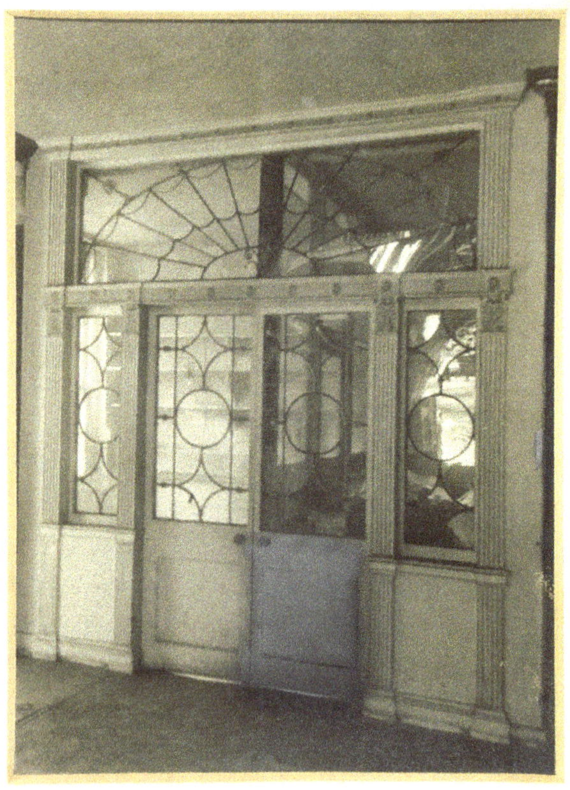

& Co. published, by 5s. subscription, a tinted lithograph printed by M. & N. Hanhart entitled *The Peace Festival at Salisbury, May 29th 1856.* The letterpress credits included 'Composed by W.F. Tiffin from photographic prints by E. Whitlock.' Walter Francis Tiffin (1817–1890) was a Salisbury artist, painter of figures and portraits, and drawing teacher. He was a keen collector of fine art prints and of porcelain, publishing a catalogue of over 1300 mezzotint portraits. The photographer was Edwin Whitlock (1825–1887), a chemist who had established his business in the Market Place in 1845. It is unclear exactly how many of Whitlock's photographs Tiffin used to create his view of the

left: Reginald Harding. Doors to the bookshop of Brown & Co, 11 New Canal. 1920s. Platinum print. The Salisbury Museum.
below: Advertisements on inside cover of *Brown's Stranger's Handbook and Illustrated Guide to City of Salisbury*, Brown and Co., Salisbury, 1866. Anthony Hamber collection

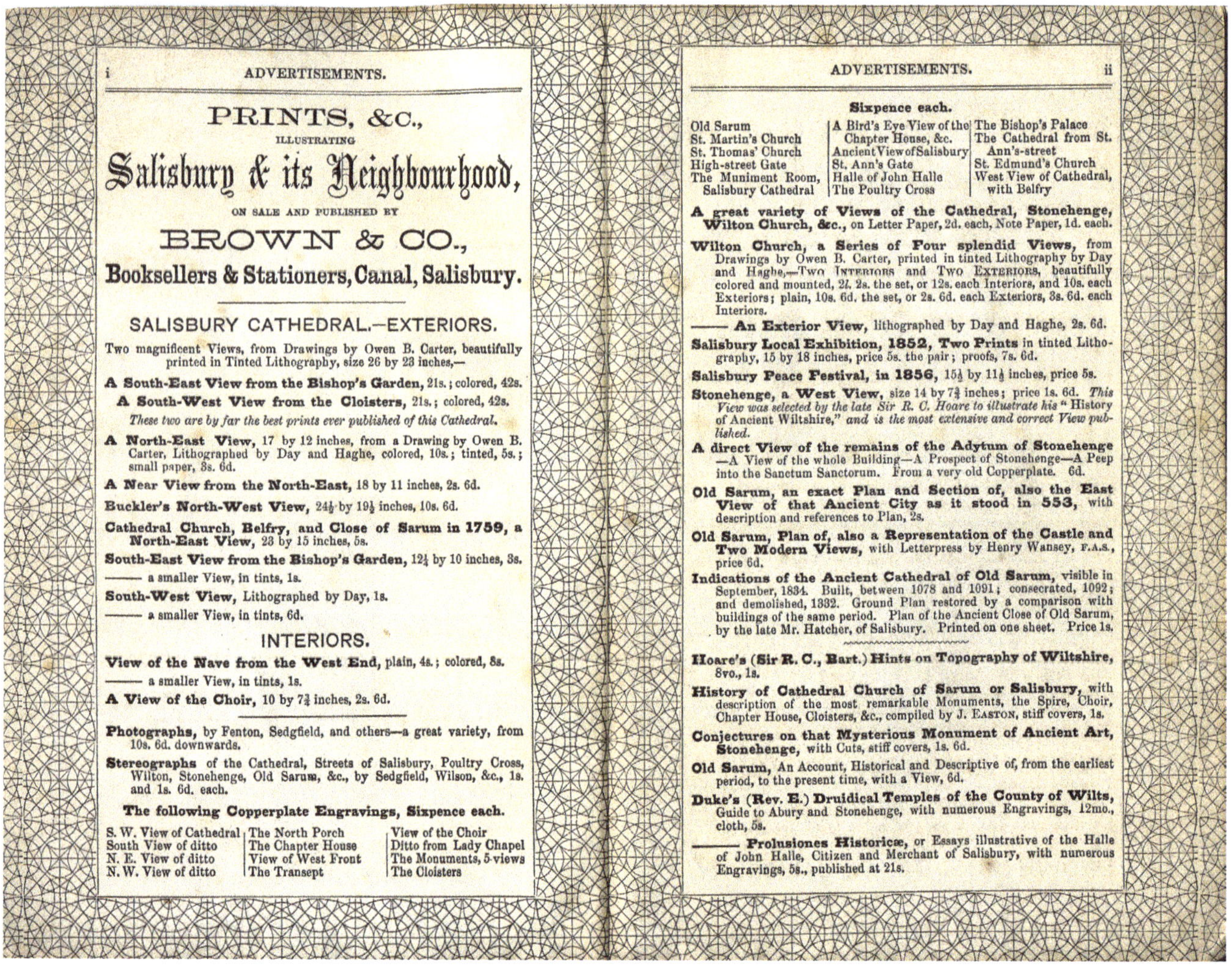

i ADVERTISEMENTS.

PRINTS, &c.,
ILLUSTRATING
Salisbury & its Neighbourhood,
ON SALE AND PUBLISHED BY
BROWN & CO.,
Booksellers & Stationers, Canal, Salisbury.

SALISBURY CATHEDRAL.—EXTERIORS.

Two magnificent Views, from Drawings by Owen B. Carter, beautifully printed in Tinted Lithography, size 26 by 23 inches,—

A South-East View from the Bishop's Garden, 21s.; colored, 42s.

A South-West View from the Cloisters, 21s.; colored, 42s.

These two are by far the best prints ever published of this Cathedral.

A North-East View, 17 by 12 inches, from a Drawing by Owen B. Carter, Lithographed by Day and Haghe, colored, 10s.; tinted, 5s.; small paper, 3s. 6d.

A Near View from the North-East, 18 by 11 inches, 2s. 6d.

Buckler's North-West View, 24½ by 19½ inches, 10s. 6d.

Cathedral Church, Belfry, and Close of Sarum in 1759, a North-East View, 23 by 15 inches, 5s.

South-East View from the Bishop's Garden, 12¼ by 10 inches, 3s.

—— a smaller View, in tints, 1s.

South-West View, Lithographed by Day, 1s.

—— a smaller View, in tints, 6d.

INTERIORS.

View of the Nave from the West End, plain, 4s.; colored, 8s.

—— a smaller View, in tints, 1s.

A View of the Choir, 10 by 7¾ inches, 2s. 6d.

Photographs, by Fenton, Sedgfield, and others—a great variety, from 10s. 6d. downwards.

Stereographs of the Cathedral, Streets of Salisbury, Poultry Cross, Wilton, Stonehenge, Old Sarum, &c., by Sedgfield, Wilson, &c., 1s. and 1s. 6d. each.

The following Copperplate Engravings, Sixpence each.

S. W. View of Cathedral	The North Porch	View of the Choir
South View of ditto	The Chapter House	Ditto from Lady Chapel
N. E. View of ditto	View of West Front	The Monuments, 5 views
N. W. View of ditto	The Transept	The Cloisters

ADVERTISEMENTS. ii

Sixpence each.

Old Sarum	A Bird's Eye View of the Chapter House, &c.	The Bishop's Palace
St. Martin's Church	Ancient View of Salisbury	The Cathedral from St. Ann's-street
St. Thomas' Church	St. Ann's Gate	St. Edmund's Church
High-street Gate	Halle of John Halle	West View of Cathedral, with Belfry
The Muniment Room, Salisbury Cathedral	The Poultry Cross	

A great variety of Views of the Cathedral, Stonehenge, Wilton Church, &c., on Letter Paper, 2d. each, Note Paper, 1d. each.

Wilton Church, a Series of Four splendid Views, from Drawings by Owen B. Carter, printed in tinted Lithography by Day and Haghe,—Two INTERIORS and Two EXTERIORS, beautifully colored and mounted, 2*l*. 2s. the set, or 12s. each Interiors, and 10s. each Exteriors; plain, 10s. 6d. the set, or 2s. 6d. each Exteriors, 3s. 6d. each Interiors.

—— **An Exterior View,** lithographed by Day and Haghe, 2s. 6d.

Salisbury Local Exhibition, 1852, Two Prints in tinted Lithography, 15 by 18 inches, price 5s. the pair; proofs, 7s. 6d.

Salisbury Peace Festival, in 1856, 15½ by 11½ inches, price 5s.

Stonehenge, a West View, size 14 by 7¾ inches; price 1s. 6d. *This View was selected by the late Sir R. C. Hoare to illustrate his* "History of Ancient Wiltshire," *and is the most extensive and correct View published.*

A direct View of the remains of the Adytum of Stonehenge—A View of the whole Building—A Prospect of Stonehenge—A Peep into the Sanctum Sanctorum. From a very old Copperplate. 6d.

Old Sarum, an exact Plan and Section of, also the East View of that Ancient City as it stood in 553, with description and references to Plan, 2s.

Old Sarum, Plan of, also a Representation of the Castle and Two Modern Views, with Letterpress by Henry Wansey, F.A.S., price 6d.

Indications of the Ancient Cathedral of Old Sarum, visible in September, 1834. Built, between 1078 and 1091; consecrated, 1092; and demolished, 1332. Ground Plan restored by a comparison with buildings of the same period. Plan of the Ancient Close of Old Sarum, by the late Mr. Hatcher, of Salisbury. Printed on one sheet. Price 1s.

Hoare's (Sir R. C., Bart.) Hints on Topography of Wiltshire, 8vo., 1s.

History of Cathedral Church of Sarum or Salisbury, with description of the most remarkable Monuments, the Spire, Choir, Chapter House, Cloisters, &c., compiled by J. EASTON, stiff covers, 1s.

Conjectures on that Mysterious Monument of Ancient Art, Stonehenge, with Cuts, stiff covers, 1s. 6d.

Old Sarum, An Account, Historical and Descriptive of, from the earliest period, to the present time, with a View, 6d.

Duke's (Rev. E.) Druidical Temples of the County of Wilts, Guide to Abury and Stonehenge, with numerous Engravings, 12mo., cloth, 5s.

—— **Prolusiones Historicæ,** or Essays illustrative of the Halle of John Halle, Citizen and Merchant of Salisbury, with numerous Engravings, 5s., published at 21s.

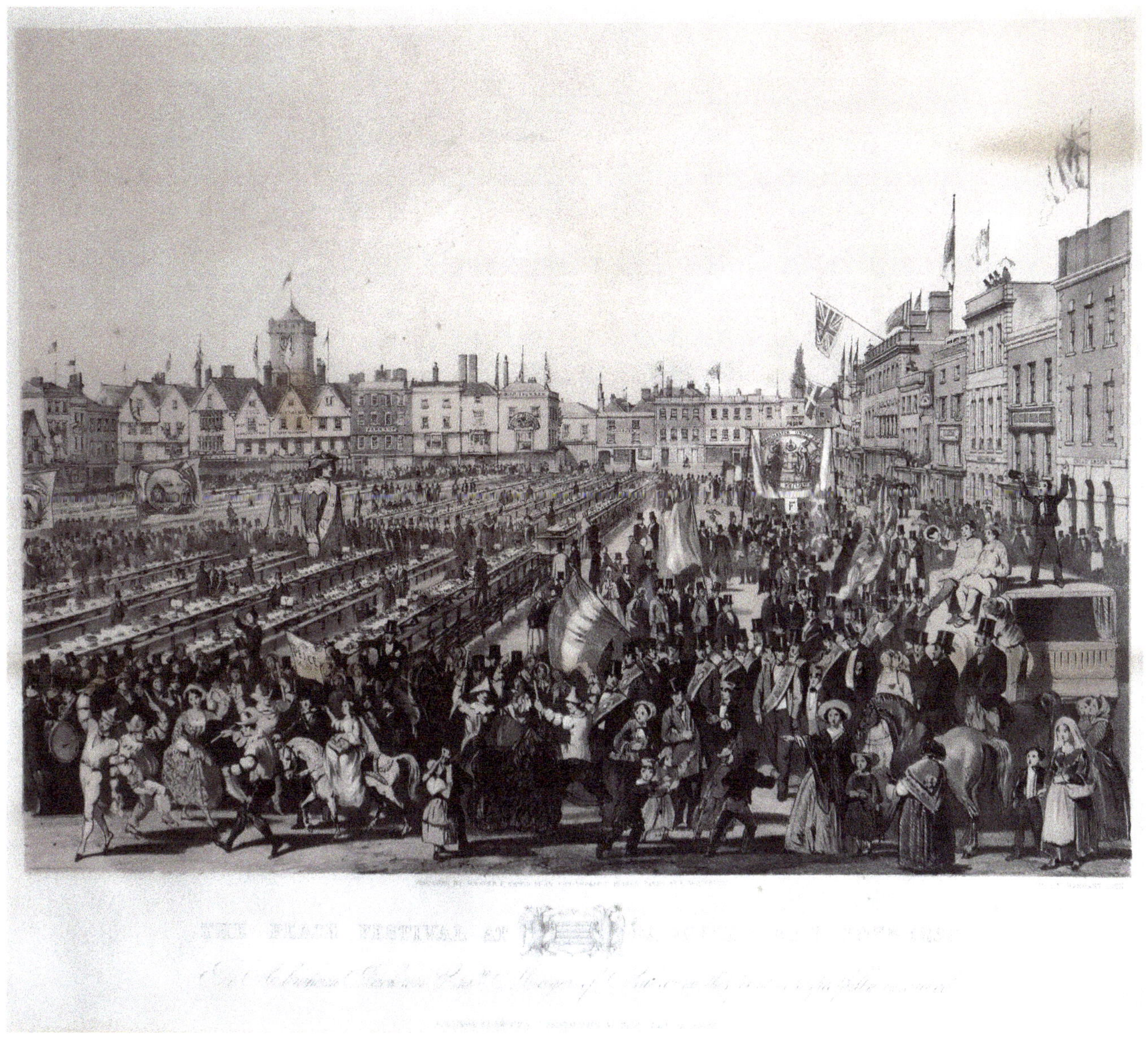

Peace Festival at Salisbury, May 29th 1856. Lithograph by M. & N. Hanhart of London from drawing by Walter F. Tiffin after photographs by Edwin Whitlock. Published by Brown & Co. Anthony Hamber collection.

Market Place. The row of figures in the foreground is Tiffin's invention, and it may be that only one photographic view of the Market Place taken from Whitlock's shop was copied by Tiffin.

In the 1857 edition of *Brown's Stranger's Handbook and Illustrated Guide to the City of Salisbury* one finds a full-page advertisement by Brown & Co. that includes:

> Photographs, by Fenton, Sedgfield, and others – a great variety, from 10s. 6d. downwards.
> Stereographs of the Cathedral, Streets of Salisbury, Poultry Cross, Wilton, Stonehenge, Old Sarum, &c., by Sedgfield, Wilson, &c., 1s. and 1s. 6d. each.

Brown's handbooks consistently had advertisements for his stock of prints and photographs placed on the inside of the front and back cover. There is evidence that he was an early stockist of the photographs of Sedgfield and George Washington Wilson. A catalogue of the photographs available at Brown and Co. has yet to be located.

By the early 1860s Brown was regularly advertising in the *SJ* a range of photographically illustrated books, frequently listed as Christmas or New Year's gift books. This decade was something of a 'golden age' for this form of illustrated publishing and evidence suggests that Brown and Co. was well stocked with titles. The firm also became a publisher of photographically illustrated books, such as The Rev. H. T. Armfield's *The Legend of Christian Art Illustrated in the Statues of Salisbury Cathedral* previously mentioned.

By 1876 Brown & Co. was advertising an extensive list of photographs of Salisbury. These included the Frith Series (both its Panoramic Series and its Universal Series), the Wormald Series, and Sedgfield's Cabinet Series. By 1880 the Valentine Series was added to the photographs available, though whether Brown had these as stock or could order them is unclear.

F. A. Blake

Frederick Augustus Blake (1820–1892) opened his establishment on Blue Boar Row on Monday 10th January 1848 in the premises formerly occupied by Mrs. Goldburn, who ran a business as a chemist and temporary surgery for a visiting dentist. Blake's services included, printing, supply of stationery and newspapers, and patent medicines. He had previously worked for fifteen years for Messrs. Brodie and Co. and had set himself up in business following Brodie's bankruptcy.[3]

Quite when Blake began stocking photographs is unclear though, as mentioned previously, by September 1853, together with Brown & Co., he was offering for sale the Russell Sedgfield set of ten photographs of views of Salisbury.[4] There is no evidence that these sets sold well and the high price of 25s., 'in a neat cover' limited their affordability.

It is difficult to gauge what level of commitment Blake made to stocking photographs during the first half of the 1850s. Realistically, photographs could not have provided significant income, but Blake was open to new opportunities. In 1855, when he arrived to start his photographic business in Salisbury, William Pitcher exhibited 'specimens of various styles' at Blake's premises. It is not clear whether these were for sale, or a marketing ploy to drive customers to his nearby studio in the Market Place.

In July 1857 Blake advertised local topographical prints and also photographs of Salisbury Cathedral, the Chapter House, Stonehenge, Wilton New Church, Old Sarum, Wilton House, The Hall of John Halle, and The Council House.[5] This was part of a campaign to target visitors of the Royal Agricultural Society's Annual show that was being held in Salisbury.

By 1862 Blake was advertising in the *SJ*, stereoscopic slides and 'Photographic Scraps' for Albums, &c., of Salisbury Cathedral, Stonehenge, Old Sarum, Poultry Cross, 'and other objects of Local Interest, in Variety'. He also acted as an outlet for at least one local photographer, Edmund Rogers [q.v.], whose photographs could be had at Blake's shop during the late 1860s.

Blake, like a number of his commercial colleagues in Salisbury sold a wide range of services and products. He acted as a subscription agent to events such as the 1851 Great Exhibition[6] and sold Keating's Cough Lozenges.[7] In 1860 Blake was selling tickets for the Last Drawing for the prizes of the Art Union of Great Britain at the Free Trade Hall in Manchester. These included 300 sets of photographs.[8]

It would appear that by the end of the 1870s he had ceased selling photographs, since he did not mention stocking them in his advertisements in the *SJ*.

Kenneth and Walter Clapperton

The Clapperton family played a particularly diverse role in the introduction and supply of photographs and photographic equipment in Salisbury.

In 1820 Kenneth Clapperton (1780–1859) bought premises in Catherine Street and traded as a bookseller, bookbinder, printer and publisher. He launched the short-lived *Wiltshire Standard* newspaper in 1833 and the following year published, together with Whittaker & Co. of London, Henry Hatcher's unillustrated *An historical and descriptive account of Old and New Sarum, or Salisbury*.

On the death of Kenneth Clapperton, his son, Walter Clapperton (*c.*1826–1881) took over his father's business. He compiled and published the first Salisbury railway timetable and in 1860 a cyclopaedia entitled *Clapperton's register of facts and occurrences relating to literature, the sciences and the arts.* He also established a commercial relationship with the firm of the leading London print dealer and publisher Colnaghi.

By at least January 1856 Clapperton was selling Brewster lenticular stereoscopes and stereo

THAT WONDERFUL DISCOVERY of SIR DAVID BREWSTER'S, which brings into one's own apartment, with the most astounding reality, the grandest works of Nature and Art from all parts of the world, will be found a charming companion in solitude, and for Evening Parties and other social gatherings, an endless source of high intellectual enjoyment. With it no company can ever be *dull*. At one moment, with this singular instrument, you are standing amidst the ruins of Pompeii, at another on the Alps, at another in Herculaneum, in Paris, at Versailles, in the French Exhibition, at the Arc de Triomph, the Place de la Concorde, in the beautiful Courts of the Crystal Palace, and hundreds of Nature's loveliest scences, modelled with her own hand, so wonderfully and so exquisitely wrought that the beholder gazes in eager delight and amazement.

The Instrument may be had, in mahogany, at 5s., 7s. 6d., 11s. 6d., to a Guinea. The Groups, Views, and Objects, 1s. to 3s. each. Lists on application.

8793] K. CLAPPERTON, Salisbury.

Walter Clapperton advertisement for Brewster's stereoscope.
Salisbury Journal, Saturday 12th January 1856 p. 2.

photographic views. The stereoscope could be had in a variety of prices; 5s., 7s. 6d., 11s. 6d., and a guinea. The slides cost between 1s. to 3s. each. and the advertisement refers to views of the Alps, Pompeii, Herculaneum, the 1855 French Exposition universelle, the Arc de Triomphe and Place de la Concorde, and the Courts of the Crystal Palace in Sydenham. As Clapperton put it, Brewster's discovery;

> brings into one's own apartment, with the most astounding reality, the grandest works of Nature and Art from all parts of the world, will be found a charming companion in solitude, and for Evening Parties and other social gatherings, an endless source of high intellectual enjoyment.[9]

The equipment and slides were from the London Stereoscopic Company, a point that Clapperton made clear in his advertisements in December 1856.[10] In these advertisements he specified that 'Twin Calotype' [i.e. paper stereoscopic photographic prints] cost 1s. to 3s. while Glass slides cost 5s. 6d. to 7s. 6d.

In August 1856 the *SJ* noted that Clapperton was selling photographs of that year's Peace Festival held in the Market Place, celebrating the end of the Crimean War, though no mention was made about the photographer.[11] It might have been William Russell Sedgfield, or Edwin Whitlock the

RAFFAELLE'S CARTOONS AT HAMPTON COURT.

WALTER CLAPPERTON respectfully announces that the above remarkable PICTURES have, by the permission of Her Majesty's Government, been PHOTOGRAPHED on an important scale by Signori Caldesi and Montecchi, and are now ON VIEW for a short time at his Shop in Catherine-street.

The Photographs are the largest that have been attempted --44 by 28 inches! The price is 14 Guineas for the Set of 7, or 2½ Guineas separately. There is also a Middle size, 29 by 18 inches, 7 Guineas the Set, or 25s. separately; and a Small size, 14 by 9 inches, 35s. the Set, or 6s. separately. They are all photographed from the sublime originals, and convey in the most impressive manner the transcendant genius of this great master of expression.

"To have these Photographs is to have the Cartoons themselves. All other copies become flat, stale, and unprofitable." --*Times*.

"They at first sight impress us more than do the famous originals."—*Critic*.

"In the tone, too, of these Photographs there is a solemnity and massive grandeur which no effect of engraving could approach."—*Illustrated News*.

WALTER CLAPPERTON, PRINT AND BOOKSELLER, STATIONER, PRINTER, AND BINDER, SALISBURY.

Walter Clapperton advertisement for Caldesi and Montecchi photographs of the Raphael Cartoons.
Salisbury Journal, Saturday 12th February 1859 p. 4.

chemist, or another local amateur or commercial photographer.[12]

Clapperton formed a significant business relationship with the leading fine art, print and photographic dealer Colnaghi of London. In February 1858 he had arranged for the celebrated painting *The Horse Fair* by Rosa Bonheur (1822–1899) to be put on display in the Assembly Rooms. Admission to view the painting cost 6d.[13] In 1863 Clapperton advertised that he would have on exhibit from the 10th to the 24th of December in his 'gallery' in Catherine Street, the celebrated picture of *Derby Day* by William Powell Frith (1819–1909). Admission to view the painting was again 6d.[14] and the painting was 'inspected by a great number of persons.'[15] These exhibitions were primarily aimed at drumming up business for the engravings of these paintings. Colossal amounts were spent by print publishers on acquiring the copyright to reproduce the painting and the subsequent engraving.

In February 1859 Clapperton advertised a temporary display of the photographs of the Raffaelle cartoons by Caldesi and Montecchi and published by Colnaghi, 'publishers to Her Majesty.'[16] These were advertised as expensive, de-luxe, prints. The set of seven prints costs 14 guineas in the largest size of 44 by 28 inches , or 2½ guineas each; middle size, seven guineas for the set; and £1 15s. for the small size set.[17] There were also some

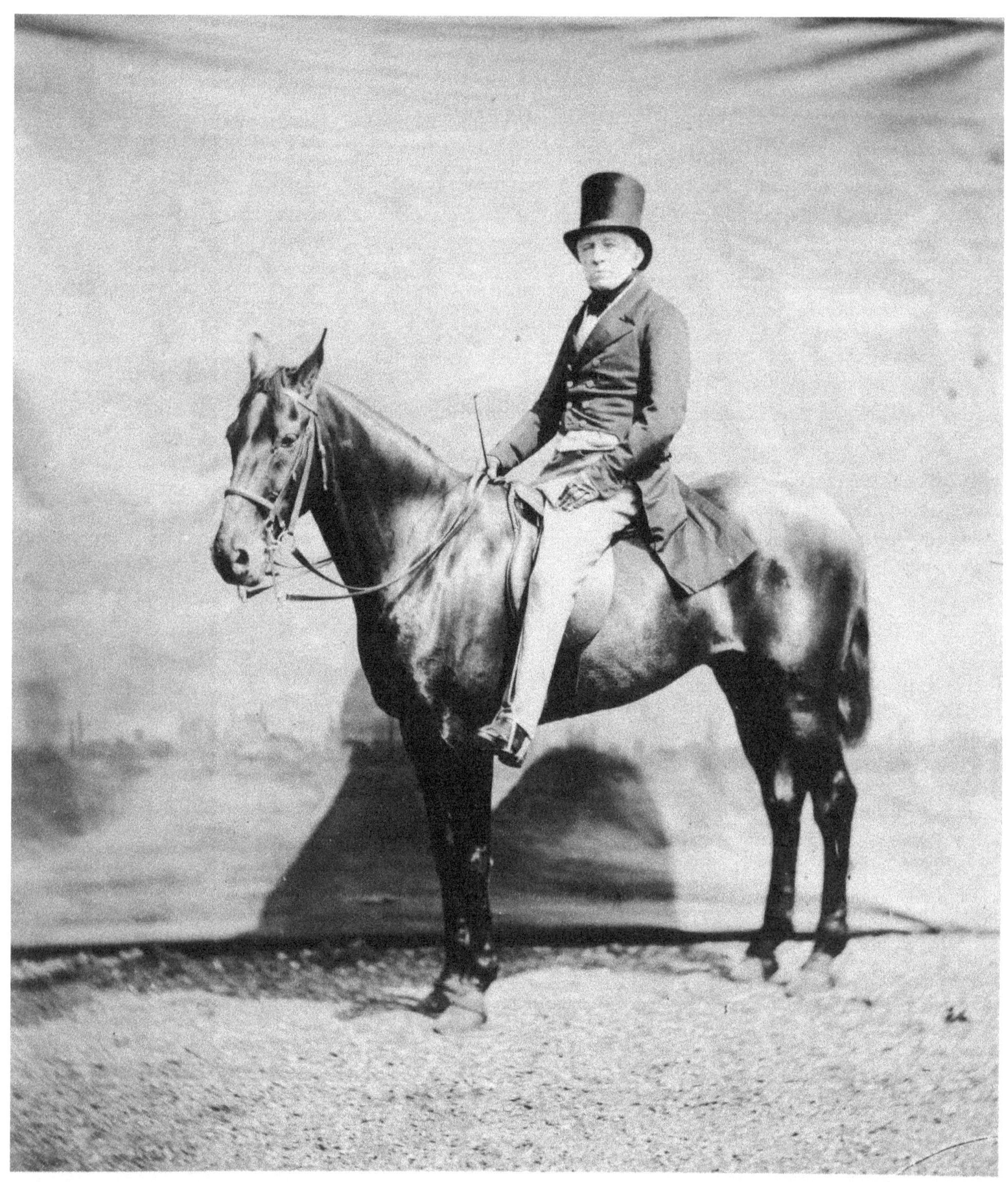

THOMAS ASSHETON SMITH, ESQ.

SALISBURY: Published by Walter Clapperton, Jan. 1, 1859.

Unidentified photographer. Equestrian portrait of Thomas Assheton Smith. 1858. Published by Walter Clapperton on 1st January 1859. Albumen print. The Salisbury Museum.

thirty-five details of figures and the 'most interesting heads', though it is unclear whether these were also exhibited at Clapperton's establishment.

In the same year Clapperton began acting as a photographic publisher when he issued two portraits of the quarry owner and sportsman Thomas Assheton Smith (1776–1858) – one an equestrian portrait.[18] While the photographer has yet to be identified, it should be noted that this was a relatively ambitious photographic portrait since camera exposure times were not instantaneous and the horse needed to remain still. It is unclear whether these were one-off publications by Clapperton or if he continued to publish photographs under his own imprint.

In October 1860 Clapperton announced that Rev. Samuel Waldegrave (1817–1869), canon of Salisbury Cathedral and bishop elect of Carlisle 'had entrusted him for publication' his portrait taken by Herbert Watkins (1828–1916) of London.[19] Clapperton stocked a range of carte de visite portraits and in the same year he was advertising a carte de visite portrait by W. Walker and Sons of London of The Right Hon. Lady Herbert of Lea (1822–1911), widow of Sidney Herbert (1810–1861), 1st Baron Herbert of Lea. This was priced at 1s. 6d.[20] Lady Herbert of Lea became a Roman Catholic convert at Palermo in 1866, practising as an 'ardent Ultramontane', under the influence of her intimate friend, Cardinal Manning (1808–1892), second Archbishop of Westminster from 1865.

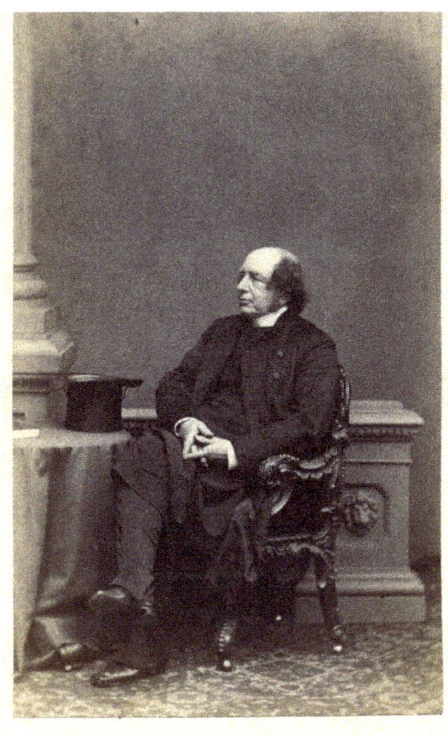

John Jabez Edwin Mayall. Portrait of Walter Kerr Hamilton. Bishop of Salisbury. Early 1860s. Carte de visite. Albumen print. Anthony Hamber collection.

The appetite for photographic portraits during the Victorian era was enormous. London photographers in particular touted for important establishment figures and celebrities to visit their studios. This included a number of bishops of Salisbury. One was Walter Kerr Hamilton (1808–1869), Bishop of Salisbury from 1854 until his death. He was photographed, probably in the early 1860s, by the leading London photographer John Jabez Edwin Mayall (1813–1901) who issued carte de visite photographs of the portrait. At least three variants of this portrait were produced by Mayall as carte de visites – including cropped and retouched versions – perhaps both before and then after Hamilton's death.[21]

Hamilton's successor, George Moberly (1809–1885), was photographed by a number of London photographers. The National Portrait Gallery holds photographic portraits of Moberly taken by Maull & Co. and Samuel Alexander Walker, 'Ecclesiastical Art Photographer', who specialised in portraits of church dignitaries. Moberly was immortalised in one of the most significant photographically illustrated publications of 'contemporary portraits of distinguished men.' This was the series *Men of Mark* published between 1876 and 1883.[22] All the portraits were taken by the studio of Lock & Whitfield and reproduced by the woodburytype photomechanical process. George Moberly's portrait appeared in the Second Series published in 1877.

The photographic piracy of high value engravings became a significant issue to photographers and printsellers in the early 1860s. In 1867 Walter Clapperton became involved in a court case examining photographic piracy. It was claimed that Clapperton had written to John William Hall, a commercial traveller, who was selling photographic piracies of copyright engravings, asking Hall to send him a photograph of the engraving after the painting *Railway Station* by William Powell Frith (1819–1909). The copyright of the engravings was owned by one of the leading London printsellers

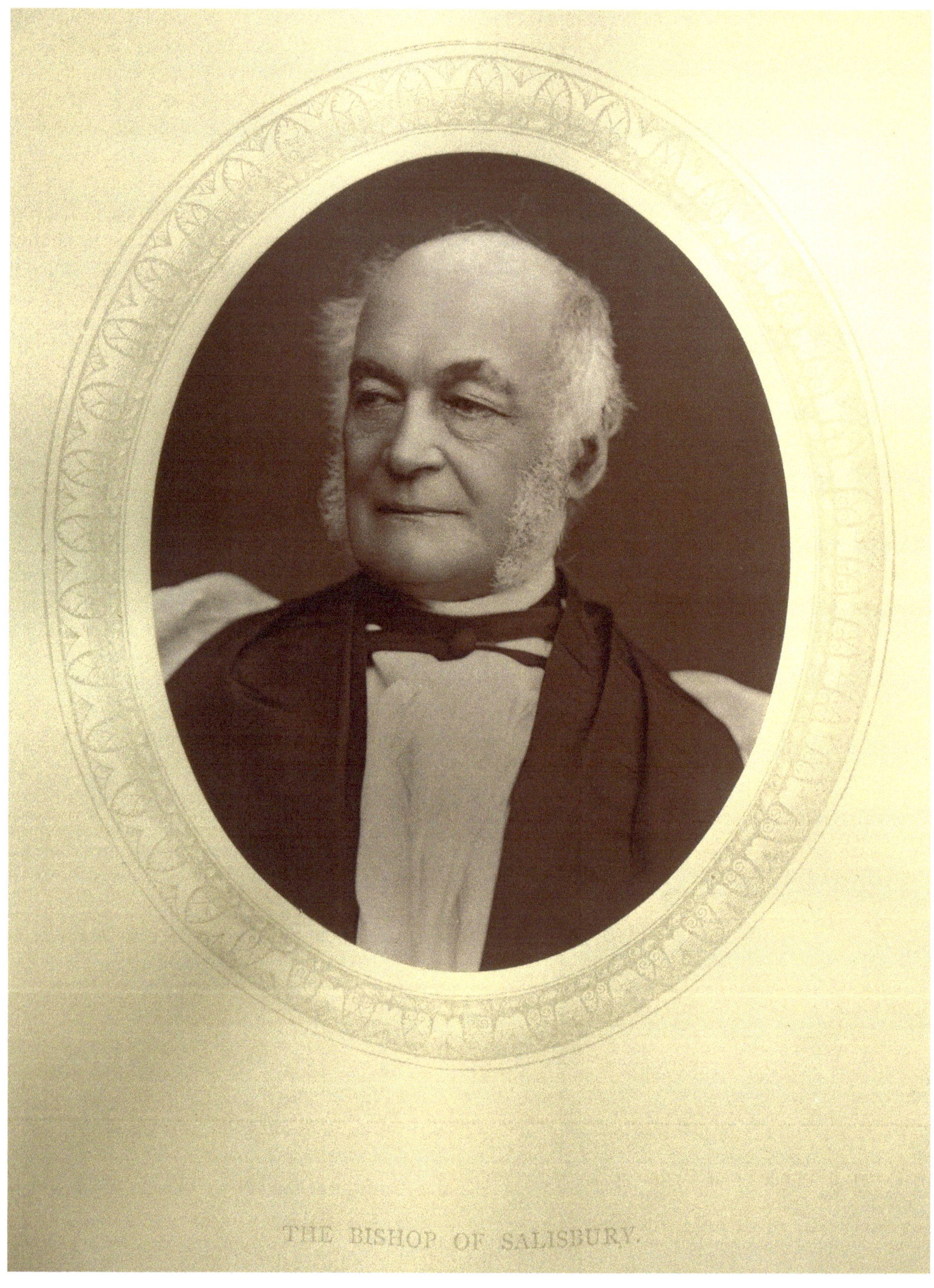

Lock & Whitfield. George Moberly, Bishop of Salisbury. 1877. Woodburytype. From *Men of Mark... Series Two.*, Sampson Low, Marston, Searle, & Rivington, London, 1877. Anthony Hamber collection.

and publishers, Henry Graves (1806–1892), who had outlaid the colossal amount of £24,200 to have the painting engraved.[23] Clapperton, as a friend of Graves, had written to Hall in order to entrap him. When the photographic prints arrived in Salisbury, Clapperton sent them to Graves, and the court case ensued. While copies of the engraving sold for five guineas, a photographic copy could be had for 1 guinea, and the cost of production so low to enable a healthy profit. Hall was fined £50, £5 for each of the photographic piracies cited.

Walter Clapperton died intestate in July 1881 and his entire stock was sold and his premises at 17 and 19 Catherine Street – consisting of his shop, a compositors' room and printing offices together with a separate house with a private entrance – were bought by C. Mabbett, a jeweller, who re-opened the premises as his shop in August 1882.

Edward Roe

EDWARD ROE (1825–?) set up his business in Queen Street in October 1849. He stated that he had gained experience 'in one of the first manufacturing houses in London and had taken over the premise of the late Mr. Truman' who sold carpets.[24] He offered a wide range of goods and services including books, almanacs, diaries, magazines, periodicals and newspapers, together with printing, bookbinding and stationery services.

In July 1857 Roe advertised in the *SJ* 'Magnificent Views of Salisbury Cathedral, Stonehenge, Wilton Church &c.' costing 1s., 6d., 2d., and 1d. each.[25] This was in connection with the Royal Agricultural Society Show being held in Salisbury though none appear to be photographs.

However, Roe seems to have ignored the commercial opportunities to sell photographs though in 1859 another member of the Roe family, Frederick, was running an upholstery and cabinet manufactory in Catherine Street and advertising 'Photographic and Artistic Decorations.'[26]

William Price Aylward

WILLIAM PRICE AYLWARD (1811–1890), set up his first music shop in Catherine Street, possibly in 1837, and he then moved into his Musical Emporium in the Canal. Aylward was also a publisher. He had been elected a councillor for St. Thomas' Ward in 1858 and was a member of the Town Council for thirty-two years. He was mayor in 1868 and in 1879 elected alderman. He founded the Salisbury Musical Society and was sometime conductor of the Sarum Choral Society.

On Friday 25th and Saturday 26th June 1869 the Royal Tycoon Troupe of Japanese Performers entertained audiences at the Assembly Rooms with their 'wonderful and astonishing feats of top-spinning, balancing, butterfly fanning' and a grand concert by Japanese ladies. A photograph of the Troup might be seen at Aylward's Music Warehouse in the Canal, though copies appeared not to be on sale. This might suggest that the photograph formed part of some marketing material aimed at increasing ticket sales.[27] It is not clear whether Aylward regularly stocked photographs of composers, musicians and entertainers.

Aylward died in Holmleigh in Elm Grove in 1890.

Watson & Godden

THE DIVERSITY OF outlets in Salisbury from which photographs might be purchased is exemplified by one example; an existing china and glass emporium. In 1861 Alfred Watson (c. 1836–1926) had succeeded to a business operating from the Halle of John Halle in the Canal. By the mid-1870s he and his partner Charles Godden (1839–?) were advertising their 'choice collections of English & Foreign china, glass and ornamental goods.' It also sold 'models and photographs of Salisbury and all other cathedrals, Stonehenge, &c.'[28]

How long Watson & Godden sold photographs for, and how successful they were in terms of sales, has yet to be established.

Photographers

WHILE THE MAJORITY of commercial photographers active in Salisbury between the mid-1850s and up to 1880 simply sold the photographs they had taken, some also sold commercially available photographs taken and marketed by others.

One of those to offer commercially available photographs other than his own was James Miell who had a studio in Catherine Street which he referred to as his 'Wholesale Photographic Warehouse.' In 1859 he was advertising that he stocked 'any article connected with photography of English, French, German, and American manufacture' that could be had.[29] Frustratingly, Miell did not detail exactly what these 'goods' were and whether they included photographs. By 1865 Miell advertised that he offered 'photographic views of Egypt, the Holy Land, Rome, London, &c., &c., lanterns and slides on sale or hire.'[30] The use of lantern projectors to project photographic glass slides supported the rise in illustrated lectures in Salisbury during the 1860s and 1870s, as referred to in the previous chapter. What subject matter Miell held amongst his glass slide stock and who bought or borrowed them remains to be unearthed.

The evidence suggests that Miell possibly had the largest stock of commercially available photographs in Salisbury up until the 1870s.

Buying

The first generation of photographers offered to photograph almost any object, though the vast majority of purchases of their services were for portraits. These could then be placed in scrap albums or special photographic albums, such as those produced to house carte de visites in window frame mounts. While this consisted of the citizens of Salisbury commissioning local photographers to take their portrait, and often those of their family, some widened their scope and collected photographs as works of art as a new form of documentation.

Establishing the scale and scope of the forming of collections of photographs by those living in and around Salisbury is problematic. The display of photographs in private soirees or conversazione in the city remains elusive. Evidence probably lies in letters and diaries yet to be unearthed. Other sources are found in the contents of the estates of the recently deceased put up for auction. These may cover photographic equipment as well as photographs themselves.

By far the most prominent purchaser of photographs with a Salisbury connection was William Blackmore (1827–1878), the subject of a previous study by the author.[31] His photographic collection of North American natives numbered more than 2,000, including many commissioned by him from leading photographers in Washington and New York. He also collected carte de visite portraits of prominent contemporaries. It is unclear whether these photographic collections were held in Salisbury at the Blackmore Museum during Blackmore's lifetime or whether any of the photographs were sourced by Blackmore through outlets in Salisbury.

The purchasing of photographs by institutions to form distinct collections is another aspect of the collecting of photographs in the city. As will be seen below, the Salisbury Literary and Scientific Institution (SLSI) was the venue of an exhibition of photographs in 1854. However, there is no evidence of the SLSI collecting photographs and it perhaps relied on loans from the Department of Science and Art's Circulating Collection.

It is possible that some professionals in Salisbury – such as architect practices – formed collections of photographs to support their businesses, though these have yet to be identified.

The display of photographs in public exhibitions in Salisbury indicates some of those who collected commercially available photographs taken by other than Salisbury photographers. A number of exhibitions held during the 1850s and 1860s either consisted entirely of photographs or contained some photographs. These are discussed in more detail in the next section.

Exhibitions

During the 1840s it would appear that the citizens of Salisbury had very limited access to formal displays of photography in the city. The odd photographic specimen might be found on display in shop windows, but no record has been found of a significant exhibition that included photographs taking place in this decade.

By at least the early 1850s, however, photography was being exhibited within a formal setting in Salisbury. This reflected the explosion of interest in photography generated by the Great Exhibition of 1851. On the 12th October 1852 an exhibition of 'local industry, amateur productions, works of art, antiquities, objects of taste, articles of vertu, etc.' opened in Salisbury. James Brown of

Silver Street included 'Photography on Glass and Paper, by the Calotype or Talbotype Processes with Collodion etc.' while Henry Neale, jun. son of the plumber and gas fitter of the Canal, exhibited 'A Series of Pictures from Nature, taken by Talbot's Photographic process called Calotype; the whole of them printed from paper negatives.'[32] The exhibits of Brown and Neale suggests they were collectors of photographs and perhaps local amateur photographers, or even both.

In late December 1852 a major exhibition of photographs opened at the Society of Arts in London. The exhibition of 'Recent Specimens of Photography' included in excess of 835 photographs by some 79 photographers. It was the largest exhibition of photographs since those displayed at the Great Exhibition the previous year, and it was to have a profound impact on the spread of photography in Britain.

A significant step took place at the General Meeting of the Society of Arts held on the 8th June 1853. The minutes recorded that:

> Suggestions made from time to time that the Society might lend useful support to Institutions, by sending to them, on special occasions, interesting objects for exhibition, have been carefully considered by the Committee. Steps have, in consequence, been taken for procuring, e.g., a collection of Photographs capable of being put into a small space for the convenience of transit from point to point, and likely to prove interesting and instructive. This collection comprises a large number of Photographs, supplied by the most accomplished practitioners of the art, and illustrating its different processes and the latest results of improvement.[33]

Already, by June 1853, it was noted in the provincial press that 'a collection of photographs has been formed by the society as a first experiment towards providing institutions with interesting objects for exhibition on special occasions, when they may wish to make a display.'[34] It remains unclear whether the Society already held such photographs – perhaps those exhibited at the exhibition held at the Society between December 1852 and January 1853 – or approached photographers to supply copies.

The following month a set of photographs had already been sent out for exhibition near Salisbury. The *SJ* of 16th July 1853 noted that 'The Society of Arts forwarded a splendid collection of photographic pictures illustrative of the vast and manifold improvements in that interesting branch of scientific art' that was currently being exhibited as part of a larger exhibition at the Mechanics' Institute in Fordingbridge.[35] This exhibition does not seem to have been a formal venue for the 1st Tour set of eighty-three photographs that started in Woburn at the Literary and Scientific Institution in mid-September 1853. The final location of the exhibition of this set was at the Ventnor & Bonchurch Literary & Scientific Institution in Ventnor on the Isle of Wight that took place in March 1854.

The success of this touring set of photographs – which did not include any photographs of Salisbury – was such that, following numerous applications from various towns, a further two sets of photographs were assembled and sent off to criss-cross the country. The itinerary of these sets was printed in the Society's journal. According to this list, the 2nd Tour, 1st Set started off in Deptford in April 1854 and was taken across central southern England and displayed in Exeter before returning across the south coast where it eventually reached Margate.[36] The 2nd Tour, 2nd Set, started off in Bury St. Edmunds and moved north, criss-crossing the country through Wrexham and Sheffield before eventually finishing north of the Scottish border in Falkirk.[37]

The Salisbury Literary and Scientific Institution (SLSI) was 'in union' with the Society of Arts and this was, in all probability, the reason why it was selected as a venue for the 2nd Tour, 1st Set of touring photographs to be exhibited at the SLSI between 6th and 14th July 1854. Previously the photographs were to be exhibited at the Literary Institution in Newbury between 25th June and 3rd July and after display in Salisbury they were then to move on to the Literary Institution in Shaftesbury to be on show between 17th and 25th July. The *SJ* reviewed the photographs on display and specifically noted that photographs by the Count de Montizon, Sir William Newton, Fox Talbot, Thurston Thompson, Delamotte, Fry, Fenton, Sandford, and others were scheduled to be exhibited.[38]

At a meeting of the committee of the SLSI held on 3rd July 1854 it was resolved that a sub-committee 'take charge of the photographs & to make necessary arrangements for the exhibitions of the same.'[39] The *SJ* of 8th July duly recorded the forthcoming exhibition of this set of photographs in the Reading Room of the SLSI.[40] Curiously, no subsequent review of the photographs appeared in the newspaper.

The significance and popularity of this exhibition is unclear. At the end of 1854 the finance committee of the SLSI reported that the total revenue for admission to the exhibition had been £1. 0s. 0d. On another occasion the finance committee reported that a bill had been received from a Mr. Beale [sic for Harry Neale], painter and glazier of the New Canal 'for glazing' for £4 11s. 2d. but noted that 'As to Mr. Beale's bill a proportion appeared to belong to the Society of Arts for glazing some of the photographic portraits which were lent by the Society to this institution and the secretary was requested to place himself in communication with the secretary of the Society upon the subject.'

James Smith, the Honorary Secretary of the SLSI wrote to Peter le Neve Foster, the Secretary of the Society of Arts, explaining his high anxiety when the framed photographs were delivered and he had found that a number had broken glasses. Smith pondered 'Who is to bear the cost [of replacing the glass]?'[41]

Curiously, the SLSI does not appear to have formed its own collection of photographs and no other institutional collection seems to have been built in Salisbury during the 1860s and 1870s.

No record has been found of any subsequent similar public exhibition of photographs in Salisbury before the 'temporary exhibition' held in January 1862, in the Council Chamber. The exhibition was held under the auspices of the SLSI and the Salisbury and South Wilts Museum and organized by Edward T. Stevens, Honorary Curator of the Blackmore Museum, his brother-in-law Dr Humphrey Blackmore, also Honorary Curator of the Blackmore Museum, and C.J. Read, musician and conductor of the Sarum Choral Society.

At this exhibition, referred to in the *SJ* as a 'Grand Conversazione', it was noted that 'a large collection of photographs' was exhibited in the Grand Jury Room.[42] A relatively detailed description of these photographs was to be found in the *SJ* for the 26th January, and readers had been informed that photographs were to be exhibited in notices in the *SJ*'s columns over the previous weeks.[43]

The Society of Arts exhibited;
Views of the Bavarian exhibition in Munich
Views of the Paris Exhibition
Views in Egypt
Panoramic view of Constantinople
Views of the Progress of the Exhibition of 1862
Photographs from the Art Union of London
Views by Stephen Thomson
Photographed engravings
Photogalvanography (Herr Paul Pretch)

E. D. Fisher
Photographs from Raffaelle's original cartoons
St. Paul Preaching at Athens
Charge to Peter
Death of Ananias
Elymas the Sorcerer Struck with Blindness
Miraculous Draught of Fishes
Paul and Barnabas at Lystria
the Beautiful Gate of the Temple
a collection of photographs of English Cathedrals and Abbeys
views in Paris, &c.

This might have been Edward D. Fisher (b. 1838), according to the 1861 census a surveyor and builder, living with his parents Frederick and Anna at 88 High Street. Frederick was a city magistrate, surveyor and builder employing 24 men.

Walter Francis Tiffin exhibited;
Portfolio of photographic copies of studies of Raffaelle, from the British and French Museums
Portfolio of photographs from Buckingham Palace, copied for Prince Albert from original drawings by Raffaelle, in the possession of Mr. W. F. Tiffin

Tiffin was a keen collector of fine art prints and of porcelain, publishing a catalogue of over 1,300 mezzotint portraits in 1883. The extent of his collection of photographs is unknown.

These photographic exhibitions mentioned in this chapter were not commercial, in that none of the photographs exhibited were for sale. However, they did act as a pump primer for those wishing to acquire copies of such photographs themselves.

It remains to be established whether local dealers of photographs, such as Brown, Blake, Roe and Clapperton increased their sales as a result.

Another consideration is how representative were James Brown, Henry Neale, E. D. Fisher and Walter Tiffin in terms of the total number of collectors of photographs to be found in Salisbury during the 1850s and 1860s? Further examination of local auction records may provide some answers, though frequently auction catalogues give few, if any, details of the photographs being offered for sale.

1 Hogarth's letter was dated 18th November 1856, and appeared in the *Journal of the Photographic Society*, no. 50, 21st January 1857 p. 209. By 1862 the London print dealer H. Hering was advertising a catalogue of 800 photographs of the works of Ancient and Modern Masters in 'different sizes and prices.' *Athenæum*, no.1832, 6th December 1862 p. 714. In France the market for photographic art reproduction was, if anything even larger. In 1863–1864 the Paris photographer Franck published a catalogue entitled *L'Art Ancien* which included 1,000 photographs of works in the collections of Napoléon III, the Musée d'Artillerie, mobilier de la Couronne, other state and private collections, and a section on the 1863 Exposition de l'Union centrale des Beaux-Arts. See Elizabeth Anne McCauley, *Industrial Madness: Commercial Photography in Paris, 1848–71*, Yale University Press, New Haven, 1994, p. 273. In 1866 the *Fine-Art Quarterly Review* (Vol.1, New Series, July 1866–October 1866 p. 431) noted that John Brampton Philpott of Florence was advertising a catalogue of some 2000 photographs of drawings in the 'Royal Gallery', Florence each costing 14d. Some of these images were taken by Fratelli Alinari.

2 *The Publishers' Circular*, 16th August 1854 p. 378.

3 *SJ*, Saturday 4th December 1847 p. 4.

4 *SJ*, Saturday 17th September1853 p. 2.

5 *SJ*, Saturday 18th July 1857 p. 5

6 *SJ*, Saturday 18th May 1850 p. 2.

7 *SJ*, Saturday 15th December 1855 p. 1.

8 *SJ*, Saturday 17thNovember 1860 p. 5.

9 *SJ*, Saturday 12th January 1856 p. 2.

10 The London Stereoscopic Company had been founded in 1854. An 1856 company catalogue advertised forty-five stereo views of the Crystal Palace in Sydenham and referred to a 'Second Series of about 200 subjects taken from the Crystal Palace.'

11 *SJ*, Saturday 2nd August 1856 p. 3.

12 Sedgfield offered copies of his photograph for 4s. unframed and 7s. framed. The exhibition was held under the auspices of the Norfolk and Norwich Fine Arts Association and the Norwich Photographic Society between 17th November 1856 and 14th February 1857.

13 *SJ*, Saturday 6th February 1858 p. 4.

14 *SJ*, Saturday 5th December 1863 p. 5.

15 *SJ*, Saturday 19th December 1863 p. 5.

16 *SJ*, Saturday 12th February 1859 p. 4.

17 As advertised in the *Athenæum*, 8th January 1859 p. 34.

18 These photographs formed part of the 1898 bequest of Job Edwards, of Amesbury, who had been the Honorary Librarian of the Salisbury Museum.

19 *SJ*, Saturday 13th October 1860 p. 5. A set of photographs loaned by the Society of Arts was exhibited in the Assembly Rooms in Beccles in April 1853 'for the benefit of the Public Library and Scientific Institution.' *The Suffolk Chronicle; or Weekly General Advertiser & County Express*. Saturday 23rd April 1853 p. 3.

20 *SJ*, Saturday 19th September 1863 p. 8.

21 The National Portrait Gallery, London has three such examples.

22 *Men of Mark. A Gallery of Contemporary Portraits of Men distinguished in the Senate, the Church, in Science, Literature and Art, the Army, Navy, Law, Medicine, etc. Photographed from Life by Lock and Whitfield, with brief biographical notices by Thompson Cooper, F.S.A.*, Sampson Low, Marston, Searle, & Rivington, London, 1876–1883.

23 'Pirating engravings', *British Journal of Photography*, 15th November 1867 p. 545 and 'Piracies of Engravings', *British Journal of Photography*, 22nd November 1867 p. 557.

24 An advertisement in the *SJ*, Saturday 27th October 1849 p.2. James Truman, who sold carpets, drapery and haberdashery, died in 1848 and his estate was auctioned at the White Hart Hotel on Thursday 15th June 1848. *SJ*, Saturday 3rd June 1848 p. 4.

25 *SJ*, Saturday 18th July 1857 p. 5.

26 *SJ*, Saturday 18th June 1859 p. 5.

27 *ST*, Saturday 19th June 1869 p. 1.

28 This information was contained in a full-page, illustrated advertisement in several of the *Brown's Stranger's Handbooks* in the mid-1870s.

29 SJ, Saturday 18th June 1859 p. 5.

30 *SJ*, Saturday 8th April 1865 p. 5.

31 Anthony Hamber, *Collecting the American West – The Rise and Fall of William Blackmore*, Hobnob Press, East Knoyle, 2010.

32 *Catalogue of the Salisbury Exhibition of Local Industry, Amateur Productions, Works of Art, Antiquities, Objects of Taste, Articles of Vertu, Etc., Opened on the Twelfth of October, 1852*, James Bennett, Salisbury, [1852] p. 9 and p. 12.

33 *Journal of the Society of Arts*, 10th June 1853, p. 342.

34 *Evening Mail*, Friday 10th June 1853 p. 7.

35 *SJ*, Saturday 16th July 1853 p. 3. See also Anthony Light

and Gerald Ponting, *Victorian Journal – Fordingbridge 1837–1901*, Charlewood Press, Fordingbridge p. 38.

36 *Journal of the Society of Arts*, 24th March 1854, p. 319.

37 For full details of these travelling exhibitions see *Photographic Exhibitions in Britain 1839–1865* at www.peib.dmu.ac.uk.

38 *SJ*, Saturday 8th July 1854 p. 3 referring to a 'small admission fee.' A listing of all the photographs in this set exhibited in Salisbury can be found at www. http://peib.dmu.ac.uk/

39 Salisbury Literary and Scientific Institution Minutes 1850–1859, Wiltshire & Swindon Archives, Chippenham G23/993/1

40 *SJ*, 8th July 1854, p. 3.

41 I thank Roger Taylor for supplying this reference.

42 *SJ*, Saturday 18 January 1862 p. 8.

43 *SJ*, Saturday 26th January 1862 p. 6

APPENDIX 1 – PHOTOGRAPHIC PROCESSES AND FORMATS

Described below are the key photographic processes and photographic print processes utilised during the period from 1839 until 1880. Not all of these were practiced by photographers in Salisbury, though examples of all would have been available through a variety of other sources, such as London or Southampton, or through photographs and photographically-illustrated publications sold through local book sellers such as Brown & Co.

This is not intended to provide a comprehensive list and many variants of these processes were created and marketed, frequently under brand names.

Readers may wish to examine other resources, particularly an increasing number of online videos that show the processes mentioned in operation.

PHOTOGRAPHIC PROCESSES

Daguerreotype

The daguerreotype was the first commercially successful photographic process and was in use between 1839 and around 1860. The process was invented by the French artist Louis Jacques Mandé Daguerre (1787–1851) and formally announced on 9th January 1839 at the French Academy of Sciences in Paris.

To make a daguerrotype required a sheet of silver-plated copper to be polished to a mirror finish. This was then exposed to vapour from iodine that reacted with the silver coating to produce silver iodide, a light sensitive compound. The plate was then exposed in a camera for as long as was judged to be necessary, which ranged from a few seconds for brightly sunlit subjects or several minutes with less intense lighting. The latent image formed was then made visible by exposing the plate to mercury vapor. The image was then chemically fixed, washed and dried before being sealed in a protective case behind glass. Daguerreotypes are sometimes difficult to view, depending on how they are lit and whether a light or dark background is being reflected in the metal. American daguerreotypists perfected the process and produced excellent, easily viewable images.

Photogenic Drawing

William Henry Fox Talbot conceived this process in 1834, and photogenic drawing was the first photographic process capable of producing negative images on paper. Talbot did not publicise his experiments until the Daguerre's process was announced in January 1839.

The paper used to create a photogenic drawing was sensitised using a two-step process. First water and table salt (sodium chloride) were applied, followed by a brushed-on coating of silver nitrate to create silver chloride. Since the silver chloride is not particularly sensitive, lengthy exposure times were required to form an image and the first photogenic drawings were obtained through direct contact with flat objects such as plant leaves, fabrics, drawings or manuscripts. The exposed paper was then stabilised in an alkaline halide solution (chloride, bromide, or iodide) and then the remaining sensitised salts were washed off the paper with water.

Photogenic Drawings are characterised by lilac, brown, and yellow shades generated by sodium chloride, potassium bromide, and potassium iodide. These tend to darken over time, and the images are relatively unstable when stored in darkness and even less stable when exposed to light.

The negative image created by the Photogenic Drawing was formed by contact printing out in direct light. This negative image could then be placed in contact with another piece of photosensitive paper in a frame in direct sunlight to produce a "positive" image – i.e. a negative of a negative.

Calotype

IN LATE 1840, Talbot worked out a very different "developing-out" photographic process, in which only an extremely faint or completely invisible latent image had to be produced on the photosensitive paper negative in the camera. Such an image might only take a minute or two if the subject was illuminated by bright sunlight. The exposed paper negative, protected from further exposure to daylight, was then removed from the camera in a dark slide and the latent image was chemically developed into a fully visible negative image. This major improvement was introduced to the public as the calotype or talbotype process and patented by Talbot on the 8th of February 1841 (Patent No. 8842).

Positive prints from calotype paper negatives followed the process for the Photogenic Drawing, with calotype negatives being placed in contact with photosensitised paper in printing frames placed in direct sunlight.

The calotype remained popular, particularly with amateur photographers until the mid-1850s, when it was replaced by the collodion on glass negative process. (see WET COLLODION)

Talbotype

An alternative name for the CALOTYPE.

Waxed Paper Negative

A VARIANT OF THE calotype process. The aim of this process was to make the paper negative more transparent, by applying wax to the paper it filled in the gaps in the paper fibres, changing the refractive qualities and allowing light to pass through more directly. The wax was melted, coated on the negative and then blotted off with successive layers of blotters. Henry Talbot mentioned the waxing of paper negatives as early as October of 1842. The French photographer Gustave Le Gray (1820–1884) published his waxed paper negative process in 1850 (an English edition appearing the following year) in which the paper was waxed before chemical sensitising it and the subsequent camera exposure.

The waxed paper negative had a number of benefits. Thinner paper could be used since the wax strengthened the paper, negatives could be prepared in advance, and following camera exposure negative developed more quickly thus enabling photographers to print more photographs each day.

The waxed paper negative remained popular during the 1850s but was replaced by the WET COLLODION on glass process.

Wet Collodion

DURING THE LATE 1840s experiments using glass to support the photographic negative, rather than paper, had been undertaken. Abel Niépce de Saint-Victor (1805–1870) first experimented in 1847 with negatives made with albumen on glass. A glass plate was coated with albumen extracted from egg white and treated with light-sensitive chemicals. However, the albumen process it was soon overtaken by the wet collodion on glass process.

This process, also called the collodion process, was invented in 1848 by Englishman Frederick Scott Archer (1813–1857) and published in *The Chemist* in March 1851. The process involved adding a soluble iodide to a solution of collodion (cellulose nitrate, also referred to as "gun cotton") and manually coating a glass plate with the mixture. The plate was then sensitised by dipping it in silver nitrate to create a coating of light sensitive silver iodide and silver bromide. The plate was inserted into a dark slide and then into the camera for the exposure to be taken.

The wet collodion process required only two to three seconds of camera exposure to produce an image. However, the process required that there could be only around ten minutes elapsed time from the moment the glass plate had been prepared and sensitised until, post camera exposure, the plate had been chemically developed. It continued to be widely used until dry plate negatives became widely available in the 1880s. Photographers often scraped off the collodion emulsion on glass negatives in order to reuse the glass plate. This followed the practice of lithographic printers reusing their lithographic stone printing plates.

Some very large wet collodion negatives were taken during the nineteenth century. In 1875 Bayliss and Holtermann of Sydney, Australia, made 160 x 96.5 cm wet collodion negatives to form a panorama of Sydney Harbour.

Dry Plate Negative

THE DRY PLATE process, also known as the gelatin process, was an improved type of glass photographic plate. The first collodion-albumen dry plates of practical utility were formulated by the French scientist Jean-Marie Taupenot (1822–1856) and manufactured in limited quantity in England in 1860.

The English photographer Dr. Richard L. Maddox (1816–1902) made a major breakthrough in 1871 when he substituted gelatin for collodion. By 1879 the new negative process was so well introduced that there were several companies making dry plates in Britain, including the Britannia Works Company, Wratten & Wainwright, Mawson & Swan and the Liverpool Dry Plate Company.

The advantages of the dry plate negative were significant: Firstly, they were around ten times more sensitive than the wet collodion plates they replaced. Photographers were able to use commercial dry plates off-the-shelf, since they did not have to prepare their own emulsions and coat the glass plates, either in a studio or in a mobile darkroom. Furthermore, negatives did not have to be developed immediately.

PHOTOGRAPHIC PRINT PROCESSES

Salted Paper Print

THE SALTED PAPER print was the dominant paper-based photographic print process for producing positive prints (from negatives) from 1839 until approximately 1860. Salted paper prints were created from photogenic drawing negatives, calotype/talbotype paper negatives, and from the early 1850s wet collodion glass plate negatives.

Good quality paper is soaked in a salt solution (sodium chloride but was often sodium citrate and ammonium chloride,) and dried. In subdued light, it is brushed with a generous coating of a silver nitrate solution and dried in darkness or very subdued light. The paper is then exposed under a negative in daylight (perhaps 10 minutes in bright sunlight) until the image is darker than required. The paper was then washed in several rinses of water to remove excess silver nitrate, fixed in sodium thiosulphate, and washed for an hour in water.

After 1850, many photographers toned their prints with gold chloride (gold toning) to produce a more desirable cool, purplish-brown color after processing. Gold toning also resulted in a more stable print. Other toning options included toning with sulfur as well a mixture of gold chloride and sodium thiosulfate, also known as sel d'or toning or toning with platinum.

The prints exhibit a diverse range of visual characteristics depending on the paper, process variations, and finishing. Since the photographic image is held in the structure of the paper fiber, it gives a "soft" visual appearance. This characteristic was in some instances considered appropriate for certain subject matter, such as reproducing Old Master drawings and engravings.

Albumen Print

THE ALBUMEN PRINT, also called the albumen silver print, was published in January 1847 by Louis Désiré Blanquart-Evrard (1802–1872), It is considered the first commercially exploitable method of producing a photographic print on a paper base from a negative. It remained the most popular print process for photographic printing between around 1855 and 1900.

The albumen process consisted of taking a sheet of paper, usually 100% cotton, coated with an emulsion of egg white (albumen) and salt (sodium chloride or ammonium chloride), then dried. The albumen seals the paper and creates a slightly glossy surface for the sensitiser to rest on. The paper was then dipped in a solution of silver nitrate and water which renders the surface sensitive to light, then dried in the dark. The dried, prepared paper was placed in a frame in direct contact under a negative and exposed to daylight until the image achieves the desired level of darkness, Since the albumen print is a printing-out process (rather than a chemically developed out process) the progress of the print could be manually checked in daylight during the exposure. A bath of sodium thiosulfate fixed the print's exposure, preventing further darkening and the print was then washed in water.

Optional gold or selenium toning was used to improve the albumen print's tone – giving it a rich purple-brown colour – and stabilised it against fading. Depending on the toner, toning could be performed before or after fixing the print.

Photolithography

PHOTOLITHOGRAPHY WAS THE first practical photomechanical printing process combining lithography, invented in 1798 by the German author Aloys Senefelder (1771–1834), and photography.

Experiments to create a photolithographic process were being undertaken in the early 1850s. In August 1855 a French chemist, Alphonse Louis Poitevin (1819–1882) perfected a photolithographic process. He coated a lithographic stone (grained for halftone picture) with a solution of potassium bichromate and albumen, spreading the coating with a towel. After drying the stone it was exposed under a photographic negative, washed with water, rolled up with greasy ink which only adhered to the parts which had become insoluble by exposure to light, but did not adhere to the moist parts. The stone was then etched and printed by the usual lithographic manner.

Photolithography had based its commercial market on the reproduction of line drawing. During the 1870s the process was increasingly used to reproduce drawings that appeared as illustrations in architectural periodicals such as *Building News.* The London trade directories of the 1870s indicate that the number of photolithographers had more than quadrupled in this decade.

Photozincography – invented by the Royal Engineers officer Colonel Henry James (1803–1877) of the Ordnance Survey in Southampton in the late 1850s – used a zinc plate rather than a lithographic stone. The process was used extensively in the reproduction of maps (saving the government thousands of pounds) and James also oversaw the production of a series of photozincographic publications of historical and national manuscripts, including the Domesday book.

Carbon Print

THE CARBON PRINT developed from the emerging need for a permanent photographic positive process given the relative lack of stability of the albumen print. It was derived from principles established by the French chemist Gustav Suckow (1803–1867) who established that chromic acid salts are light sensitive, even without silver. Alphonse Poitevin invented a "black-and-white" carbon process in 1855.

In this printing process, carbon tissue (a temporary support sheet coated with a layer of gelatin mixed with a pigment—originally carbon black, from which the name derives) was bathed in a potassium dichromate sensitising solution and then dried. When exposed to strong light through a photographic negative the gelatin hardens in proportion to the amount of light reaching it. The tissue is then developed by treatment with warm water, which dissolves the unhardened gelatin. The resulting pigment image is physically transferred to a final support surface, usually a sheet of paper. The carbon print is permanent and not liable to fading.

Carbon tissue was introduced by British physicist and chemist Joseph Swan in 1864 and marketing began in 1866. Initially, Swan's ready-made tissues were sold in only three colors: black, sepia and purple-brown. The process was largely directed towards the commercial market of art reproductions and professional portraits. Variants of the carbon print process were produced, such as the chromotype.

Collotype

THIS DICHROMATED COLLOID process used the tanning effect of light on dichromated gelatin, whereby the hardened parts retain greasy ink that can be transferred onto paper, porcelain, or a variety of other supports. This planographic process was invented by Alphonse Poitevin in 1855 and can be considered the first practical process of photolithography.

The collotype was used for large-volume mechanical printing before the introduction of cheaper offset lithography. The first rotary offset lithographic printing press was created in England and patented in 1875 by the Englishman Robert Barclay (1833–1876), a member of the celebrated banking family and partner of the London printing house of Barclay and Fry.

Woodburytype

A PHOTOMECHANICAL REPRODUCTION PROCESS, producing continuous tone images that resemble carbon prints, though are often differentiated by showing relief between the highlight and shadow areas. It was patented in 1864 by its inventor Walter Bentley Woodbury (1834–1885).

The woodburytype process is based on the exposure and development of a positive relief image in a thick film of dichromated gelatin. The sensitised gelatin hardens in proportion to the density of the photographic negative. The gelatin is then developed by washing away the unexposed parts in warm water. This master relief is then used to produce a shallow negative intaglio printing mould with the highlights as hills and the shadows as hollows, usually by sandwiching the dried, hardened relief against a sheet of lead in a powerful hydraulic press. This was a concept that Woodbury took from nature printing developed in the 18th century. Massive pressure was required to create the master relief: about 4 tons per square inch, or 500 kilograms per square centimeter, depending on the thickness and hardness of the lead, and the size and nature of the image.

To produce the woodburytype print, a small amount of warm pigmented gelatin "ink" was poured onto the centre of the lightly greased, carefully leveled mould placed on a special press, and covered with a sheet of specially-prepared, waterproof paper. The press was then closed, forcing the gelatin into the contours of the mould. After about a minute (to allow the gelatin to set and adhere to the paper), the print was peeled out of the press, plunged into an alum bath to harden, rinsed, dried, and finally trimmed before being mounted onto either a book page or printed card mount.

At its peak in the 1870s and 1880s, woodbury type was extensively used to photographically illustrate books and journals, particularly for works of art and portraits of contemporary celebrities. However, as the above indicates, the woodburytype was a time consuming and thus expensive process and would be increasingly displaced in the high-quality sector of the market by collotype and photogravure processes.

Photogravure

AN INTAGLIO PHOTOMECHANICAL printing process in which the lines, dots, grain or other elements of the printing plate, are sunk in the plate so that the depressions are filled with ink for printing. Henry Talbot developed a photogravure process in stages taking out two patents, for photographic engraving (1852 – Patent No. 565), and photoglyphic engraving (1858 – Patent No. 875). However, Talbot failed to commercialise his process that was was instrumental in the development of the modern photogravure process, perfected by Karl Klíč (1841–1926) of Vienna in 1879. The process became increasingly popular during the 1880s.

APPENDIX 2 – SALISBURY PHOTOGRAPHERS AND COMMERCIAL PHOTOGRAPHIC STUDIOS

THIS APPENDIX DOCUMENTS the photographers who worked in Salisbury from the 1840s until 1880. It is made up, almost exclusively, by commercial photographers, existence of whom is known through extant photographs, advertisements in local newspapers and trade directories. However, this leaves a very significant gap in terms of the amateur photographers who practiced in and around the city during this period, and whose careers and history remains obscure.

Other than one failed attempt to set up a commercial photographic portrait studio in the High Street in 1846, nothing has been established about the amateur or commercial photographers active in and around Salisbury during this decade.

During the first half of the 1850s a number of photographers were operating from rented space within existing commercial premises across Salisbury. These include itinerants such as John Clarke, Mr. Shoosmith and Philip Monson. By the mid-1850s permanent commercial photographic studios began to appear and by 1856 there were already at least four "permanent" commercial photographic studios operating in Salisbury, those of Philip Monson, William Pitcher, Witcomb Brothers and James Miell. By the following decade there were some twelve commercial photographic studios operating in Salisbury, far more than any other town in Wiltshire.

The earliest photographic studios of the mid-1850s were primarily clustered in the city centre, Market Place and the High Street in the 1850s. Catherine Street became particularly popular for commercial photographic studios during the 1860s and 1870s. Other studios were to be found in Exeter Street, Bridge Street, Milford Street, De Vaux Place and Harnham Bridge. As the ribbon development from Fisherton Anger along the Wilton Road and Devizes Road began, a few photographers set up studios there.

The following is a list of photographers active in Salisbury from 1846 and follows a chronological view. It has not always been possible to establish the first date at which the photographer started working in Salisbury. This is a complex area since some well-established photographers would in later life state in their advertisements in local newspapers certain dates at which they claimed they had founded their commercial studios, many referring to the mid-1850s. These dates are not always supported by contemporaneous newspaper advertisements and beg the question as to how these photographers promoted their products and services if they did indeed start trading in the mid-1850s.

Richard Beard (1801–1885)

Photographic Portrait Rooms, Close Gate, High Street, June 1846.

AN ADVERTISEMENT PLACED by Beard, the holder of the English patentee for the daguerreotype, in the *SJ* (Saturday 6th June 1846 p. 4.) noted that this studio was open for business. This is the only reference found to date for these "Portrait Rooms", probably Salisbury's first commercial photographic studio, that also offered classes teaching photography, and it is presumed that it closed soon afterwards. Whether any portraits were actually taken in Beard's Photographic Portrait Rooms in the High Street is open to conjecture. Beard himself would not necessarily been either the camera operator or even present. Who Beard employed to operate the studio may never be known.

Mr. Shoosmith

"Mr Roe's, Printer, Queens Street", 1855.

THIS WAS PROBABLY Decimus Shoosmith (1832–1922), who may have worked in a London studio as an operator before setting off into the provinces as an independent. In his advertisements in which began to appear in the *SJ* in the summer of 1855 he referred to six years of experience as a photographer. He advertised that specimens of his photographs were on display at "Mr Roe's, Printer, Queens Street". A framed daguerreotype portrait cost 2s. 6d.

Shoosmith set up his studio next to the "Roman Catholic Chapel" (St. Osmund) in Exeter Street where he stated he took portraits "by his celebrated coloured photographic process", which were probably hand-coloured photographic originals. (*SJ*, Saturday 27th October 1855 p. 2 – "positively the last week")

He was in Frome from December 1855 until the end of March 1856 and advertised in the *Somerset & Wilts Journal* in December 1855.

By 1860 Shoosmith was working in Canterbury, Kent. The 1871 Census found him still living with his family in St George's Place, Canterbury with a profession of "Artist & Photographer." In the 1881 census he was listed as living in Camberwell, South East London as an "Artist Portrait Painter." Shoosmith died in Surrey in 1922.

William Thomas Pitcher (1828–1909)

"next the Council Chamber", Market Place, 1855–1859.
St. Ann Street, 1859.

PITCHER'S ADVERTISEMENTS IN the *SJ* that he had previously been for "many years" a camera operator in the studio of Richard Beard, and a "Photographist" in London at the Royal Polytechnic Institution. Pitcher's first advertisement in the *SJ* for Saturday 21st July 1855 stated that he intended "practising... the Beautiful Art in this city for a short time" and that "specimens of various styles are on view at F.A. Blake's, booksellers, Market Place." So, Pitcher, like a number of his contemporary photographers, initially intended to undertake seasonal photography in Salisbury, possibly to establish the size of the market in the city.

In his advertisement in the *SJ* for 8th September 1855, Pitcher included, for the first time, a line which read "Paintings, Prints, Models, Articles of Virtu etc. etc. copied." Such a service offering was common amongst the first generation of photographers who were generalists, though earned most of their income through portraiture.

At the end of the first year he operated in Salisbury he claimed he had taken "1000 very accurate portraits during his residence in Salisbury for a period of four months." (*SJ*, Saturday 8th December 1855 p. 3.) He announced he was closing his studio for the season on 22nd December 1855 in an advertisement place in the *SJ* on the 8th December. He reopened in March the following year. (*SJ*, Saturday 8th March 1856 p. 3.) By the end of the following year, in an editorial piece, it was stated that Pitcher had taken in total some 5000 portraits during his residency in Salisbury and his studio would be open during the Christmas period. (*SJ*, Saturday 26th December 1857 p. 5.)

Pitcher widened his services and offered to teach photography and supply photographic apparatus.

In late March 1856 Pitcher displayed in the window of his studio, "a miniature photographic copy" of *The Times* newspaper announcing that the peace treaty to end the Crimean War had been signed. (*SJ*, Saturday 5th April 1856 p. 2.) Quite what the point was of this display remains unclear, since many walking past Pitcher's studio would already have read of the event in national and local newspapers, and this application of photography had no ready market.

Pitcher also set up temporary studios in neighbouring towns. In November 1856 it was noted that he had been taking portraits in Fordingbridge, but that it was his last week and it was recommended by the editor "that those who have not yet availed themselves of his services to do so at once." (*SJ*, Saturday 1st November 1856 p. 3.) He continued to set up temporary studios in neighbouring towns and in May 1858 it was noted that he intended to set up a portrait studio in Warminster (*SJ*, Saturday 22nd May 1858 p. 8.) Whether this would be a permanent subsidiary to his Salisbury studio is unclear.

By 1859 Pitcher claimed to have taken nearly 9,000 portraits since arriving in Salisbury, the equivalent of a photograph for each of three-quarters of the population. However, while a probable exaggeration, Salisbury's catchment area meant that he might have taken a significant

IT HAS BEEN FOUND
BY MR. PITCHER
FAR MORE CONVENIENT TO CARRY ON HIS PROFESSION IN A PRIVATE HOUSE; he, therefore, begs to inform his numerous Patrons and the Public that he has REMOVED to a MOST CONVENIENT HOUSE on the north side of ST. ANN'S-STREET, where those persons who honour him with their support will meet with the comfort of Waiting and Dressing Rooms, and the advantage of a GLASS HOUSE, specially erected for operating.

Mr. P. embraces the present opportunity of thanking those parties who have so liberally supported him the last four years, during which time he has executed nearly 9,000 Portraits, and to inform them that as he has now superior advantages for taking Pictures, he is desirous that all should share in the improvement. He will, therefore, readily exchange any of them done during that time, at a mere nominal charge.

Mr. P. trusts that this offer, and his efforts to study the comfort of his patrons, will not fail to be appreciated.

St. Ann's-street, Salisbury, March 19th, 1859. [616

Advertisement of William Pitcher.
Salisbury Journal, Saturday 18th June 1859 p. 5.

number of portraits of those visiting the city, either local residents of Wiltshire, and neighbouring Hampshire and Dorset, or travellers and tourists. In this year he relocated his studio to the north side of St Anne Street since it was "far more convenient to carry on his profession in a private house." (*SJ*, Saturday 11th June 1859 p. 5.) The move away from the busy Market Place may indicate the beginning of the decline of his photographic business and in March 1861 his household furniture and effects were auctioned by J. Sutton, without reserve, perhaps an indication that his business had finally failed. (*SJ*, Saturday 9th March 1861 p. 4.)

The 1861 census – taken on the 7th and 8th April – found Pitcher as a "photographic artist" lodging in the Morepack Inn at 26 Endless Street. A decade later the 1871 census found him living at 128 Dorset Road, Lambeth in central London where he was married and was given the profession of commercial traveller.

Pitcher's demise reflected the increased competition by other Salisbury photographers. He seems to have failed to build on his position as one of the earliest professional photographers in Salisbury.

Edwin Whitlock (1825–1887)

WHITLOCK WAS THE son of Thomas Whitlock, a farmer, of Winterslow.

The 1841 census found Edwin as a "Chemist Apprentice" living in the house of the chemist and dentist William Buckell, in Silver Street. Probably around 1845 he set himself up as a chemist with premises on the corner of Queen Street and the Market Place. In 1846 he married Julia Mary Jane Kelly.

Whitlock was active as an amateur photographer by at least the mid-1850s. It is unclear whether he ever acted as a professional photographer. In 1856 Brown & Co. published, by 5s. subscription, a tinted lithograph printed by M. & N. Hanhart[1] entitled *The Peace Festival at Salisbury, May 29th 1856.* The letterpress credits included "Composed by W.F. Tiffin from photographic prints by E. Whitlock." The print was available from Brown and Co. of New Canal and was sold for 5s. Whether Whitlock intended to set up a commercial photographic business is unknown.

How many other photographers may have documented the 1856 Peace Festival is unknown. William Russell Sedgfield exhibited "Dinner in the Market Place, Salisbury, to celebrate the Peace of 1856" (Cat. No. 89) at the exhibition held by the Norwich and Norfolk Fine Arts Association between 17th November 1856 and 14th February 1857. The photographic view exhibited by the Salisbury postmaster William Toomer (1820–1887) may have been taken by another, as yet unidentified, photographer.

Other photographs by Whitlock are unrecorded and it may be that like other amateur photographers of the 1850s he gave up taking photographs as commercial photography took hold in the early 1860s.

In 1862, as a widower, he married Emily Targett, whose father was also a farmer. In March 1867 his business was taken over by his friend Edwin J. Orchard. Whitlock went bankrupt in 1869.

Thomas Edwards (1822–?)

St. Ann Street, 1850s–1870s.
30 St. Ann Street 1870s and 1880s (next door to St Ann's Street Brewery)

In an advertisement in the *ST* in 1880, Edwards claimed that his business had been established in 1854, though this may not have been his photographic business.[2] Establishing the exact date he commenced commercial photography in Salisbury was further brought into question in 1868 when he advertised that he had established his business in 1855. (*ST*, Saturday 11th April 1868 p. 1.)

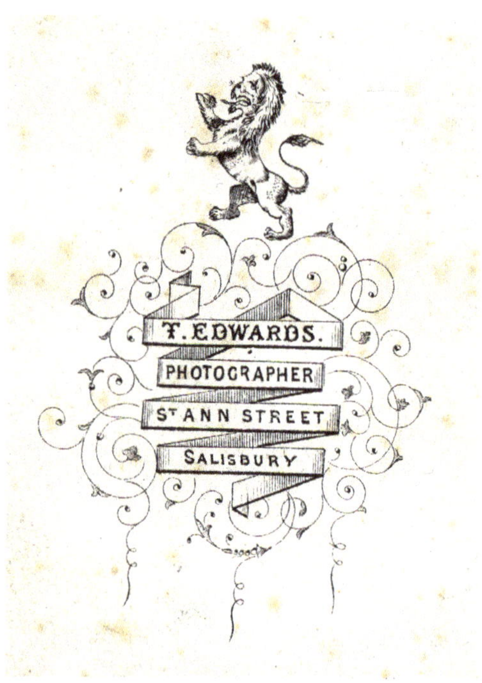

Etiquette of Thomas Edwards. Verso of a carte de visite. Anthony Hamber collection.

"LIFE IS BUT A SHADOW."

IMPORTANT NOTICE!

T. EDWARDS,

PHOTOGRAPHER,

NO. 30, ST. ANN'S ST., SALISBURY,

(Next door to St. Ann's St. Brewery.)

IN returning his sincere thanks to his numerous friends and the public generally for the support accorded to him during the past 20 years, begs to inform them that he has secured all the latest improvements in the optical and chemical departments of his business, and as in the past, so in the future, he will spare no effort to merit a continuance of their patronage.

CARTE-DE-VISITES, CABINET PORTRAITS, AND PERMANENT AUTOTYPE ENLARGEMENTS,

☞ Please observe particularly the Address:

T. EDWARDS,

30, ST. ANN'S ST., SALISBURY.

Advertisement of Thomas Edwards. *Salisbury Times*, 11th September 1875 p. 1.

In the *SJ* for Saturday 11th June 1864 (p. 4.) there was an advertisement stating that the house that Edwards occupied would be sold in one or four lots. It was held at the time under a term of 39 ½ years from the Vicars of Salisbury Cathedral.

Edwards was advertising his "Permanent Autotype Enlargements" from the summer of 1874. (*ST*, Saturday 4th July 1874 p. 1.) "Autotype" was a generic brand name of the Autotype Company founded in 1868, with a factory initially in Brixton, South London. It could refer to a number of permanent or photomechanical processes, such as carbon prints, woodburytypes or collotypes.

In advertisements placed in the *ST* in 1875 under the heading "Life is but a Shadow", Edwards thanked his "numerous friends and the general public generally for the support accorded to him during the past 20 years" thus indicating that he had commenced business around 1855, though not advertised at the time in the columns of the *SJ*.

In 1877 Edwards was advertising in the *ST* that "Cameras and Photographic apparatus of every description made to order or repaired." Also, "Cabinet work or all kinds repolished and repaired. Picture Frames made to order."[3] In 1880 he was advertising his services as a "Photographer and Carver" including "Antique carving, marquetry & fretwork,"

It is unclear when Edwards ceased practising as a professional photographer in Salisbury. His advertisements in Salisbury newspapers appear to have ceased in 1885.

Philip Monson (1828–1905)

St Ann Street, 1856.

MONSON WAS BORN in Colchester, one of four brothers, all of whom became photographers. Edward Monson was operating a studio in Ipswich from 1849.

The 1851 census found Philip Monson living in Chapel Terrace in Wolverhampton with a listed profession as an "Artist. Portrait Painter." In 1853 Philip set up a temporary photographic studio at Mr Francis' Nurseries in Hertford, in partnership with his brother Charles. In May he was operating in Queen Street, Colchester and in September of this year he advertised that he would be operating for a fortnight in a studio at Wind Hill, Bishop's Stortford. In April 1854 he was operating in Warwick Row, Coventry.

In 1855 he was operating in Reading, at 161 Friar Street, and then at Bedford. (See advertisement in *Bedfordshire Mercury* of Saturday 17th March 1855 p. 1 and in *SJ* Saturday 12th April 1856 p.2 citing the *Reading Mercury* of 21st April, 1855; *Bedford Mercury* of 10th February, 1855; *Berkshire Chronicle* of 9th June, 1855.

FOR A SHORT TIME ONLY.
DAGUERREOTYPE PORTRAITS.
MR. P. MONSON, Artist in Daguerreotype, Collodion, and Talbotype, respectfully announces a short Visit to Salisbury, and that his PORTRAIT ROOMS will open on Monday next, at St. Ann's Street, opposite Brown Street, and that he can supply PORTRAITS, singly or in groups, in the first Style of the Art (taken with one of the largest and most perfect Apparatus in use, in a Glass Room built and fitted up expressly for the purpose), and coloured, if required, by Mr. Monson. [8666
Prices from 3s. 6d.

Advertisement of Philip Monson. *Salisbury Journal*, Saturday 5th January 1856 p. 2.

Monson advertised in early January 1856 that he would be in Salisbury "For A Short Time Only" and would be taking Daguerreotype Portraits in his Portrait Rooms in St Ann Street, opposite Brown Street. Prices from 3s. 6d. (*SJ*, Saturday 5th January 1856 p. 2.) What is significant is that Monson claimed that he had had a purpose built "Glass Room" constructed which perhaps indicated that he intended to establish a permanent studio in Salisbury. By March of the same year he changed photographic process and he was advertising his collodion portraits for one shilling, which appeared to be the going rate, as also advertised by Witcomb (*SJ*, Saturday 29th March 1856 p. 2.)

In 1856 Monson advertised in the *SJ* in March 1856 that his portraits were priced from 3s. 6d. (*SJ*, 29th March 1856 p. 2.). Monson's advertisements in the *SJ* stop in mid-1856 and he does not seem to have returned to the city. Whether he lost money as a result of building a "Glass House" in his St Ann Street studio and not securing enough business must be left to conjecture. In October 1856 he advertised in the *Western Gazette* that he would "For A Short Time Only" be taking photographs in Yeovil in his Princes' Street studio next door to the Western Flying Post Office. This advertisement included a quotation from the *SJ* of the 19th January 1856 (p. 2.) that described Monson as "unquestionably one of the greatest masters of this beautiful art that has ever visited this city."

In 1859 a trade directory lists him as operating a studio at 40 Newland, Northampton.

Henry Brooks (1825–1909)

60 High Street, 1859–1880.
45 High Street, 1897–1913.

BROOKS WAS BORN in Britford on 23rd March 1825, the son of William, a horsehair weaver. He married Caroline Coombs in 1847. In 1851 the couple were living in Salt Lane and his occupation was listed as a turner. A decade later he and his family were living at 60 High Street, above his photographic studio.

An obituary appeared in the *SJ* (Saturday 26th June 1909 p. 5.) in which it was stated that he began his "study and practice of photography at the Old

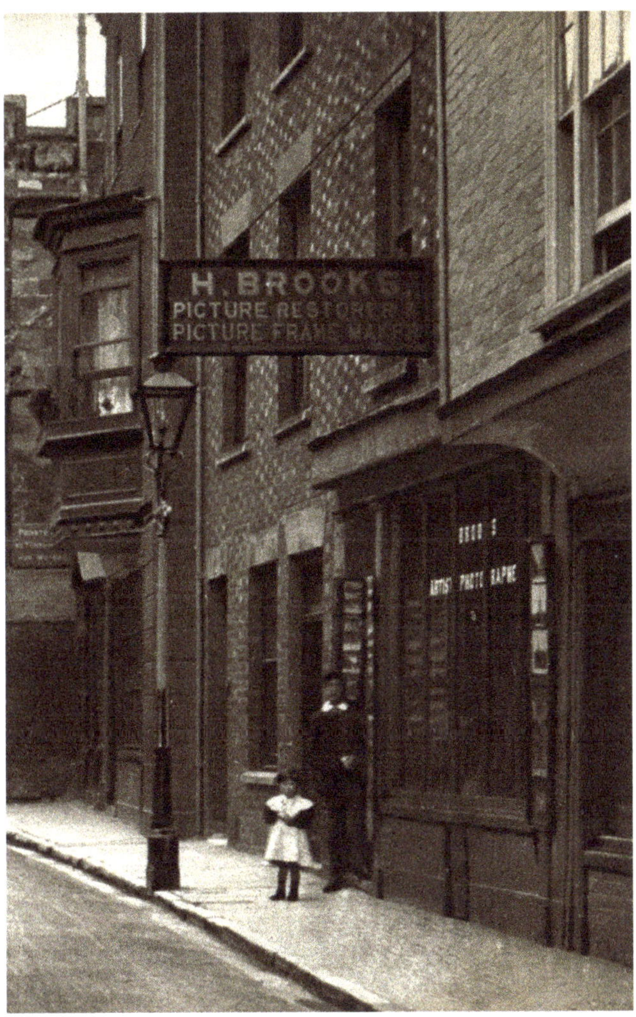

Exterior view of Henry Brooks shop and studio at 60 High Street. c.1900. Detail of a postcard published by A. Smee. Anthony Hamber collection.

George, High-Street" "about 1850" and that he was "the first person in Salisbury to produce a photograph on paper. He ground and polished his own lenses and made his own camera." It also stated that "one of his most noted photographs at that time was of the Cathedral, showing the top of the spire, which had not hitherto been produced." This was primarily a result of the limited angle of view of photographic lenses and the need for camera movements – of the front element holding the lens, and the back element holding the negative "dark slide". The latter needed to stay vertical and perpendicular with the building in order to prevent a distorted view with "converging verticals."

It is reasonable to assume that Brooks took the portraits of various prominent members of Salisbury society. One of these was Mrs Lear, a member of the family living in the Close that included the Dean of the cathedral, Francis Lear (1789–1850), Dean of Salisbury from 1846 until his death and the Rev. Francis Lear (1823–1914), Archdeacon of Sarum from 1875 until his death. In 1845 Isabel Elizabeth Lear, married Walter Kerr Hamilton, who became Bishop of Salisbury in 1854. Isabella Lear paid for the construction of All Saints Church, Harnham, consecrated in 1854.

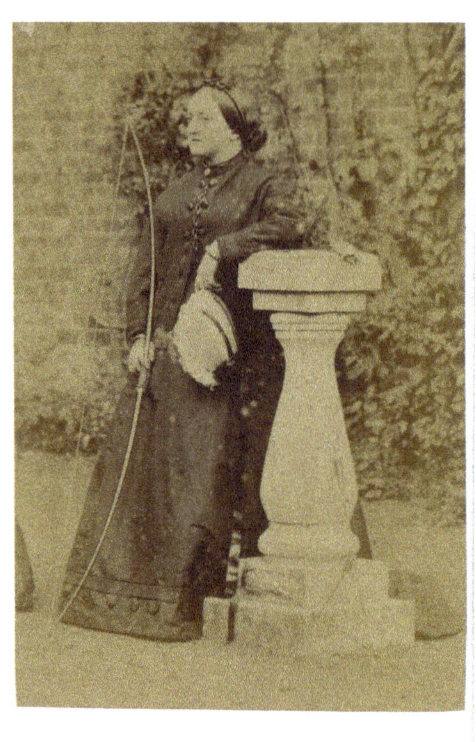

Henry Brooks. Portrait of a woman archer. c. 1865. Carte de visite. Albumen print. Anthony Hamber collection.

Brooks took portraits away from his studio, including one of a woman archer.

Brooks had extensive set of photographs for sale at the first Royal Agricultural Society Show

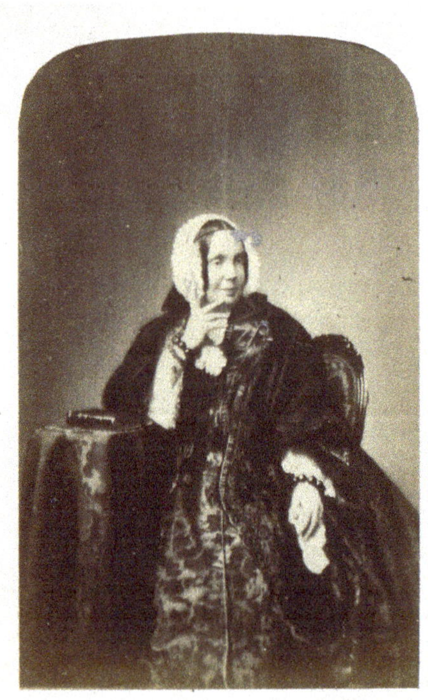

Henry Brooks. Portrait of Mrs Lear. 1860s. Carte de visite. Albumen print. Anthony Hamber collection.

H. BROOKS,

PHOTOGRAPHIST,

HIGH STREET, SALISBURY,

Begs to return thanks for past favours, and to say he has a fine Selection

OF

Views of Salisbury and Vicinity

CONSTANTLY ON SALE.

Gentlemen's Residences taken in any Part of the Country

PORTRAITS, &c. &c.

Henry Brooks advertisement in *Brown's Stranger's Handbook and Illustrated Guide to Salisbury Cathedral,* Brown and Co; Simpkin and Co., Salisbury; London, 1858.

held in Salisbury in July 1857. Perhaps as a result of increased sales, in 1858 he advertised in that year's edition of *Brown's Strangers' Handbook and Illustrated Guide to Salisbury Cathedral* targeting visitors to Salisbury.

As mentioned previously, an illustration of an interior view of the "Salisbury New Market" that appeared in the *Illustrated London News* of 18th June 1859 was credited to "H. Brooks of Salisbury". This was also mentioned in the *SJ* (18th June 1859 p. 8.)

In January 1860 it was noted that full-length portraits by Brooks of officers and non-commissioned officers of the Salisbury Rifle Corps (1st Company of the Wiltshire Rifle Volunteers) had been copied to form the illustrations of a lithographed title page illustration of "The Rifleman's March" by J. E. Richardson, Assistant Organist at the Cathedral. (*SJ*, Saturday 28th January 1860 p. 5.)

In August 1860 Brooks photographed a meeting of around fifty members of the Southampton Medical Society at Laverstock House Asylum, whose proprietor was Dr. Stephenson Bushman, whose important book *Cholera and Its Cure: An Historical Sketch* had been published in 1850. (*SJ*, Saturday 11th August 1860 p. 7.)

In May 1863 Brooks felt it necessary to address rumours in Salisbury, and he placed an advertisement in the *SJ* stating that "having heard that there is a Report set on foot, by some Person or Persons, that he has GIVEN UP TAKING PORTRAITS, he begs to inform his friends and the public that such is not the case." (*SJ*, Saturday 23rd May 1863 p. 5.)

In December 1864 Brooks advertised that he had moved his studio to new premises near the Close Gates in the High Street (*SJ*, Saturday 17th December 1864 p. 4.). This can be seen on the right-hand side of a postcard in the Anthony Hamber collection (p. 109 above)

Brooks was listed as a "photographist" in the 1861 census, and a "photographer" in the 1871 census, but within the decade had ceased this profession.

Brooks took the opportunity to take large format views of the Cathedral prior to the restoration of the West Front and the addition of 63 statues installed between 1867 and around 1871 from the workshops of James Redfern (1838–1876). (Anthony Hamber Collection, p. 50 above) He also took stereoscopic views of the city from the late 1850s.

By 1873 Brooks was advertising that he held the exclusive license for "Salisbury and its Neighbourhood" for the Patent Vander Weyde Process for finishing photographs, also known as the "Atmospheric stippled effect."

Brooks, like a number of other commercial photographers in Salisbury, changed the etiquette he placed on the verso of his carte de visite. Three of these are illustrated below.

Probably as a result of their increasing popularity in the late 1850s, Brooks began taking stereoscopic views of the city. Not all were of the usual subject matter, such as the one below of the entrance to a courtyard, perhaps off Winchester Street.

Brooks had a number of other interests, he studied microscopy and made microscopes. He built himself an observatory, making his own

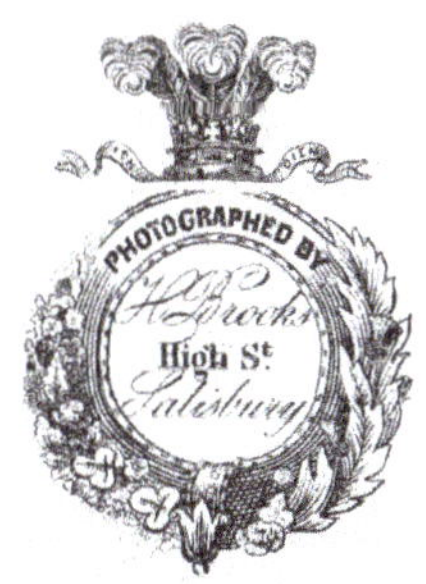

Etiquette of Henry Brooks. Verso of a carte de visite. Late 1850s to early 1860s. Anthony Hamber collection.

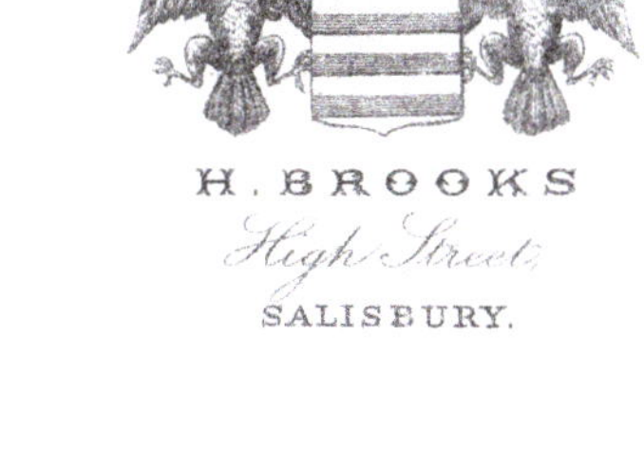

Sarum coat of arms etiquette of Henry Brooks. Verso of a carte de visite. 1860s. Anthony Hamber collection.

H. BROOKS
ARTIST
60 High Street
SALISBURY

Etiquette of Henry Brooks. Verso of a carte de visite. 1870s. Anthony Hamber collection.

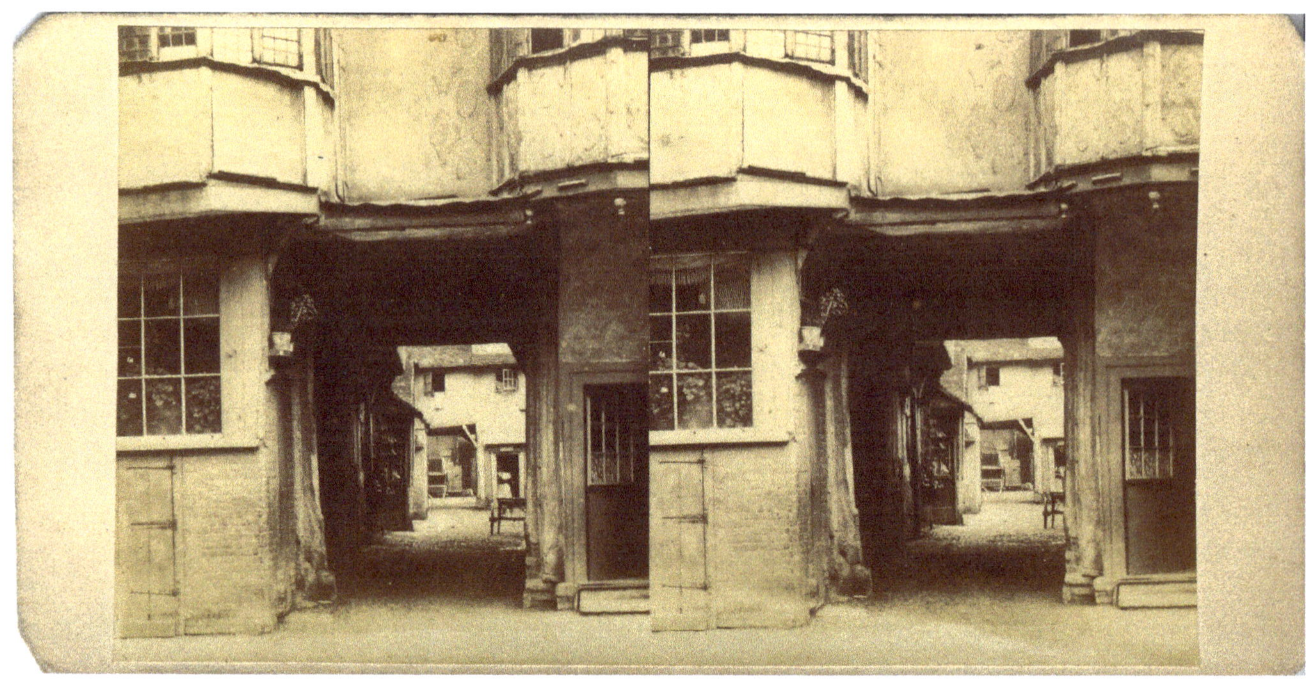

Henry Brooks. Entrance to a courtyard, perhaps off Winchester Street. Late 1850s. Stereoscopic view. Albumen print. Anthony Hamber collection.

equatorial telescope, which was driven by clockwork. He took many photographs of the moon from which he made a large map, showing the mountains, valleys, and plains which were sold to all the leading astronomers, including the Astronomer Royal. In 1909 a copy of the map could still be seen hanging in the shop of his son at 60 High Street.

In 1880 Brooks retired from photography and returned to painting, making watercolour and oil studies of the New Forest that were exhibited at the Royal Academy, Birmingham Art Gallery, the Crystal Palace in Sydenham, and other London and provincial galleries. The 1881 and 1891 censuses list Brooks as an "Artist painter", still living in the High Street, his photographic business having been taken over by his son. In 1885 Brooks painted a posthumous portrait of Edward Thomas Stevens (1828–1878), FSA, the Director of the Salisbury & South Wiltshire Museum (1860–1878). This may have been based on a portrait photograph, perhaps by Brooks, who donated the painting to the museum.

An obituary of Brooks appeared in the *Salisbury Journal* (*SJ,* Saturday 26th June 1909 p. 5.)

James Wesley Miell (1837–1901)

31 Catherine Street, 1856.

21 Catherine Street, 1859 (Opposite Lewis' Carriage Factory, and near the White Hart hotel).

45 Catherine Street, 1872.

West End Studio, (Opposite the South Western Railway Station) Fisherton, 1879.

St. John's Street 1885–1889.

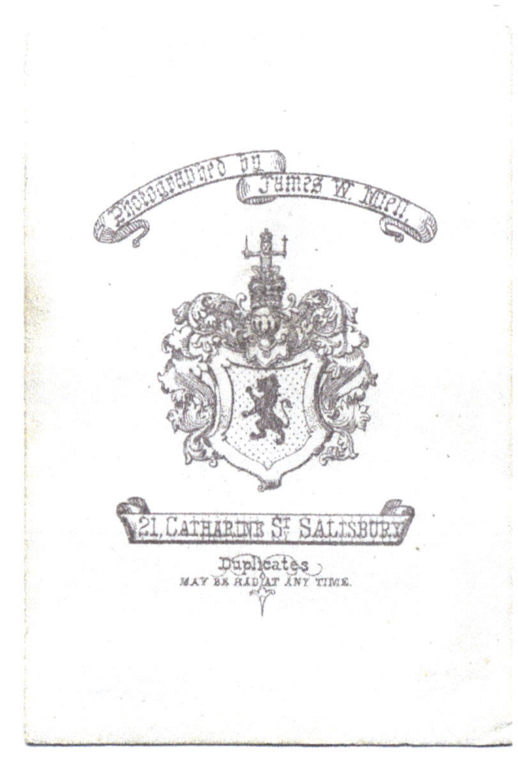

Etiquette of James Miell. Verso of a carte de visite 1860s. Anthony Hamber collection.

Son of Thomas Miell, picture dealer, 37 Catherine Street, as listed in *Kelly's Directory of Wiltshire* 1855 edition.

Quite when Miell set up his "Photographic Portrait Rooms" is not documented in advertisements in the *SJ* during 1855 or much of 1856. In December 1856 Miell did place an advertisement in the *SJ* in which thanked a range of inhabitants of Salisbury for their "very liberal Patronage" bestowed on him.

PHOTOGRAPHIC PORTRAIT ROOMS,
37, CATHERINE-STREET, SALISBURY.

J. W. MIELL, ARTIST in COLLODION and TALBOTYPE, in tendering his sincere thanks to the Nobility, Clergy, Gentry, and Inhabitants generally of SALISBURY and its Vicinity for the very liberal Patronage bestowed upon him, begs to inform them that his ROOMS ARE OPEN DAILY, having had considerable IMPROVEMENTS made for the convenience of Parties during the WINTER MONTHS.

PORTRAITS (Frames included) from ONE SHILLING EACH.——BROOCHES, LOCKETS, &c. &c., for receiving Portraits, in great variety.

VIEWS taken of Buildings, Landscapes, &c. &c.
Families waited upon at their own Residences.
Dull or *Wet Weather* of no consequence.

The ART TAUGHT, and Apparatus supplied, on reasonable terms.—THE TRADE SUPPLIED. [902

Observe—37, *Catherine street, Salisbury.*

James Miell advertisement. *Salisbury Journal.* Saturday 20th December 1856 p. 2.

The advertisement included advertisements for J.W. Miell's studio in which he stated that he would reproduce buildings, drawings, and oil paintings, and visit families at their own residences.

By 1859 Miell was described as a photographic materials dealer in 1859 and then as a "Dealer in photographic goods" in the 1861 census. In April 1859 Miell was advertising "American Excelsior Collodion" used to coat glass plate negatives (*SJ*, Saturday 9th April 1859 p. 5.) Holmes & Company's American Excelsior Collodion had been marketed in 1858 and the sole agent for England was Messrs. Squier and Co., of King William Street in London. An advertisement in the *Photographic News* in 1859 listed Miell's "photographic warehouse" as an agent for this important periodical which had commenced publication the previous year. (*Photographic News*, 8th October 1859 p. viii.).

In 1860 Miell was advertising that he was an importer of "French, Germans and American Photographic Goods" (*SJ*, Saturday 23rd June 1860 p. 5.) During 1862, Miell mentioned in his regular advertisements in the *SJ*, that he had employed a first-class artist to colour his photographs in oils.

In the *Illustrated London News* for the 11th July, 1863, an illustration of the Inauguration of a Memorial Statue to the Late Lord Herbert of Lea was credited as being "from a photograph by J.W. Miell, of Salisbury". This followed a note in the *SJ* for Saturday 4th July 1863 p. 5:

> THE HERBERT STATUE.
> We have had an opportunity of inspecting some very excellent photographs of the inaugural ceremony, on Monday last, executed by Mr. James. W. Miell, of 21, Catherine-street, in this city. He has also taken a good photograph of the statue, which is a most faithful representation of this integrating work of art. Mr. F. Treble, of Catherine-street, has also photographed the statue, in good style, by order of Baron Marochetti.[5]

On Thursday 22nd September 1864 Miell photographed "several good photographs… during the visit of the British Association to Stonehenge." "One of these was taken during the discussion, and Dr. Thurnam is seen in the act of addressing members from the impost of the great trilithon. Considering the great difficulty of obtaining pictures under such circumstances, the photographs are well executed." (*SJ*, Saturday 24th September 1864 p. 5.)

Miell also ventured from Salisbury to document the surrounding area. For instance he published a series of carte de visite on the Priory Church, Christchurch.

In May 1869 Miell registered for copyright a photograph of the Bishop of Salisbury, from a painting by Robert Kemm (1830–1895). However, on the 25th June, Miell was declared bankrupt, though this may well have been a financial instrument to assist his continuing his business, which he did.

In August 1871 he advertised photographs of the First Battalion of Wilts Rifles Volunteers at an encampment on Homington Down, "by the Special Permission of Colonel Everett" (*SJ*, Saturday 12th August 1871 p. 5.)

The 1875 *Kelly's* directory lists him as "Miell, James, photographer to the Queen & the Royal Family, photographic apparatus & material dealer, Catherine street."

In 1875, Private Maidment won "6 large

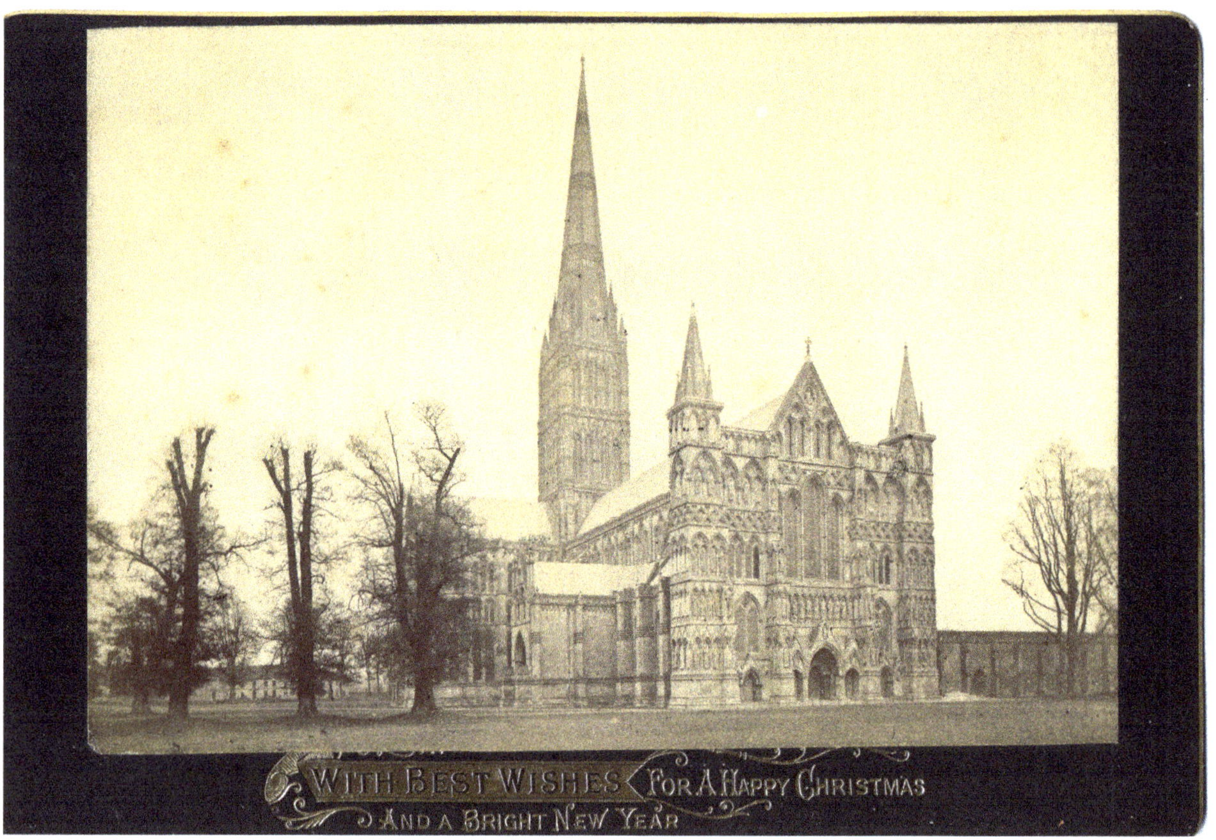

James Miell. View of Salisbury Cathedral Christmas card. Late 1870s. Cabinet card. Albumen print. Anthony Hamber collection

photographic views" donated by Miell as a prize at the Christmas Rifle Competition, held on the Laverstock Down on Saturday 27th December 1874. Private Giddings won "6 photographs from life" presented by Mr. Dunmore of Wilton Road. *(ST*, Saturday 2nd January 1875 p. 4.) Dunmore also provided 6 photographs for the 1876 Christmas Rifle Competition. In late December 1879 Owen presented 6 Cabinet photographs and Witcomb 12 Chromotype photographs as prizes at a meeting of the First Wilts Rifle Volunteers. The following year, photographic prizes for this event were donated by Miell, Owen, Targett and Witcomb.[6]

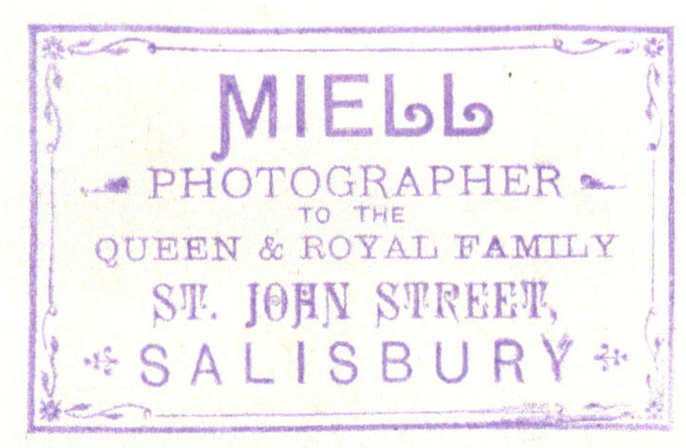

James Miell stamp. 1885–1889. Verso of a cabinet card. Anthony Hamber collection.

In February 1879 Miell moved from Catherine Street to the West End Studio, Fisherton, opposite the South Western Railway Station and advertised that his studio had been "Established 1855". (*ST*, Saturday 22nd February 1879 p. 4.) The background to this relocation is unknown but points to Miell having to find cheaper studio space.

Miell was an innovator and in the late 1870s issued a cabinet card view of Salisbury Cathedral as a Christmas card – "With Best Wishes for a Happy Christmas and a Bright New Year" stamped in gold lettering on the front bottom edge.

By 1889 he was listed in Kelly's directory as a photographer based in St. John's Street, Salisbury, which might point to an improvement of Miell's fortunes and in July 1890 Miell registered for copyright "Photograph of the Cathedrals of England, with their respective Bishops."

James Miell died in 1901, his wife Ellen Sophia dying on 24th September 1901 aged 64.

Charles John Witcomb (1835–1913)

Bridge Street (trading as Witcomb & Parker) [See also Parker]
Probably Milford Street (as one of Witcomb Brothers) 1856
47 Catherine Street, 1865.
10 Catherine Street, 1870s–1900s.

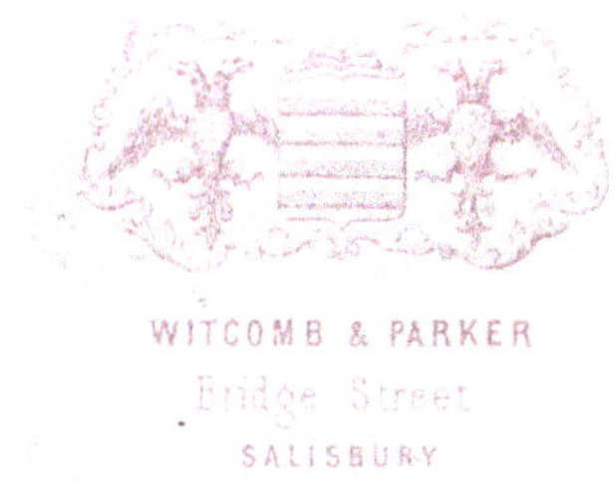

Etiquette of Witcomb & Parker. Verso of a carte de visite. 1864–1865. Anthony Hamber collection.

The studios run by various members of the Witcomb family are instructive from a variety of viewpoints.

Henry Witcomb (c.1801–1868), father of Charles, was a confectioner master who ran fruit shops in Fish Market and Milford Street.

Witcomb Brothers were advertising in 1856 that they took photographic portraits by the collodion process for one shilling at their studio in Milford Street and "Families Waited on at their own Residences." They also supplied photographic apparatus and taught "the Art on the most reasonable terms." (*SJ*, Saturday 29th March 1856 p. 2.) This photographic partnership does not seemed to have lasted for very long.

Charles John Witcomb was active as a photographer by at least 1860 when he was recorded as working with Miell [q.v.] – perhaps as his assistant – and that they had "succeeded in taking a good photograph, on a large scale, of the whole of the Band of the First Wilts [Volunteer Rifles], 28 in number" in the Market Place prior to it marching to Clarendon Park. (*SJ*, 29th September 1860 p. 8.)

In October 1860 Charles Witcomb had set up his own photographic studio in Milford Street and advertised in the *SJ* (Saturday 17th October 1860 p. 5.) in a glass house that enabled portraits to be taken "irrespective of Wet or Dull Weather."

In 1861 was living with his wife Eliza, who he had married in 1856, and two children at 2 Milford Street. He was described as a tobacconist, stationer and photographer. He advertised that he photographed on "glass, paper, or leather" as did James Miell (*SJ*, Saturday 23rd March 1861 p. 5.)

In February 1862 Witcomb advertised his Milford Street studio which had a "conveniently fitted up Glass House, with Waiting Room adjoining." The advertisement also mentioned "a large selection of Brooches, Lockets, &c. for Portraits" pointing to this significant element of the commercial market for portraiture. (*SJ*, Saturday 1st February 1862 p. 5.)

In December 1863 Witcomb "exceedingly well photographed" a heifer belonging to J. D. Allen of Pyt House Farm, Tisbury that had been considered best animal of its class in the Christmas Show of Meat in the Market Place and had been bought by Snook and Son of Butcher Row. (*SJ*, Saturday 19th December 1863 p. 8.)

In May 1864 Witcomb was advertising reductions in price of his carte de visite portraits and that his "Portrait Rooms re now open as early as seven o'clock in the morning, for the convenience

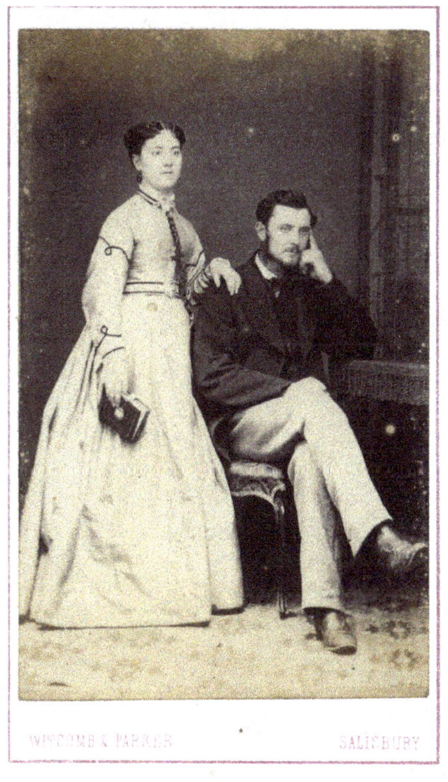

Witcomb & Parker. Portrait of a couple. 1864–1865. Carte de visite. Albumen print. Anthony Hamber collection.

of parties who are unable to attend during the day." (*SJ*, Saturday 7th May 1864 p. 5.) Perhaps as a result of the expanding market for photography, Witcomb placed an advertisement in the *SJ* in October 1864 notes that a "branch" studio, "conducted by S. Parker" would be opened on Bridge Street. (*SJ*, Saturday 22nd October 1864 p. 4.) However, this partnership seems to have lasted only until the end of 1865 when Witcomb moved his studio from Milford Street to 47 Catherine Street where he traded as "C. J. Witcomb."

Witcomb had an interesting commercial side line for his studio. In April 1866 an advertisement in the *SJ* stated that each Tuesday, Maurice Harvey, a "surgical and mechanical dentist" of 13 Portland Terrace, Southampton, would be in attendance between ten and four at Witcomb's studio.

PERMANENT PHOTOGRAPHIC ESTABLISHMENT
10, *CATHERINE-STREET, SALISBURY.*

C. J. WITCOMB begs to inform the inhabitants of Salisbury and vicinity that he has purchased the SOLE RIGHT for the production of the whole of the LAMBERTYPE PATENT PROCESSES for Salisbury, and to inform them that he is now working the never-fading CHROMOTYPE PORTRAITS, which are considered by all who have seen them to be perfect wonders. Specimens and prices on application. The Patent Chromotype Portraits have the following advantages: —1st. They will not fade as Silver Prints. 2nd. They are much more brilliant. 3rd. By making a previous appointment any number can be sent out the same day as taken.

Charles Witcomb advertisement for the Lambertype and Chromotype processes. *Salisbury Journal*, Saturday 15th July 1876 p. 5.

In *Kelly's Directory of Wiltshire* for 1867 Witcomb is described as a "photographer, & berlin & fancy repository" of 47 Catherine Street. In 1872 he moved his studio to 10 Catherine Street. Parker continued to operate the studio in Bridge Street.

In July 1876 Witcomb was advertising that he had purchased the sole rights for the Lambertype Patent Process.[7] The Lambertype was a method of retouching negatives and positives invented by Claude Leon Lambert of Paris. Lambert produced his own version of the carbon print process which he christened "Chromotype" and Witcomb also purchased a 13 year licence for this process. In an editorial piece, the *SJ* stated it had inspect some examples of Witcomb's Chromotypes and that "These specimens, which are permanent in character, are of great beauty and exquisite finish, and its appears as if the new process was about to revolutionise the art of photography. The portraits are very superior in brilliancy of tone and effect to anything yet produced by the ordinary modes".[8] In December 1876 Whitcomb had an article entitled "Hints on Permanent Chromotype Printing" published in the *British Journal of Photography* in which he stated that he had been trained on the Chromotype at the Autotype Company, who held the UK license for the process. In the same issue an editorial note stated that Witcomb had sent to the journal's editor "three charming cartes." (*British Journal of Photography*, 1st December 1876 p. 570 and 576.)

The issue of the *British Photographic Journal* for the 1st December, 1876 stated "We are favoured by Mr. Witcomb, of Salisbury, with charming card portraits printed in chromotype." "Thanks for the portraits; they are brilliant, and the tone excellent." G. Wharton Simpson, the Editor of the *Photographic News*, stated in the issue of 15th December 1876 "The success of Mt. Witcomb is apparent enough in his communication, but the confirmation he send us in examples of his work is in the highest degree satisfactory; they are among the best chromotype we have seen." The chromotype was a contact-printed carbon print.

One of those particularly interested in permanent photographic print processes was Sir Thomas Parkyns (1820 1895) of Harnham Cliff, elected a member of the Photographic Society of London in 1874 and remained a member (bar the years 1876, 1877 and 1881) until 1895.[9] A reference from the issue of *Photographic News* March 9th 1877 where in a letter from, who had visited the studio of Mr Witcomb in Salisbury, Wiltshire, to see how easy it was to make carbon prints using the Autotype company's tissue, he found that "A youth of sixteen years of age had management of the production of the prints" and "A young lady" had taken the negatives. The prints were put in the printing frame at 10.55 and Mr Witcomb delivered them to Sir Thomas by 12.12. The prints were judged successful. There was much fuss going on at the time as the Autotype patents were about to expire. Many were saying that the process was difficult to operate, Sir Thomas delivered fine carbon prints to the *British Journal of Photography*'s editorial offices where anyone could examine them, while a gentleman from Ceylon, where he was making 11 x 14 enlargements in tropical conditions, pointed out that in order to get the process to work properly, all one had to do was follow the instructions.

During 1877 Parkyns wrote repeatedly to the British photographic press regarding permanent photographic processes. He also exhibited "a new process, permanent colours" at the 1877 exhibition of the Photographic Society of London as noted by *The Times,* though these may not have been his own prints.[10] He had previously invented a camera stand, which he described in a letter to the *British Journal of Photography.*[11] Parkyns left Salisbury in 1878, moved to Kent and died in Italy.[12]

In 1876 Witcomb advertised that he was the only person who could work the Patent Lambertype, Chromotype and Contratype Portraits as he had purchased the sole right for Salisbury for 13 years.[13] In the following year Witcomb was inserting a royal reference into his advertisements:

> THE QUEEN AND FADING PHOTOGRAPHS
> Her Majesty has commanded an eminent Court photographer to reproduce by the new permanent chromotype process the pictures in the royal albums. Our patrons are recommended to follow suit.[14]

It would seem his business prospered, for in May 1877 Mrs Witcomb placed an advertisement in the *SJ* stating that "in consequence of a portion of the premises [10 Catherine Street] being required for the Photographic Business" she had disposed of the Berlin Wool and Fancy Needlework branch of the Witcomb establishment to Miss Hookway of 17 Queen Street. However the Jewellery and General Fancy Business would be carried on as usual.[15]

By at least July 1877 Witcomb had set up a branch studio in Silver Street in Warminster.

In 1878 he was advertising the "Salisbury and Warminster Permanent Photographic Establishments" and "For children's photographs, and other difficult subjects, M. Scotellarie's Patent Opturateurs [sic]" that reduced camera exposure times.[16] This was an opaque lens- system developed and patented by an Italian photographer, Scotellari, who also introduced the use of a violet varnish on the glass of the studio to reduce camera exposure times.

In 1880 Witcomb advertised that his studios were open from 7 a. m. until 6 p. m. "for the convenience of Parties unable to attend during the Day." (*ST,* Saturday 3rd July 1880 p. 1.)

Charles' son, Sidney George (1860–1947), original trained as a watchmaker's apprentice, joined him and the two were in partnership with Harry Alfred Meill as photographers from around 1884 at The Royal Studio, 9 The Triangle, Bournemouth, the former studio of George Nesbitt. The partnership was dissolved by mutual agreement in December 1890 and by 1903 Witcomb & Son were established in Middle Street, Yeovil. The Yeovil studio was run by Sidney.

Thomas Keynes (1807–?)

Brown Street, 1858–1859.

THOMAS AND HIS brother William ran auction rooms in Brown Street.

"FAITHFUL REMEMBRANCER OF ONE SO DEAR."
PHOTOGRAPHY.
THOMAS KEYNES, having Practised PHOTOGRAPHY from its first introduction to this country, begs to Give Notice to the Public that he can supply them with PORTRAITS that cannot fail to give satisfaction.
Family Groups of four, six, ten, or more persons can be beautifully executed in a first-rate style, and to which he would particularly call the attention of his Friends.
T. K. is fully prepared to state that his productions in the art of Photography may be equalled but cannot be surpassed either in this or any other country.
Brown-street, Salisbury, August 21, 1858. [8333

Thomas Keynes advertisement. *Salisbury Journal,* Saturday 21st August 1858 p. 5.

Probably the same "T. Keynes" who lectured on the daguerreotype at the Town Hall in Shaftesbury in October 1852. He may also have been the Thomas Keynes who was a curator of the collections of the Salisbury Mechanics Institution in the late 1830s.

His advertisement in the *SJ* in September 1858 stated that he had "practiced photography from its first introduction to this country." (*SJ,* Saturday 21st August 1858 p. 5.) If this were the case, Keynes was one of the earliest photographers in Salisbury. His studio was at his Auction Rooms in Brown Street, though he somewhat curiously stated "No Specimens are Exhibited in the Window." (*SJ,* Saturday 22nd January 1859 p. 4.)

William Keynes and Thomas Cusse Keynes, auctioneers of Brown Street, had been declared bankrupt in February 1858 and while the business was resurrected, it is possible that Thomas Keynes considered that commercial photography would be a significant supplement to the company's income. No advertisements for this studio have been found after 1859 and thus it is presumed that it had ceased operating.

William Dubisson (b. 1785)

IN THE 1861 census William Dubisson and his wife Elizabeth Mary were lodgers in the house of James Webb, Gunmaker, in Catherine Street. Dubisson, who was born in Dublin in 1785, gave his profession as photographic artist. He may have been a camera operator working for a Salisbury studio, but no record that he traded in Salisbury as a photographer under his own name has been found.

Edmund Rogers (1828–1878)

East Harnham (Britford), 1861.
De Vaux Place, 1864–1878.

ROGERS WAS BORN in Salisbury, the son of William Rogers, a publican, and his wife Sarah.

The 1851 census found Edmund and his wife Marianne (also known as Mary Anne), a school teacher, living in St Thomas Church Yard. His profession was given as a wood and general turner. A decade later the census found Edmund living in Britford with Marianne and their children. He was still a wood and general turner.

Edmund, having taught himself photography, set up as a photographer in Britford by at least September 1861. His advertisements were short and referred to "carte de visite and album photographs" and "Portraits taken in various positions." No prices were given. An advertisement in the (*SJ*, 28th December 1861 p. 4) refers to a cottage to let next to Rogers photographic studio in East Harnham (Britford), This was a boom time for commercial photography in Great Britain and clearly Edmund had identified the opportunity and somehow acquired the necessary knowledge, associated craft skills and financial wherewithal to set up in business. However, he seems to have had at least one side line, that of selling English and Belgian canaries and a few mules! (*SJ*, Saturday 8th February 1862 p. 5 and 15th February p.5)

SPECIMENS of the CARTE DE VISITE or ALBUM PHOTOGRAPHS ON VIEW at E. ROGERS'S, PHOTOGRAPHER, EAST HARNHAM, SALISBURY, taken with Dallmeyer's Improved Apparatus, especially constructed for this purpose.
SINGLE COPIES, ONE SHILLING EACH. 10s. PER DOZEN
SECOND DOZEN, 7s. 6d. [4284

Edmund Rogers advertisement. *Salisbury Journal*, Saturday 12th April 1862 p. 3.

By the spring of 1862 Rogers appears to have identified the market price in Salisbury and the need to provide more information in his advertisements. He advertised his studio at East Harnham where he would take carte de visite portraits using Dallmeyer's "Improved Apparatus" for one shilling for a single image. 10s per Dozen and 7s. 6d. for the second dozen. (*SJ*, Saturday 12th April 1862 p. 3.) In January 1864, Rogers announced that he was moving to the Corner House of De Vaux Place. (*SJ*, Saturday 2nd January 1864 p. 5.) This may have been a result of business being slow, particularly in East Harnham. It is not clear whether Rogers actually operated a studio in the High Street premises he traded from, but he appreciated that he needed to operate a studio close to the city centre. Rogers noted for portraits that there was an "Extra charge for children under ten" underlining an age old maxim.

In 1865 Rogers was advertising in the *SJ* that the studio would only be open on Mondays and Tuesdays, suggesting that he had another line of business or profession.

In 1867 Rogers advertised that since Frederick Treble was selling his negatives, he would be happy to print copies from the same. (*SJ*, Saturday 14th December 1867 p. 4.)

In the same year Rogers was registering some of his photographs for copyright purposes. These included "Two portraits of Mrs Walter Kerr Hamilton and Miss Constance Hamilton", the wife and daughter of the Bishop of Salisbury (*British Journal of Photography* 1st February 1867 p. 58) and "Group of the choristers of Salisbury Cathedral". (*British Journal of Photography*, 31st May 1867 p. 262.)[17]

Rogers died in 1878 but his wife Mary Ann (c. 1828–1911) continued the photographic business until around 1890.[18] It is likely Mary Ann worked as an assist to her husband photographer for several years before his death. Attributing work to Mary Ann

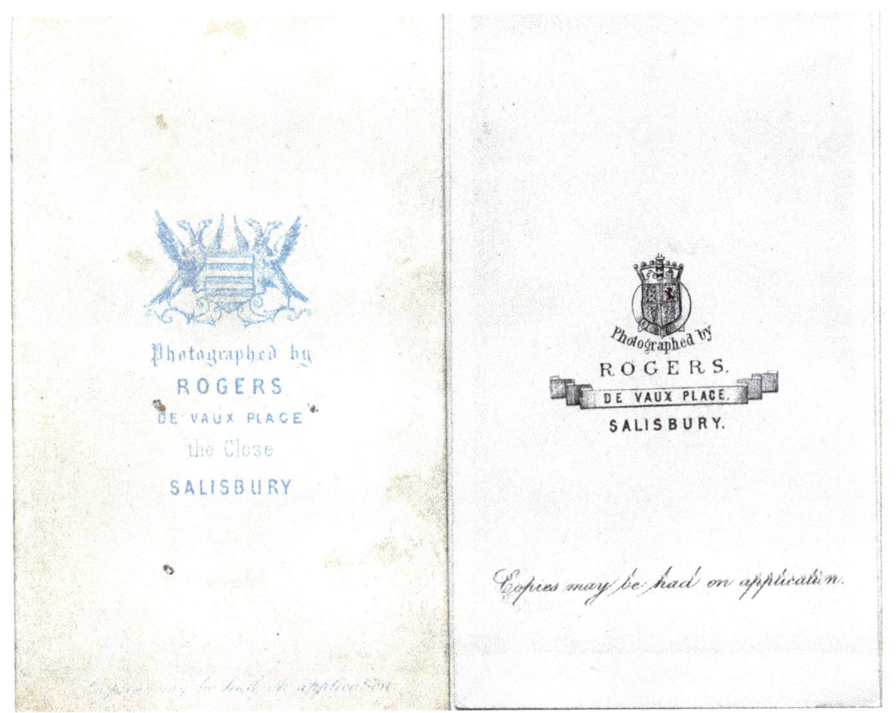

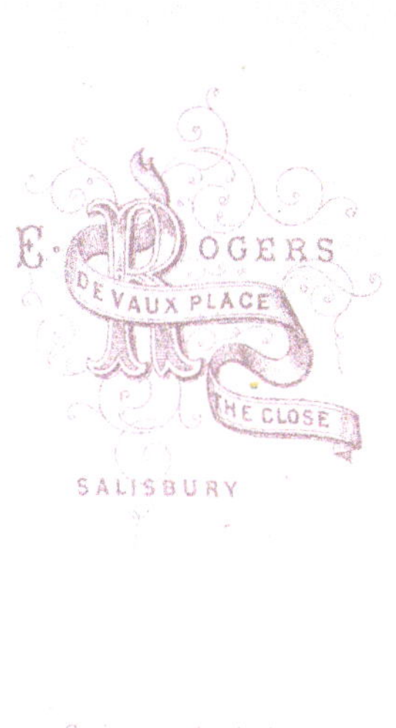

Etiquettes on verso of three Rogers carte de visite. 1860s and 1870s. Carte de visite. Anthony Hamber collection.

is made difficult since the etiquettes on the verso of the carte de visites produced by this commercial photographic studio either refer to "E. Rogers" or just "Rogers", the latter inferring that both Edmund and Mary Ann took photographs.

Frederick Treble (c.1832–1915)

14 Catherine Street, 1862.
High Street, 1865.

TREBLE WAS BORN in Paddington, London, the son of artist Benjamin Treble and his wife Eliza.

When Treble started his professional career as a photographer is unknown, though this was probably in the second half of the 1850s. He was reported to have gone bankrupt in 1857. Treble worked briefly as a photographer in Catherine Street in 1858 before moving to Yeovil, working as a partner to an artist named John Swatridge. The 1861 census found Frederick Treble and his wife Elizabeth living at 17 Middle Street, Yeovil. He was described as an "artist in painting. Practicing photography."

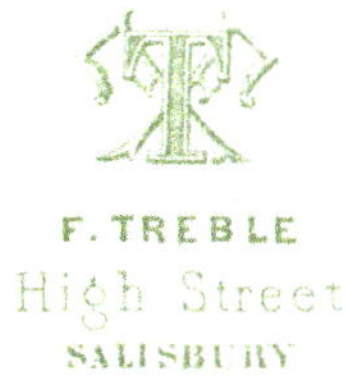

Etiquette of Frederick Treble. Verso of carte de visite. Early 1862–1865.
Anthony Hamber collection.

An advertisement in the *SJ* in April 1862 noted that Treble was a photographer and miniature portraitist and his premises were next to Mr Beach's Cutlery Establishment, located in Catherine Street. (*SJ*, Saturday 12th April 1862 p. 5.) with a note that the establishment appears to have opened on the 5th April. Treble stated he would take "Large Views of Gentlemen's Residences" and "Stereoscopic Portraits."

In June 1863 Treble advertised a "Series of Photographic Views of Wilton House and Grounds" and in September 1864 he took two views of a fete held at Wilton Park.[19]

In 1865 Treble moved from Catherine Street to the High Street, taking out a three year lease on a property until 1868 for which he paid £37 per annum.

In 1867 Treble's photographs of the interior and exterior of Salisbury Cathedral taken using J. H. Dallmeyer's new wide-angled rectilinear lens

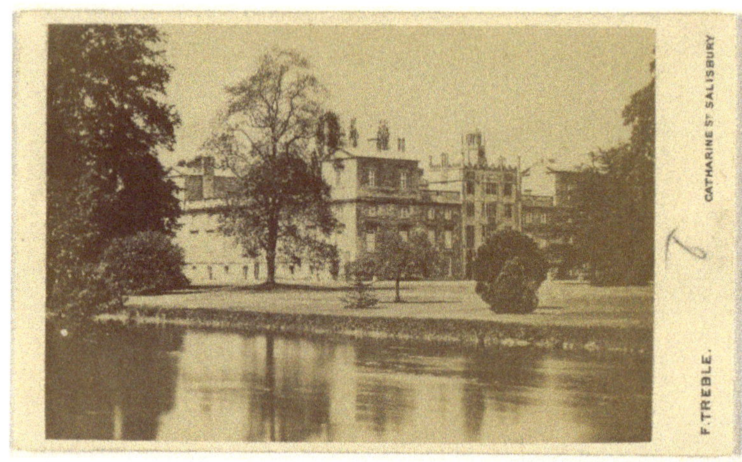

Frederick Treble. View of Wilton House from across the Nadder river. 1863. Carte de visite. Albumen print. The J. Paul Getty Museum 84.XD.1157.1069.

was noted in an article by Dallmeyer in the *British Journal of Photography* (*BJP*, 21st June 1867 p. 291.) These had been exhibited at an ordinary monthly meeting of the Photographic Society of London (later the Royal Photographic Society) held on the 11th June 1867. (*The Photographic Journal*, 15th June 1867 p. 54.) Treble must have been well connected to have had his photographs exhibited at such a prestigious gathering.

Carte de visite format images are known of some of these images, one having on its verso a printed credit to "Mr. F. Treble, Artist". This is a curious description of Treble's profession since it seems to imply that his primary profession was as an artist, rather than a photographer. He listed as "Artist & Photographer" in *Kelly's Directory for Wiltshire* for 1867, presumably compiled in 1866.

As mentioned previously, Treble also ventured out to Stonehenge and took a number of views of the monument which he published in carte de visite, and perhaps larger, formats. It has yet to be established how far from Salisbury Treble ventured to take photographs.

Treble left Salisbury in the autumn of 1867 though it is unclear whether this was the result of competition from other photographers. He placed an advertisement (*SJ*, Saturday 26th October 1867 p. 5.) stating that all correspondence should be addressed to 21 White Rock Place, Hastings.

In December 1867 Treble advertised in the *SJ* that ladies and gentlemen whose portrait he had taken might "possess themselves of the negatives on moderate terms", seemingly announcing that he had already left Salisbury. It also referred to a Mr Cupper, who would "undertake the printing from any of Mr. Treble's negatives." Immediately below Treble's advertisement, Edmund Rogers advertised that he would be happy to print copies from Treble's negatives. (*SJ*, Saturday 14th December 1867 p. 4.)

Treble appears to have sold his Salisbury negatives, and these may have been acquired either by Edwin Macy, who had previously worked for Treble, or Edmund Rogers. [q.q.v.]

However, in March 1871, Elizabeth, Treble's wife, previously referred to as a "Professor of Music and Language", had to return to Salisbury to defend a court case regarding Treble's alleged overcharging for some carte de visite photographs. She won the case and was awarded 35s. costs since she had to travel from Hastings and the judge considered the round trip would have taken 3 days.

Treble continued to describe himself as a photographic artist. He is cited as also operating studios in Nottingham, Yeovil, Hastings, London, Brighton and Norwich during his career.[20]

J. F. Hassett (actually John Frederick Blenner-Hassett) (1834–1904)

Robert Rhoades, Gun-maker, Market Place, 1864 – a temporary studio.

Hassett ran two studios in London, one at 62 Upper Street, Islington and another at his home address, 1A Vernon Street, Pentonville. He

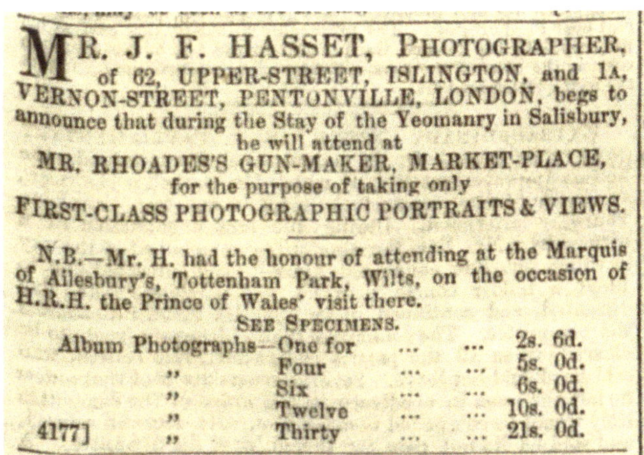

MR. J. F. HASSET, PHOTOGRAPHER, of 62, UPPER-STREET, ISLINGTON, and 1A, VERNON-STREET, PENTONVILLE, LONDON, begs to announce that during the Stay of the Yeomanry in Salisbury, he will attend at
MR. RHOADES'S GUN-MAKER, MARKET-PLACE,
for the purpose of taking only
FIRST-CLASS PHOTOGRAPHIC PORTRAITS & VIEWS.

N.B.—Mr. H. had the honour of attending at the Marquis of Ailesbury's, Tottenham Park, Wilts, on the occasion of H.R.H. the Prince of Wales' visit there.

SEE SPECIMENS.

Album Photographs—One for	... ...	2s. 6d.
" Four	... ...	5s. 0d.
" Six	... ...	6s. 0d.
" Twelve	... ...	10s. 0d.
4177] " Thirty	... ...	21s. 0d.

J. F. Hasset advertisement. *Salisbury Journal*, Saturday 7th May 1864 p. 5.

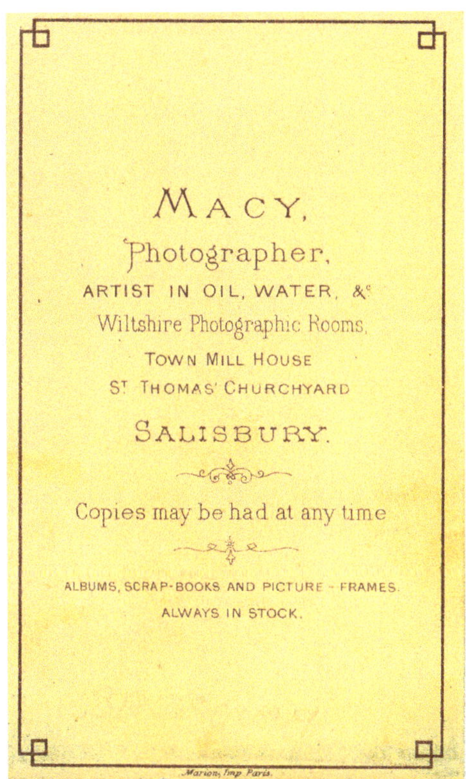

Etiquette of Edwin Macy. Verso of a carte de visite. 1864–1865. Anthony Hamber collection.

advertised in May 1864 that he would be taking "first-class portraits and views" based at Robert Rhoades (died 1866), the gun-maker in the Market Place, during the stay of the Yeomanry in Salisbury. He also noted that he had "had the honour of attending at the Marquis of Ailesbury's, Tottenham Park, Wilts , on the occasion of H. R. H. the Prince of Wales' visit there." (*SJ*, Saturday 7th May 1864 p. 5.)

Such a visit from a professional photographer from outside Salisbury was unusual for this date.

Edwin Horatio Macy (c.1834–1926)

Wiltshire Photographic Rooms, Town Mill House, St. Thomas, 1864 to 1881.

MACY WAS BORN in Whitechapel in London. He appears to have arrived in Salisbury in the early 1860s, possibly to work in the studio of Frederick Treble, who had set up a studio in Catherine Street in the spring of 1862.

Macy claimed to have been the "late operator and sole printer for Mr. Treble." (*SJ*, Saturday 9th July 1864 p. 4.) However, in the summer of 1864 he set up his first establishment, the Wiltshire Photographic Rooms at Town Mill House, St. Thomas Churchyard. This he stated had been "specially adapted for children and dull

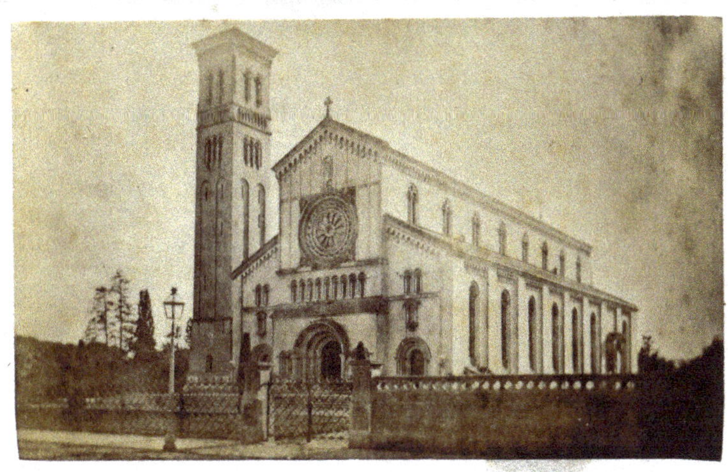

Edwin Macy. Exterior view of St Mary and St Nicholas, Wilton.1870s. Carte de visite. Albumen print. Anthony Hamber collection.

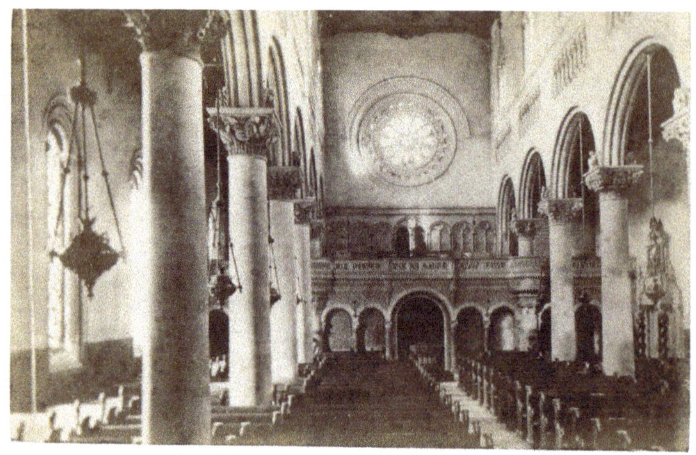

Edwin Macy. Interior view of St Mary and St Nicholas, Wilton.1870s. Carte de visite. Albumen print. Anthony Hamber collection.

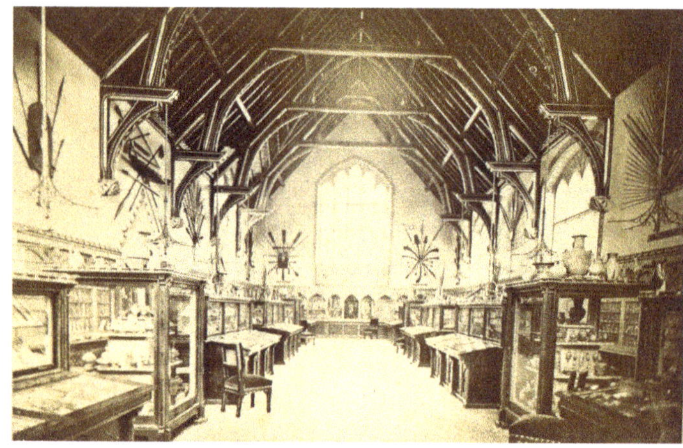

Edwin Macy. Interior view of the Blackmore Museum, Salisbury. 1870s. Carte de visite. Albumen print. Anthony Hamber collection.

weather." He offered to print for amateur and the professional photographers. By December 1864 he was advertising that he had "discovered a chemical that enables him to take photographs in one-fourth the usual time." And this coupled to "the reduction in the price of photographic materials" enabled him to take photographs "at greatly reduced charges." (*SJ*, Saturday 17th December 1864 p. 4.)

During the 1870s Macy published a number of carte de visites of Salisbury Cathedral, and exterior and interior views of the Church of St. Mary and St. Nicholas in Wilton. He also published an interior view of the Blackmore Museum.

Macy married Rosina Louisa, third and only surviving daughter of John Coombs of Minster Street, on 18th December 1864 at St. Thomas' Church (*SJ*, Saturday 24th December 1864 p. 8.)

In 1877 his advertisement in the *SJ* referred to him as an "Artist, Photographer, Picture Dealer and Picture Frame Maker." (*SJ*, Saturday 29th December 1877 p. 5.)

In the 1881 census Macy was still resident in Mill Yard House with an occupation of an "Artist Photographer". By 1891 he had moved to 21 High Street and was a fancy goods dealer.

In 1901 Macy was listed as a shopkeeper and in 1912 he was listed as a subscriber to Charles Haskins' *The Ancient Trade Guilds and Companies of Salisbury* published in that year. His address is given as 21 High Street.

In the 1911 census Macy was described as running an artists' suppliers and fancy goods shop.

Edwin Macy died in 1926.

Charles Pembroke Gearing (b. 1820)

Photographic Gallery, High Street, 1865.

London and Parisian Portrait Rooms, High Street, 1866

PHOTOGRAPHIC GALLERY, HIGH STREET, (Two Doors from Mitre Corner), SALISBURY.

MR. GEARING, from REGENT-STREET, London, begs to announce that he has ELEGANTLY FITTED-UP the above GALLERY with every requisite for the production of FIRST-CLASS PORTRAITS in every branch of the Art, including the New Beautiful Process of PRINTING on OPAL GLASS. [1575

Prices as Moderate as First-class Photography will permit.

Charles Gearing advertisement, *Salisbury Journal*, Saturday 14th October 1865 p. 4.

LITTLE HAS BEEN established about Gearing and his career in Salisbury. He advertised the opening of his studio on the High Street "Two Doors from Mitre Corner" in the *SJ* in October 1865 (*SJ*, Saturday 14th October, 1865 p. 4.) in which he claimed he was from "Regent-Street, London", though there is no record on the PhotoLondon web site http://www.photolondon.org.uk probably indicating that he had worked as an assistant or camera operator in a larger Regent Street studio. He appears to have been living in Beresford Street, Lambeth in 1861.

In May 1866 he advertised in the *SJ* his premises as the "London and Parisian Portrait Rooms" and also "attends personally to take Portraits at the Residences of Invalids or others who are unable to bear the fatigue of a Journey to his Studio." He also offered to photograph "Noblemen's and gentlemen's Mansions and Seats" on moderate terms. (*SJ*, Saturday 12th May 1866 p. 5.)

It has yet to be established when Gearing closed his studio, and he is recorded as a photographer in Cheshire in 1871.

J. E. Nevill

High Street, 1865.

DESCRIBED AS A "photographic artist" on the back of his carte de visite, and also in the 1865 *Harrod's Postal and Commercial Directory of Wiltshire.* Nevill was listed in the *Kelly's Directory for Wiltshire*

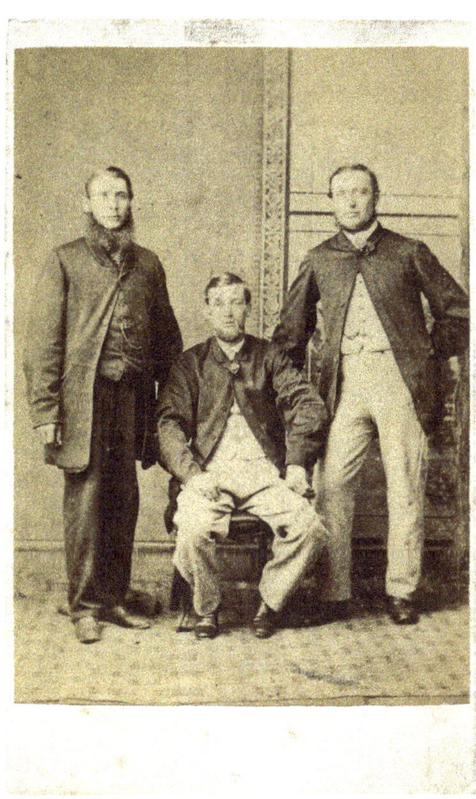

J. E. Nevill. Portrait of three men. 1865–1867. Carte de visite. Albumen print. Anthony Hamber collection.

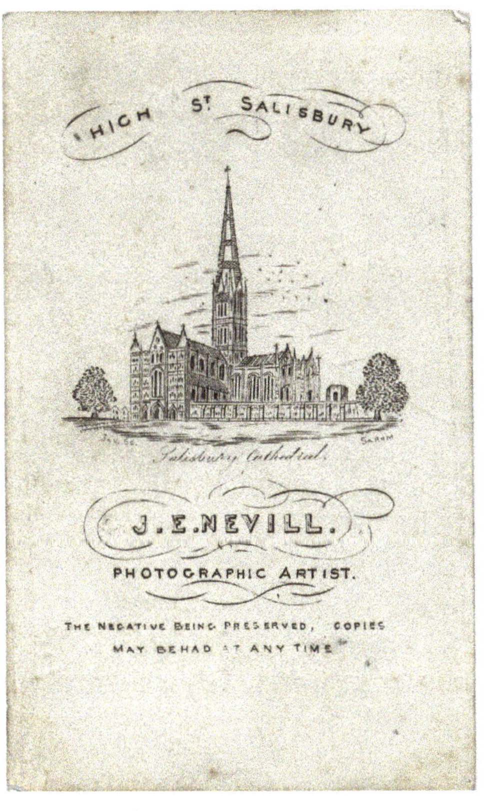

Etiquette on verso of J. E. Nevill. Portrait of three men. 1865–1867. Carte de visite. Albumen print. Anthony Hamber collection.

for 1867.

Little more has been found about Nevill. He is not recorded in the 1861 census for Salisbury and did not advertise in the *SJ* during this period.

Edward Leman (1827–1894)

Harnham Studio, Harnham Bridge in 1865.

Harnham Bridge & Queen Street, 1867 [*Kelly's* 1867]

13 St Ann Street, 1871.

IN 1861 EDWARD Leman was listed as a photographic artists living in St. Pancras, London. He operated two studios in Camden town until 1864 when he presumably moved to Salisbury.

In a very basic advertisement, Leman introduced his Harnham Photographic Studio, next to Harnham Bridge, in the *SJ* in April 1865 (*SJ*, Saturday 8th April 1865 p. 5.), his "Superior" carte de visite portraits costing six shilling per dozen.

In the 1871 census Leman is recorded as an "Artist Photographer" living at 12 St. Ann Street with his wife Mary and five children. In this year he unsuccessfully applied to be the Clerk of the Salisbury School Board.

By 1881 he had returned to London and was living in Camberwell and then moved to Battersea.

Samuel Parker (1839–1897)

Bridge Street, 1868.

PRESUMABLY THE SAME S. Parker who had been a partner of Witcomb & Parker at the same Bridge Street address. S. Parker ran a wholesale and retail tobacconists from premises in Catherine Street and Bridge Street.

Parker's Photographic Studio was opposite the Judge's Chambers in Bridge Street. He advertised it in the *ST* in March 1868.

Arthur Foley (1831–1894)

Fisherton Cabinet Works, 39–43 Fisherton Street, 1870s to 1890s.

ARTHUR FOLEY & Son, cabinet maker and furniture manufacturer of the Fisherton Machine Cabinet Works. On 9th February 1870

BY ROYAL LETTERS PATENT.

SPECIMENS of FOLEY'S New Patented Process for PRINTING PHOTOGRAPHIC PRODUCTIONS on Wood, for Cabinet Work, and Fancy Wood Articles, may be seen as applied to Cabinet Furniture, at ARTHUR FOLEY'S, PATENTEE and MANUFACTURER, *FISHERTON CABINET WORKS, SALISBURY,* and in the Fine Arts Furniture Court at the International 274] Exhibition (Catalogue No. 3130, C).

Arthur Foley advertisement. *Salisbury Journal*, Saturday 12th August 1871 p. 5.

Foley was issued Letters Patent (No. 3843) for "Improvements in the production of photographic pictures or designs on veneers and solid woods." Specimens were available for inspection at his Fisherton Street works. He exhibited a ladies' toilet table and a canopy bedstead, containing panels of his recently patented photographic pictures on wood at the 1871 International Exhibition in London. In 1873 he sent a lady's boudoir table designed by H. Dickenson to the International Exhibition being held in Vienna.

H. Foley (fl. 1875)

86 Fisherton Street

FISHERTON GAOL.—A Series of VIEWS of the INTERIOR, which have been recently taken, can be obtained for [1661
1/- Single Large Copy, and 6d. Small, or 7 Various Ones for 6/- and 3/-,
at H. Foley's, Photographer, 86, Fisherton-street, Salisbury.

H. Foley advertisement. *Salisbury Journal*, Saturday 10th July 1875 p. 8.

POSSIBLY HENRY FOLEY, brother of Arthur Foley [q.v.], cited in the 1871 and 1881 census as an "upholsterer" by profession

In July 1875 Foley advertised a series of recently taken views of the interior of Fisherton Gaol, which was in the process of being sold. [21] These cost 1s. for a single large copy, and 6d. for a small copy, or 7 various ones for 6s. and 3s.[21] Foley was probably an amateur photographer and does not seem to have operated as a commercial photographer past this date.

Alfred Dunmore

Wilton Road, 1875.

117a Fisherton Street 1877 ("New Studio and Fancy

Repository" advertisement in *ST*, Saturday 24th March 1877 p. 4.)

The Poplars, London Road, 1880.

IMPORTANT NOTICE.

MR. ALFRED DUNMORE, ARTISTIC LANDSCAPE, PORTRAIT AND ARCHITECTURAL PHOTOGRAPHER (Licensee for the Permanent Carbon Process), begs to thank the Public generally for the liberal support accorded him since his commencing business in Salisbury, and to inform them that he is now prepared to execute every description of OUT-DOOR PHOTOGRAPHY in Town or Country, at moderate charges for first-class work. *Satisfaction guaranteed.*

THE POPLARS,

LONDON-ROAD, SALISBURY. [1974

Alfred Dunmore advertisement, *Salisbury Journal*, Saturday 2nd August 1879 p. 5.

In 1878 described as an artist, photographer, fancy repository and licensee for the new patent Carbon photograph.

It has yet to be established when Dunmore opened his first studio and how long he operated for in Salisbury. He advertised in both the *SJ* and the *ST*.

In August 1879 Dunmore was located at The Poplars on the London Road and was describing himself as an "Artistic Landscape, Portrait and Architectural photographer" with a license for the Permanent Carbon Process. He appears to at this point be pushing his services for "every description of Out-Door Photography in Town or Country", perhaps finding commercial portraiture too competitive.

Mary Ann [Marianne] Rogers (1828–1911)

De Vaux Place, The Close, c.1870–1899.

The wife, then widow of Edmund Rogers. In the 1861 census, Mary Ann was listed as a schoolmistress. In July 1868 Marianne advertised that she wished to open a school at their home in July 1868. Whether this reflected Edmund's business falling on harder times as a result of the economic recession between 1867 and 1869 brought about by the impact on exports due to the American recession post-civil war is unclear.

The 1871 census provides the following information about Edmund and Marianne from the Harnham Bridge Road District 4 Salisbury who were living in De Vaux Place.

Edmund Rogers, Head, 43, Photographer, b Salisbury
Marianne Rogers, Wife, 43, Photographer's wife b Oxfordshire
Edith Rogers, daughter, 9, b East Harnham
Charles Rogers, son, 7, b —
Florence M. Rogers, daughter, 6, b Salisbury
Annie Rogers, daughter, 4, b Salisbury

It is likely that Marianne Rogers had assisted her husband in running his photographic business during the 1860s. Yet it remains significant that she gave her profession as a "photographer" in the 1871 census, indicating that she took photographs, rather than operated in processing and printing the negatives taken by her husband. Edmund died in 1871, though Marianne was recorded in the 1881 census, still listing her profession as "photographer"

GREAT ATTRACTION!

AN OPPORTUNITY NOT TO BE LOST!!!

NOW SELLING OFF at ROGER'S Photographic Establishment, De Vaux House, the Close, Salisbury, 100,000 PORTRAITS AT ONE PENNY EACH. [706

Rogers advertisement for sale of carte de visite stock. *Salisbury Times*, 29th April 1876 p. 4.

and was listed as such in Kelly's Directory for 1880 and 1889.

However, in the 29th April 1876 issue of the *ST* Rogers had advertised the sale of his stock of some 100,000 portraits – presumably carte de visite – that were being offered at one penny each.

Mary Ann appears to have had a long career as a photographer, though no advertisement for her commercial services have been found in the *SJ* or *ST* during the 1880s. However, when she was recorded as a visitor in the Southampton suburb of Millbrook in the 1891 census, she still listed her profession as a photographer. She was also listed as a photographer in the 1898 *Kelly's Directory for Wiltshire.* The 1901 census recorded Mary Ann, aged 73, still living in De Vaux Place, though she seems to have retired. Her profession was recorded as managing "let apartments", together with one of her daughters, Edith. A decade later the 1911

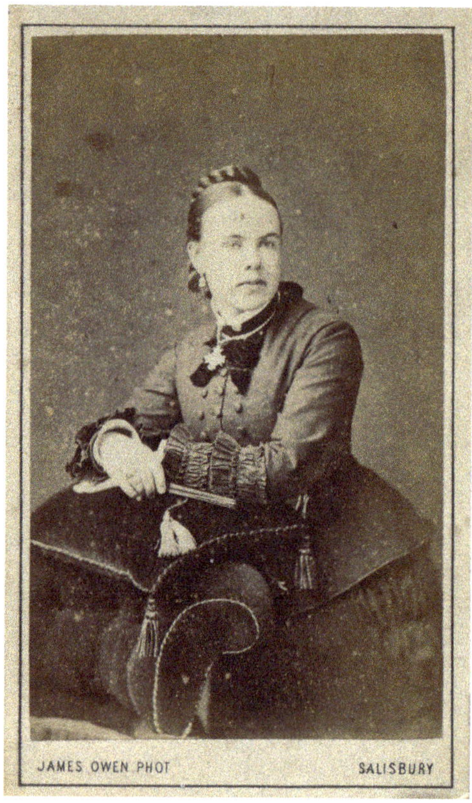

James Owen. Portrait of a Woman. c. 1880. Carte de visite. Albumen print. Anthony Hamber collection.

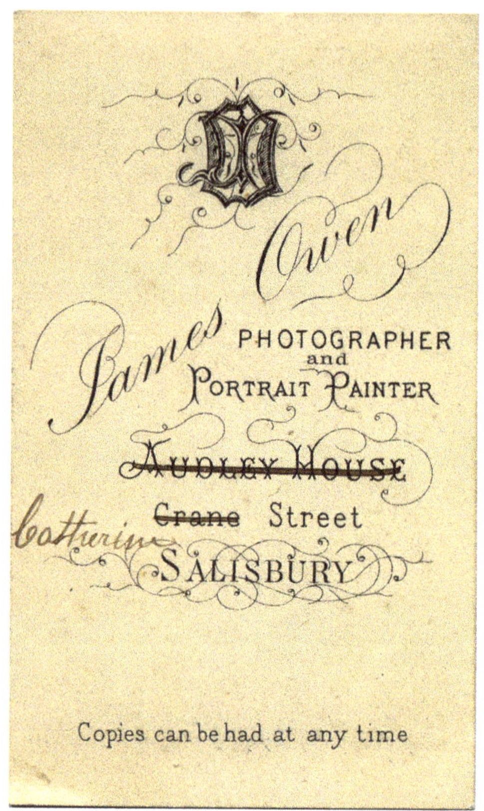

Etiquette of James Owen for his Crane Street studio. Verso of Portrait of a woman. carte de visite. Anthony Hamber collection.

census recorded she was still living in De Vaux Place with her three spinster daughters who were running a school in the house. No profession is recorded for Mary Ann who is simply described as a widow. Mary Ann died in the same year.

James Owen (1848–1903)

The Studio, Audley House, Crane Street 1876.
29 Catherine Street, 1878–1903.

IN 1871 OWEN was listed as a photographer living as a boarder at 34 South Grove, Camberwell, south London. He advertised as a "photographer and portrait painter" in the *ST* issue of Saturday 21st October 1876 (p. 4.) that his studio in Audley House, Crane Street would be "open in a few days." The advertisement also stated "For many years Principal Operator to Messrs. Adams and Stilliard of Southampton." One presumes that he moved to Southampton from London in the early 1870s. Adams & Stilliard had been operating the South of England Photographic Institution at 9 Bernard Street, Southampton from the early 1860s, both having worked as camera operators in the studio of one of the earliest photographer's in Southampton, Samuel Wiseman (1831–1914).

Owen gave details of his studio that included a private dressing room for ladies, and a lady attendant in the reception room; and "is also admirably adapted for photographing children." He also stated that "the chemical room is quite away from the studio, thus preventing any unpleasant odour from chemicals, which is so often a cause of complaint from visitors to photographic studios."[22]

Described as a portrait painter and photographer in 1878. In that year he advertised a portrait of George Moberly, the Bishop of Salisbury; 1s for a carte de visite, 2s 6d. for a Cabinet. Owen advertised that he would take photographs from nine until dusk, daily.

By 1881 he was living at 64 Brown Street. This was listed as the studio of Mrs. Owen in 1897.

In the 1891 census James (aged 42) and his wife Sarah (36) and their eight sons were living at Domini House on the London Road.

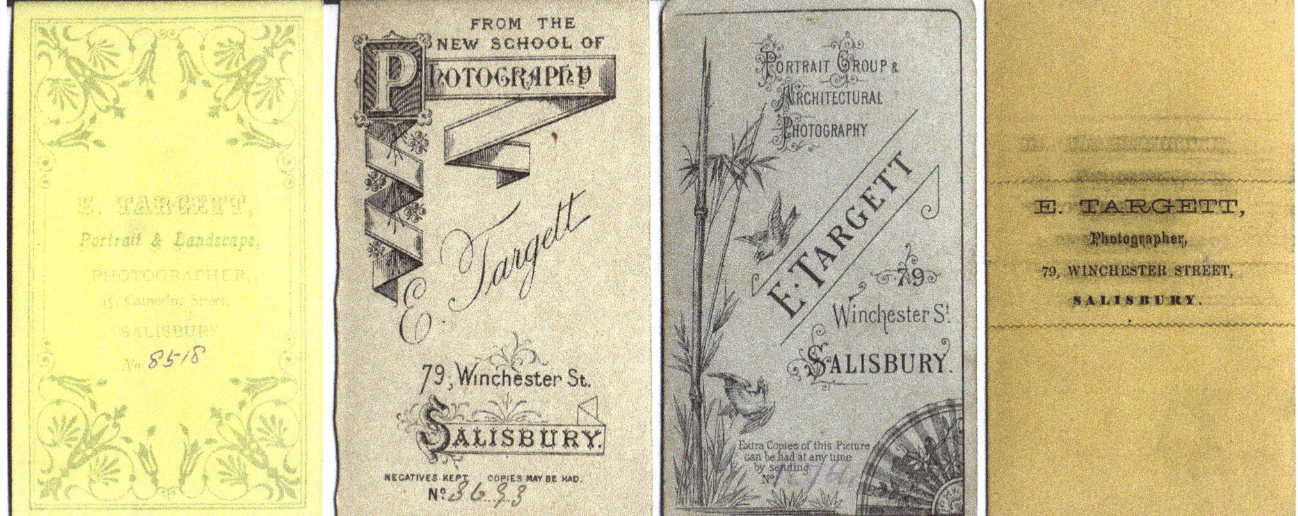

Edwin Target etiquettes on verso of four carte de visites. Anthony Hamber collection.

Edwin John Targett (c.1850 – after 1909)

79 Winchester Street, 1875–1911.
43 Catherine Street, 1880–1885.
29 Winchester Street, 1899.

NOTICE OF REMOVAL.

E. TARGETT,

PORTRAIT AND LANDSCAPE PHOTOGRAPHER AND PICTURE FRAME MANUFACTURER,

BEGS to inform his numerous Patrons and the Inhabitants of Salisbury and Neighbourhood, that he has now removed to more central premises,

45, CATHERINE STREET, SALISBURY,

Where he has erected a spacious Studio, replete with every requisite for the production of the highest class Portraiture, and hopes by sending out nothing but the best work to merit a continuance of their patronage and support.

12 Copies, 5s. 6 Copies, 3s. 3 Copies, 1s. 6d.

Wedding and Family Groups and Gentlemen's Residences Photographed on the shortest notice.

Enlargements to Life Size, coloured or plain.

E. T. would call special attention to his 30s. Enlargement, which for quality and price defies competition.

All kinds of Photographs, Prints and Drawings Framed and Glazed.

Views of Salisbury and Neighbourhood, and all kinds of Fancy Goods and Stationery always on Sale.

ONE TRIAL SOLICITED.

[1900

Edwin Targett advertisement. *Salisbury Times*, 2nd August 1879 p. 1.

EDWIN TARGETT MAY have been related to the photographer T. G. Targett who left Warminster in 1863, the final auction of his household and shop took place on 7th May, 1863 at Cruse's auction house, Market Place, Warminster. A T. G. Targett was listed as an artist a picture dealer on Blue Boar Row in January 1867. (*SJ*, Saturday 12th January 1867 p. 4.) though he gave up the shop and retired the same year.

However, in 1868 T. G. Targett advertised a photograph of a painting of the Church of St. Andrew, Bemerton – where George Herbert had preached – prior to its restoration. Targett copyrighted this image, and the copyright could be seen at Targett's office at Silverthorn's in the Canal on Tuesday 16th June. Targett also acted as an agent for a photograph of the painting by Henry Leonidas Rolfe (1823–1881) – the socalled "Landseer among fishes" – of the "Freshwater Fishes of Great Britain." Copies cost one guinea uncoloured; £2 12s. 6d. tinted in watercolours; £4 14s. 6d. highly finished in tinted watercolours; and additional 20s. 6d. if framed. Every photograph would be signed by the artist "to prevent piracy." (*SJ*, Saturday 15th June 1868 p. 4.)

Edwin Targett was advertising in the *Salisbury Times* during the second half of 1875 that he had "commenced business" at 79 Winchester Street, which he named the "New School of Photography", including supply of the new "cameo vignette" portrait.

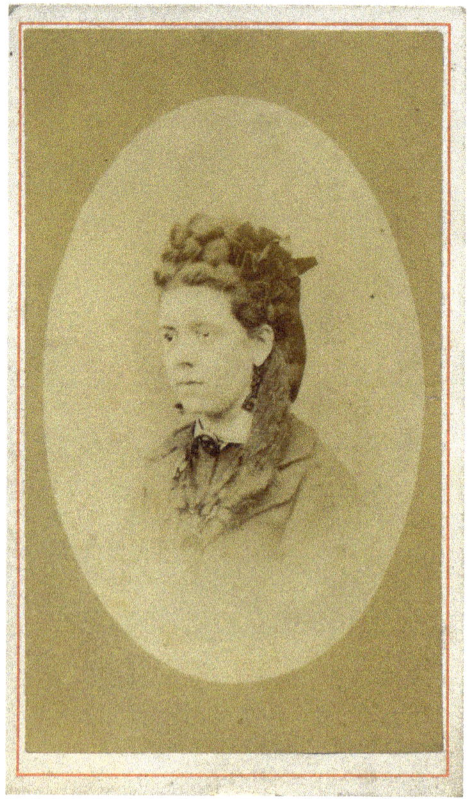

Edward Sanger. Portrait of a woman. Late 1870s. Carte de visite. Albumen print. Anthony Hamber collection.

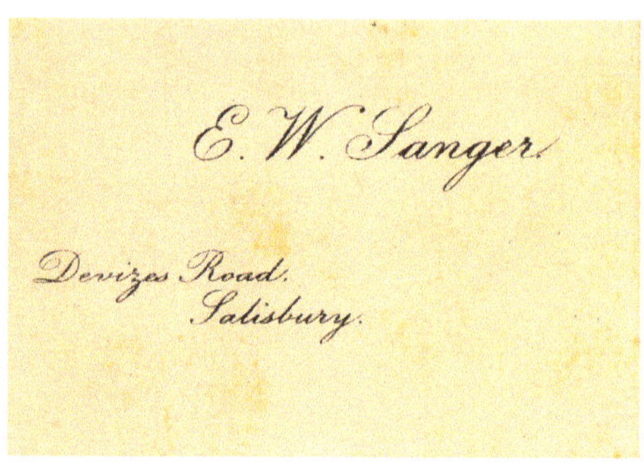

Etiquette of Edward Sanger. Verso of carte de visite. c. 1880. Anthony Hamber collection.

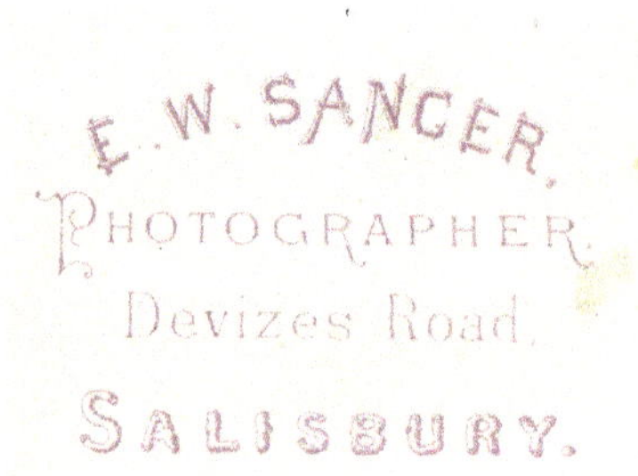

Etiquette of Edward Sanger. Verso of carte de visite. c. 1877. Anthony Hamber collection.

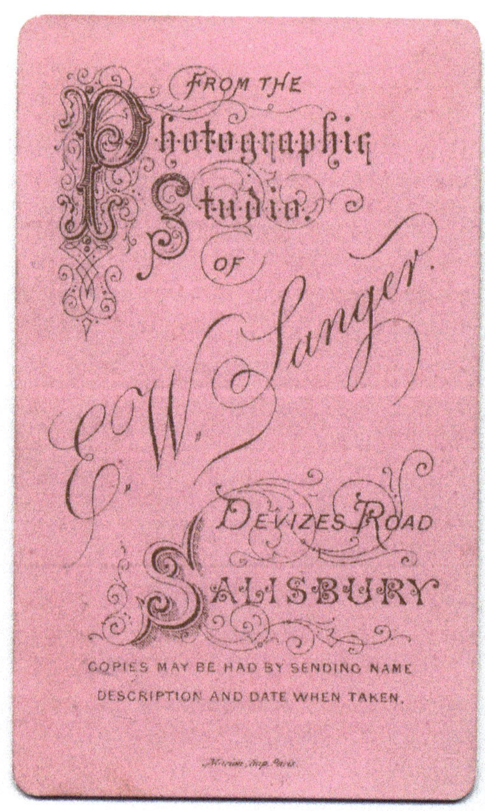

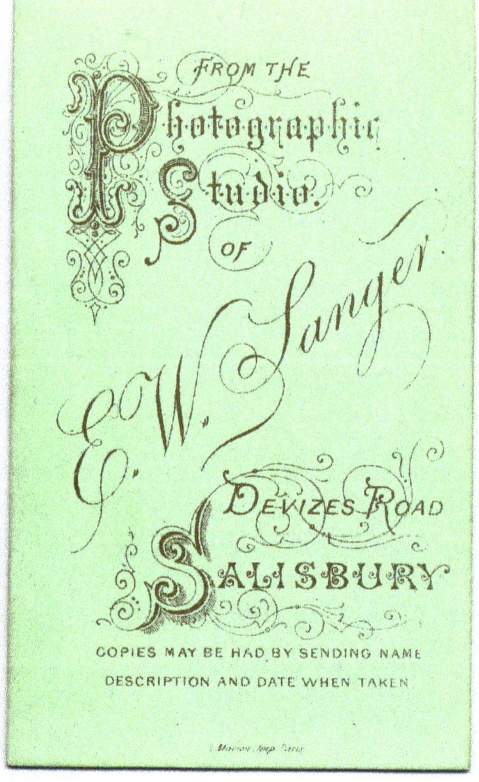

Etiquettes of Edward Sanger. Verso of two carte de visites. 1880s. Anthony Hamber collection.

Edward Wynne Sanger (1849–1883)

Devizes Road, 1877–1885.

SANGER WAS BORN in Lambeth, south London in 1849.

He was described as a photographer and bookbinder in 1877 in advertisements in the *ST*.

In January 1877, Sanger advertised "the only complete series of Photographs of the Floods in Fisherton Street." A series of 24 views costing 10 shillings (or 6d. each) obtainable from his studio in Devizes Road; Mr. Jarratt [q.v.], the Infirmary; or Mr. Hiller, News Office, Fisherton Street.[23]

It has yet to be established when Sanger ceased his commercial photography and he was described as a bookbinder living in Devizes Road in the 1881 census.

Thomas Jarratt

Fisherton Street, 1877.

THOMAS JARRATT, AGED 36, is listed in the 1871 census as a "Dispenser of Medicines" living with his wife Hannah (aged 38) and four children at 66 Milton Place, Fisherton Anger.

That Jarratt was a photographer can be established through his printed credit on the verso of carte de visites in Anthony Hamber collection.

In May 1877 an advertisement appeared in the *ST* for a series of twenty-four view by E. W. Sanger of the floods that had taken place in Fisherton Street. The set cost 10s. and could be had from "Mr. Jarratt, The Infirmary" or "Mr. Hillier, News Office, Fisherton Street".

No other information has been found confirming Jarratt worked as a commercial photographer.

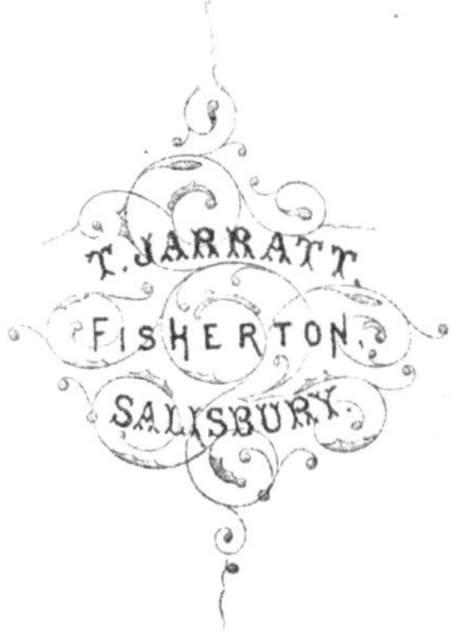

Etiquette on verso of carte de visite of Thomas Jarratt. c. 1877. Anthony Hamber collection.

1 *SJ*, Saturday 9th and 30th August 1856 p. 2. Michael and N. Hanhart were litho printers active during the 1850s and were located at 64 Charlotte St, Fitzroy Square, London.

2 *ST*, Saturday 4th September 1880 p. 1.

3 *ST*, Saturday 22nd September 1877 p. 1.

4 *SJ*, Saturday 31st May 1873 p. 5.

5 The statue was of Sidney Herbert, Baron Herbert of Lea, born 16th September 1810, died 2nd August 1861, who was the only son of the eleventh earl of Pembroke and his second wife. He had a distinguished public career, both nationally and locally. He was elected MP for South Wiltshire in 1832 and held the seat until his ennoblement in 1861 a few months before his death. Among the offices he held were joint Secretary to the Admiralty, 1841–45 and Secretary at War 1845–6, 1852–5 and 1859–61. He was also instrumental in Florence Nightingale's expedition to provide nursing care for the Crimean War. Locally, because the twelfth earl lived abroad, it was his half-brother who lived in and maintained Wilton House. His contributions to local life and society included the building of the Italianate parish church in Wilton, charitable help for clergy families and the founding of a cottage hospital at Charmouth, Dorset. With his wife he founded the Female Emigration Fund in 1849, and in 1859 Herbert was the first president of the National Volunteer Association.

Herbert's statue, by Baron Marochetti, was unveiled by Earl de Grey and Ripon on 29th June 1863 before an audience of thousands. The statue was about 30 feet to the north of the colonnade on the front of the Guildhall, hence almost equidistant between it and the War Memorial: just how short the space was between Guildhall, statue and memorial is evident from a photograph of VE-Day celebrations published in Newman and Howells' *Salisbury past*, and that gives the clue as to why the statue came to be moved.

The City Council decided in principle in November 1952 that the statue would have to be moved in the course of preparations for Coronation celebrations. On that occasion, Alderman E.J. Case, chairman of the City Lands Committee argued that removing the statue would give more space in front of the Guildhall for civic and state occasions. An alternative to Victoria Park was a location in the grounds of the Council House. Alderman Wort argued strenuously against the removal expenditure of £110, but the decision in favour was carried by 18 votes to 7, and the statue was moved on Tuesday 12th May 1953. See http://history.wiltshire.gov.uk/community/getfaq.php?id=435

6 *ST*, Friday 24th December 1880 p. 5.

7 *SJ*, Saturday 15th July 1876 p. 5. The Lambertype was a method of retouching negatives and positives invented by Claude Leon Lambert of Paris. Lambert's produced his own version of the carbon process which he christened "Chromotype".

8 *op. cit*, p. 8.

9 Although he was listed as an underwriter at Lloyds, Parkyns was also an inventor and in 1881 showed his steam driven tricycle at the 1881 Stanley Club Show at The Athenaeum in London's Camden Road.

10 *The Times*, Saturday 20th October 1877 p. 4.

11 *British Journal of Photography*, 4th February 1876 p. 50.

12 *SJ*, Saturday 14th September 1878 p. 4. Advertisement by Winstanley & Godwin of the auction of elements of Parkyns estate and household furniture.

13 *ST*, Saturday 11th November 1876 p. 1. The Lambertype and Chromotype were carbon print processes. The Lambertype was an enlargement, and had an enamelled surface, while the Chromotype was a contact print. The Contratype (or Contretype) was a process of producing a coloured, laterally corrected, copy negative from an original negative.

14 *SJ*, Saturday 25th August 1877 p. 5. It is unclear who the Court photographer may have been but Queen Victoria employed the firm of Hughes and Mullins, based in Ryde near Osborne House, on the Isle of Wight, to undertake the copying work and printing of carbon photographs that were then pasted over the original photographic print.

15 *SJ*, Saturday 13th June 1863 p. 5 and *SJ*, Saturday 12th May 1877 p. 5.

16 *ST*, Saturday 2nd March 1878 p. 1.

17 Hamilton, as with other prominent members of Salisbury society, had his portrait taken by leading London photographers. In Hamilton's case this included Mason & Co. of Old Bond Street and Mayall of Regent Street.

18 See Anthony Hamber, "Women and Early Photography in Salisbury", *Sarum Chronicle 17*, Salisbury, 2017 pp. 116–128 and see https://lynnswaffles.com/2016/09/12/salisbury-victorian-photographer-edmund-rogers/

19 *SJ*, Saturday 24th September 1864 p. 5.

20 See http://freepages.genealogy.rootsweb.ancestry.com/~brett/photos/emtreble.html

21 *SJ*, Saturday 10th July 1875 p. 8.

22 *ST*, Saturday 16th December 1876 p. 1.

23 *ST*, Saturday 13th January 1877 p.4. There was a note in the Local News section of this issue referring to this set of photographs "obtained at a cheap rate" and Sanger's advertisement. (p.5).

APPENDIX 3 – PHOTOGRAPHY PRICES

THIS APPENDIX EXAMINES the change in prices charged by photographers in Salisbury from the 1850s to the late 1870s, and the prices of photographs on sale through outlets such as bookshops and print sellers. The former is taken from advertisements in Salisbury newspapers, while the latter uses the advertisements within the front covers of the range of handbooks and guidebooks published by Brown & co. of the Canal.

Photographic Portraiture

ESTABLISHING THE SPECIFICS of the commercial market for photography in Salisbury during the period 1855 to 1880 relies almost exclusively in the advertisements place by photographers in local newspapers. References to prices are, however, sporadic and limited. Prices sheets were available at the photographers and there may well have been "deals" done at the studio.

The table gives an indicative overview of the prices charged by commercial photographers in Salisbury for photographic portraits, primarily in the carte de visite format.

YEAR	PHOTOGRAPHER	PRICES	SOURCE - SJ or ST
1855	Shoosmith	2s. 6d. for a framed Daguerreotype portrait "Great Reduction in the Price of Photography" – also coloured collodion portraits	*SJ*, 4th August 1855 p. 2.
1856	Witcomb	One shilling for a collodion portrait	*SJ*, 29th March 1856 p. 2
1864	Witcomb & Parker	Carte de visite. 1 copy 1s. 3 copies 2s. 6d. 6 copies 4s. 6d. 12 copies 7s. 6d. Glass portraits from 1s. each.	*SJ*, 22nd October 1864 p. 4.
1876	Owen	Carte de visite. Two positions. 6s. per dozen.	*ST*, 30th December 1876 p. 1.
1877	Witcomb	Carte de visite. Two positions, any style 5s. per dozen.	*ST*, 20th January 1877 p. 8.
1878	Edwards	Carte de visite 12 copies – 5s. "two position if required."	*ST*, Saturday 6th July 1878 p. 1.
1878	Owen	Portrait of Bishop of Salisbury. Carte de visite 1s. Cabinet 2s. 6d.	*SJ*, Saturday 31st August 1878 p. 5.
1879	Miell (no opposite South Western Railway Station)	Carte de visite 12 copies – 5s. 6 copies – 3s. 3 copies – 1s 6d.	*ST*, 22nd February 1879 p. 4.

The competitive nature of commercial photography in Salisbury was, to some degree, accelerated by the reduction in the price of photographic materials. By 1864 Macy was advertising in the *SJ* that "on account of the reduction in the price of photographic materials, he is now able to take photographs at a greatly reduced charge." (*SJ*, 22nd October 1864 p. 4.) Significantly, he did not publish these reduce charges in the columns of the *SJ*.

There were sudden drops in trade prices of photographic materials. One instance took place In June 1871 when the Hill Norris Patent Dry Plate Company reduced the price of its dry collodion plates by 15 to 20 percent. This helped dry plate negatives to overtake the use of wet collodion glass plate negatives.

Commercial Photograph Prices

These details are representative only of the stock of Brown & Co. of the Canal.

What is significant, is that as late as 1866 Brown & Co. was still advertising on the inside covers of his guide and handbooks the same range of tinted lithographs, copper engravings as he had a decade previously. His prices for photographs had also not changed. This seems to indicate Brown & Co. considered that traditional prints represented an important part of its business.

YEAR	PHOTOGRAPHERS	FORMAT	PRICE
1857	Fenton, Sedgfield, and others	Not specified	From 10s 6d. downwards
1857	Sedgfield, Wilson &c.	Stereographs	1s. and 1s 6d. each.
1866	Fenton, Sedgfield, and others	Not specified	From 10s 6d. downwards
1866	Sedgfield, Wilson &c.	Stereographs	1s. and 1s 6d. each.
1874	Wormald's Series	20 x 24 inches	14s. unmounted; 15s. mounted
1874	Frith's Panoramic Series	10¼ x 6 ¼ inches	2s. unmounted; 2s. 6d. mounted
1874	Frith's Universal Series	8¼ x 6 ½ inches	1s. 9d. unmounted; 2s. mounted
1874	Frith's Cabinet Series	6¼ x 4 inches	10d. unmounted; 1s. mounted
1874	Sedgfield's Cabinet Series	7½ x 4 inches	10d unmounted; 1s. mounted
1874	Sedgfield	12 x 10 inches	3s. 6d. unmounted; 4s. 6d. mounted.

Fenton's photographs were probably the most expensive on sale at Brown & Co. in 1857. Fenton retired from photography in 1862 and his negatives were purchased by Francis Frith (1822–1898) who later printed some as part of portfolio publications. In 1860 Frith had started a project to photograph every town and village in the United Kingdom. By the late 1860s his photographs were available in a variety of formats and widely commercially available through outlets such as Brown & Co. The Frith Universal Series was international in geographic scope and Frith built commercial relationships with a number of other photographers include Robert Napper (who photographed Andalusia), Frank Mason Good (Egypt) and Frederick William Sutton and Hugo Lewis Pearson (Japan). The Victoria and Albert Museum has a collection of Frith's Universal Series which consists of over 4000 whole-plate albumen prints. Both Frith's Panoramic Series and Cabinet Series were also international in their respective coverage.

Edmund Wormald (b. 1829–) was a Leeds photographer who has set up in Partnership with William Child in July 1856. This partnership ended in 1859 and Wormald continued in business and had a particular interest in buildings and architecture. He may have had some business relationship with the firm of architectural photographers Bedford Lemere & Co, possibly during the 1870s. By the early 1870s Wormald's large format photographic prints of cathedrals were commercially available.

The continued interest in Sedgfield's views of the cathedral and city continued way past the end of this study. One of Sedgfield's stereo views in the author's collection has the stamp of P. H. Thomas, a chemist of 6, High Street, Purton and is dated "28 Oct 1965."

By at least 1874 photographs offered by Brown & Co. had become cheaper than some of the traditional lithographs and copperplate engravings within its stock. However, this is not a like-for-like comparison. Prints by traditional graphic processes have invariably commanded high prices than "mass produced" photographs. Tinted lithographs were a de luxe item with short print runs and commanded still higher prices.

APPENDIX 4 – TIMELINE OF THE EVOLUTION OF PHOTOGRAPHY

1839 – Daguerre introduces his daguerreotype process, based on silver-plated copper sheets. Talbot publicly introduces his photogenic drawing paper-based process.

1841 – Talbot introduces his patented calotype process based on a paper negative from which salted paper positive prints could be made.

1846 – Richard Beard, the patent holder for the daguerreotype in England and Wales, sets up the first commercial photographic studio in Salisbury. It fails immediately.

1847 – Louis Désiré Blanquart-Evrard publishes the albumen photographic print process. From the mid-1850s this became the dominant photographic print process.

1851 – The Great Exhibition held in London's Hyde Park and boosts the progress of photography. The stereoscopic photographic view makes an impact. Frederick Scott Archer introduces the collodion process based on glass photographic negatives.

1853 – Richard Beard's patent for the daguerreotype in England and Wales expires, and the process becomes free to use. Commercial photographers begin to visit and document Salisbury.

1854 – Talbot's patent for the calotype expires and negative-positive process photography becomes free to use. André-Adolphe-Eugène Disdéri credited with introduction of the carte de visite.

1864 – Sir Joseph Wilson Swan patents the carbon permanent photographic print process. Walter Bentley Woodbury patents his Woodburytype photomechanical print process.

1866 – The cabinet card photographic format introduced. There are now **12** commercial photographic studios in Salisbury.

1871 – Dry plate negatives introduced.

1873 – Hermann Wilhelm Vogel discovers dye sensitization enabling photographic emulsions for the first time to be made sensitive to green, yellow and red light.

1878 – Heat ripening of gelatin emulsions is discovered and greatly increases film sensitivity enabling very short "snapshot" exposures.

1895 – Auguste and Louis Lumière credited with the invention of cinematography, a combination camera and projector named the cinématographe.

1896 – Société Pathé Frères founded in Paris, the first commercial cinema newsreel.

1910 – British Pathé founded.

SELECT BIBLIOGRAPHY

Contemporary Newspapers and Periodicals

Salisbury and Winchester Journal
Salisbury Times
Art Journal
Athenaeum
British Journal of Photography
Illustrated London News
Journal of the Photographic Society
Penny Magazine
Photographic News
Saturday Magazine
The Salisbury Guide: giving an account of the antiquities of Old Sarum, and the ancient and present state of New Sarum, or, Salisbury, J. Easton, Salisbury [multiple editions]
Brown's stranger's handbook and illustrated guide to the City of Salisbury, Brown & Co., Salisbury [multiple editions]
Brown's stranger's handbook and illustrated guide to Salisbury Cathedral, Brown & Co., Salisbury [multiple editions]
Kelly's Directory of Hampshire, Wiltshire and Dorsetshire [multiple editions]

Online Resources

The Correspondence of William Henry Fox Talbot – www.foxtalbot.dmu.ac.uk
The William Henry Fox Talbot Catalogue Raisonné – http://foxtalbot.bodleian.ox.ac.uk/
The William Henry Fox Talbot Catalogue Raisonné Blog – http://foxtalbot.bodleian.ox.ac.uk/blog/
Photographic Exhibitions in Britain 1839–1865 – www.peib.dmu.ac.uk
Journal of the Photographic Society – www.archive.rps.org
Daguerreobase – www.daguerreobase.org
Midley History of Early Photography – www.midley.co.uk
The Daguerreotype: An Archive of Source Texts, Graphics, and Ephemera – www.daguerreotypearchive.org
The Database of 19th Century Photographers and Allied Trades in London: 1841–1901 – www.photolondon.org.uk
Sussex PhotoHistory – www.photohistory-sussex.co.uk
Queen Victoria's Journals – www.queenvictoriasjournals.org
The Times Digital 1785–1985 – www.gale.cengage.co.uk/times.aspx
British Newspaper Archive – www.britishnewspaperarchive.co.uk
www.jstor.org
www.ancestry.co.uk
www.archive.org

Secondary Sources

Adamson, Keith. "Early Provincial Studios". *The Photographic Journal*, Vol. 127, No. 2, February 1987, pp. 74–78.
Adamson, Keith. "More Early Studios [Part 1]". *The Photographic Journal*, Vol. 128, No. 1, January 1988 pp. 32–36.
Adamson, Keith. "More Early Studios [Part 2]". *The Photographic Journal* Vol. 128, No. 7, July 1988 pp. 305–309.
Ansell, Robin (with Allan Collier and Phil Nichols). *Secure the shadow – Somerset Photographers 1839–1939*, Somerset & Dorset Family Historical Society, Yeovil, 2018.
Backinsell, William G. C. *Salisbury Railway and Market House Company*, South Wiltshire Industrial Archaeology Society, 1977.
Beegan, Gerry. "The Mechanization of the Image: Facsimile, Photography, and Fragmentation in Nineteenth-Century Wood Engraving". *Journal of Design History*, Vol. 8, No. 4, 1995 pp. 257–274.
Bloore, Carolyn. "Photography and Printmaking 1840–1860". PhD dissertation, Department of Typography and Graphic Communication, University of Reading, 1991.
Brettell, Richard R., ed. *Paper and Light. The Calotype in France and Great Britain, 1839–1870*, David R. Godine; Kudos & Godine, Boston; London: in conjunction with The Museum of Fine Arts, Houston, and The Art Institute of Chicago, 1984.
Bridson, Gavin, and Geoffrey Wakeman. *Printmaking & Picture Printing: A Bibliographical Guide to Artistic & Industrial Techniques in Britain 1750–1900*, The Plough Press, Oxford, 1984.
Burnett, David. *Salisbury – The History of an English Cathedral City*, Compton Press, 1978.
Chandler, John. *Endless Street – A History of Salisbury and Its People*, Hobnob Press, Salisbury, 1983 p.137.
Coe, Brian. *Cameras from Daguerreotypes to Instant Pictures.*

Nordbok, Gothenburg, 1982.

Coke, Thomas, and Peter Kidson. *Salisbury Cathedral. Perspectives on the Architectural History*, The Stationary Office, London, 1993.

Crittall, Elizabeth (ed.). *A History of the County of Wiltshire: Volume 6*, Victoria County History, London, 1962.

Daniels, Peter. *Salisbury in Old Photographs – A Second Selection*, Alan Sutton Publishing, Stroud, 1988.

Daniels, Peter. *Around Salisbury in Old Photographs*, Alan Sutton Publishing, Stroud, 1989.

Daniels, Peter. *Salisbury – A Third Selection in Old Photographs*, Alan Sutton Publishing, Stroud, 1992.

Daniels, Peter. *Salisbury from Old Photographs*, Amberley Publishing, Stroud, 2015.

Dyson, Anthony. *Pictures to Print: The Nineteenth-Century Engraving Trade*, Farrand Press, London, 1984.

Fisher, Robert B. "The Beard Photographic Franchise in England: An Overview of Richard Beard's Licensed Daguerreotype Portrait Galleries and Their Products in the 1840s", *The Daguerreian Annual 1992: Official Yearbook of The Daguerreian Society*, pp. 73–95.

Griffiths, Antony. *The Print Before Photography: An Introduction to European Printmaking 1550–1820*, British Museum Press, London, 2016.

Hall, The Rev. Peter. *Picturesque memorials of Salisbury: a series of original etchings and vignettes, illustrative of the most interesting buildings, and other remains of antiquity, in that city and neighbourhood, to which is prefixed a brief history of Old and New Sarum.* W. B. Brodie, Salisbury, 1836.

Hamber, Anthony. "The Daguerreotype and the 1851 Great Exhibition". In *Daguerreian Annual 2016: Official Yearbook of The Daguerreian Society*, pp. 83–107.

Hamber, Anthony. *"A Higher Branch of the Art": Photographing the Fine Arts in England 1839–1880*, Gordon & Breach, Amsterdam, 1996, pp. 255–267.

Hamber, Anthony. "Photography and the West Front in the Mid-Nineteenth Century", in Ayres, Tim (ed.). *Salisbury Cathedral – The West Front.* Philimore & Co., Chichester, 2000 pp. 131–138.

Hamber, Anthony, and Jane Howells. "Salisbury and the 1851 Great Exhibition". *Sarum Chronicle*, No. 14, 2014 pp. 112–128.

Hamber, Anthony. *Collecting the American West; The Rise and Fall of William Blackmore*, Hobnob Press, East Knoyle, 2010.

Anthony Hamber. "Edward Thomas Stevens: museums and education in mid-Victorian Salisbury", *Sarum Chronicle 11*, Salisbury, 2011 pp. 79–90.

Hamber, Anthony. "Women and Early Photography in Salisbury", *Sarum Chronicle 17*, Salisbury, 2017 pp. 116–128.

Hamber, Anthony. *Photography and the 1851 Great Exhibition*, Oak Knoll Press; V&A Publishing, New Castle and London, 2018.

Howells, Jane. "'By her labour': working wives in a Victorian Provincial City", in Christopher Dyer et al. eds, *New Directions in Local History Since Hoskins*, University of Hertfordshire Press, Hatfield 2011 pp. 143–158.

Knight, Hardwicke. *The Life and Work of William Russell Sedgfield Pioneer Photographer*, University of Otago, Otago, 1998 (2 vols.)

Little, Monte. *Salisbury Mechanics Institution 1833–41*, Wiltshire Library & Museum Service, 1982.

Lush, John. "The Lost Dedication of the Church at Winterbourne Dauntsey", *Wiltshire Archaeological and Natural History Magazine*, Vol. 99, 2006 pp. 249–250.

Mitchell, Sally. *Daily Life in Victorian England*, Greenwood Publishing Group, Westport, 1996.

Moody, Robert. "The Easton Family of Salisbury: booksellers, printers and publishers c.1720–1839", *Wiltshire Archaeological and Natural History Magazine*, Vol. 101, 2008 pp. 237–250.

Newman, Ruth, and Jane Howells. *Salisbury Past*, Phillimore & Co Ltd, Chichester, 2001

Northy, T. J. *The Popular History of Old & New Sarum*, Published by the "Wiltshire County Mirror & Express Co., Ltd.", Salisbury, 1897.

Norgate, Martin (assisted by Judith Blades and Pamela Slocombe), *Photographers in Wiltshire*, Wiltshire monograph No. 5, Library & Museum Service, Trowbridge, 1982.

Norgate, Martin. *Directory of Hampshire Photographers*, Hampshire County Council Museum Services, Winchester, 1995.

Pritchard, Michael. "The Development and Growth of British Photographic Manufacturing and Retailing 1839–1914", PhD dissertation, De Montfort University, 2010.

[RCHM] *Ancient and Historical Monuments in the City of Salisbury*, Her Majesty's Stationary Office, London 1981. Volume 1.

Richardson, Mrs Herbert. "Wiltshire Newspapers – Past and Present. Part III. *(Continued)*. The Newspapers of South Wilts", *Wiltshire Archaeological and Natural History Magazine*, No. CXXX, Vol. XL, June 1919 pp. 318–351.

Richardson, Mrs Herbert. "Wiltshire Newspapers – Past and Present. Part III. *(Continued)*. The Newspapers of South Wilts", *Wiltshire Archaeological and Natural History Magazine*, No. CXXXII, Vol. XLI, June 1920 pp. 53–69.

Richardson, Mrs Herbert. "Wiltshire Newspapers – Past and Present. Part III. *(Continued)*. The Newspapers of South Wilts", *Wiltshire Archaeological and Natural History Magazine*, No. CXXXVI, Vol. XLI, June 1922 pp. 479–501.

Richardson, Mrs Herbert. "Wiltshire Newspapers – Past and Present. Part III. *(Continued)*. The Newspapers of South Wilts", *Wiltshire Archaeological and Natural*

History Magazine, No. CXLII, Vol. XLIII, June 1925 pp. 26–38.

Saunders, Peter. *Salisbury in Old Photographs*, Alan Sutton Publishing, |Stroud, 1987.

Slade, J. J. "Wiltshire Newspapers – |Past and Present. Part I.", *Wiltshire Archaeological and Natural History Magazine*, No. CXXVII, Vol. XL, December 1917 pp. 37–74.

Stannard, William John. *The Art-Exemplar; A Guide to Distinguish One Species of Print from Another, with Pictorial Examples and Written Descriptions of Every Known Style of Illustration, whether executed on gold, silver, brass, iron, tin, stone, wood, leather, steel, zinc, lead, pewter, glass, type metal, ivory, paper, plaister, antimony, fusible metal . . . To which are added "cautions in collecting prints, " "print cleaning and restoring, " "tinting and colouring prints, " "splitting paper, " "of proofs, " "of re-touching, " "of print publishing, " &c.*, Privately Printed, London, 1859.

Stevens, Frank (ed.). *The Festival Book of Salisbury. Published to commemorate the Jubilee of the Museum 1864–1914*, Salisbury, South Wilts & Blackmore Museum, Salisbury, 1914.

Taylor, Roger, and Larry Schaaf. *Impressed by Light: British Photographs from Paper Negatives, 1840–1860*, Metropolitan Museum of Art, New York, 2007.

Turley, Raymond V. *Isle of Wight Photographers 1840–1940*, University of Southampton Libraries, Southampton, 2001.

Twyman, Michael. *A History of Chromolithography: Printed Colour for All*, The British Library; Oak Knoll Press, London; New Castle, 2013.

[Victoria County History]

"Salisbury: The expansion of the city; Milford", *A History of the County of Wiltshire: Volume 6*, ed. Elizabeth Crittall, Victoria County History, London, 1962 pp. 90–93.

'Salisbury: Economic history since 1612', *A History of the County of Wiltshire: Volume 6*, ed. Elizabeth Crittall, Victoria County History, London, 1962 pp. 129–132.

Wakeman, Geoffrey. *Victorian Book Illustration: The Technical Revolution*, David & Charles, Newton Abbot, 1973.

Warrell, Ian. *Turner's Wessex: Architecture and Ambition*, The Salisbury Museum, Salisbury, 2015.

Werge, John. *The Evolution of Photography. With a Chronological Record of Discoveries, Inventions, etc. Contributions to Photographic Literature, Personal Reminiscences Extending over Forty Years*, Piper & Carter; John Werge, London, 1890.

Wilson, John Lambert. "Publishers and Purchasers of Photographically-Illustrated Books in the Nineteenth Century", PhD dissertation, University of Reading, 1995.

Wiltshire Newspapers: A Guide, Wiltshire Local History Forum, 2003.

Wood, R. Derek. "The Daguerreotype in England: Some Primary Material Relating to Beard's lawsuits". *History of Photography*, Vol. 3, No. 4, 1979, pp. 305–309.

INDEX

Note: endnote references to the *Salisbury Journal* and *Salisbury Times* have not been indexed

www.ingramcontent.com/pod-product-compliance
Lightning Source LLC
LaVergne TN
LVHW070500120826
845154LV00020BA/109
9781906978730